From the Silver Czech Tolar to a Worldwide Dollar

The Birth of the Dollar and its Journey of Monetary Circulation in Europe and the World from the 16th to the 20th Century

Petr Vorel

EAST EUROPEAN MONOGRAPHS
COLUMBIA UNIVERSITY PRESS
2013

EAST EUROPEAN MONOGRAPHS NO. DCCXCVIII

ISBN: 9780880337052

Library of Congress Control Number: 2013934443

Printed in the United States of America

Contents

Foreword

During recent decades personal genealogy – the quest for the identity and origin of our individual ancestors – has been increasingly gaining in popularity. So contrary to the historians' suggestion that it is the pedigree of the Royal Dynasties or of the famous personalities of World History that most influenced the causation of various past events, it is rather the "family history" of each one of us. If your ancestors came from Central Europe, you can usually trace their destinies in the surviving archival sources back to the 17th Century. If you are even more fortunate, they may take you back to even more ancient times when the original inhabitants of the vast plains of Utah and of the mountains of Peru had no conception that, somewhere in the east, one ship after another was arriving at the shores of their continent from far-away across the great water. It is surely not simply coincidence that the interest in finding one's individual historical roots flourishes most in those countries in which, during the centuries, huge migration and the blending of different cultures have taken place. The perception of an individual's historical roots obviously takes on a different standard and frequently it is only an inherited surname that suggests from which corner of the world our ancestors came.

Perhaps by now the reader is already shaking his head in disbelief. How is all this related to the dollar or to money at all, about which this book is concerned? But there is a relationship. There are many different types of currency in the world, just as there are people. We can trace the origins of a person and of his or her ancestors according to their names. In each country the currency also, has its own name, which was given to it within a certain context and not usually randomly. The term "dollar" (adopted in various languages) is used currently, at the beginning of the 21st Century, or has previously been used, for several dozens of different currencies all around the world, starting with the most common and the oldest in terms of its permanent continuity, i.e. the U.S.

dollar (dating back to 1792), and concluding with the youngest, the tolar, which was used by Slovenia in Central Europe as its currency during its modern history in the years 1991-2006.

Much has been written about money, and especially about dollars, in many different publications. In writing this book I have tried to present the life story of the dollar from a slightly different perspective by compiling its history using genealogical methods. To understand this mutual relationship it is necessary to delve deeply into the past. You can easily find the whereabouts of all those who are now paid in dollars simply by looking at a websites or catalogs of collectibles. But why just dollars and not zloty, pounds, francs or rupees?

It is common knowledge that the U.S. dollar was introduced sometime in the late 18th Century and that its name originated in Europe. But why was this when, much earlier on, other coinage from different monetary systems had been utilized on the American Continent? In most numismatic manuals you will read, of course, that the word "dollar" originated as a derivative of the name tolar (taler), given to a coin produced in the 16th Century in the West Bohemian mining town of Jáchymov, known as "Saint Joachim Valley" (or in German as St. Joachimsthal). In 1503, the year in which in Seville, in Spain, the Casa de la Contratación was established for trading with its overseas colonies, in the deep forest dales of the Ore Mountains, where Jáchymov was later founded, however, you risked, encountering only a stray fox. Nevertheless, just half a century later the largest silver coins that were minted in Central Europe were already called after this place. How did that become possible?

The very long history of the dollar as a unit of currency was symbolically initiated on the 9th January 1520, in the Czech Provincial Assembly in Prague. The representatives of the Czech Estates at that time ordered the Schliks family to produce silver coins of a high weight from the precious metal ore extracted in the mines that they operated, in order to prevent the illegal export of metallurgical silver. The word "taler" (or dollar) did not yet exist then and one of the many decisions made by the highest legislative body in the Kingdom of Bohemia (today's western part of the Czech Republic) certainly did not immediately reach the most distant outposts of the Caribbean, African Liberia nor New Zealand, where today everything is paid for with dollars. The causality is absolutely unmistakable, however. The common ancestor of every coin, past and present, that has borne the name of dollar originated in Bohemia. It has had a far-reaching progeny that, during the course of five centuries, has found its way, in various forms, to nearly every corner of the world.

The rich "family history" of the dollar has had both its periods of glory and its dramatic twists, the historical context of which is worthy of attention. Let us, therefore start in the conceptual heart of Central Europe, where the history of today's most common monetary unit of the world had its birth.

1

European Silver and Coins at the Turn of the 15th and 16th Centuries

In 1986, the public was commemorating worldwide the symbolic 500th birthday of the dollar.[1] This centenary, based on the ancient coins of the thaler type is, however, open to question in my opinion. It is true that dating from that year are the earliest European silver coins that featured an unprecedented weight and size, however, during the period of their production nobody called them thalers.[2] And even many years later, when the Habsburg Archduke Charles became the King of distant Spain (1516), in a pub near the bridge in the village Absam, situated on the Alpine slopes of the left bank of the River Inn, they would perhaps have just shaken their heads in disbelief about your asking what you could buy there for a thaler. Below the village in the Tyrolean town called Hall in Tirol (today part of Austria), although similar coins had already been made there for thirty years, they were named differently.[3] In terms of our quest for the origin of the dollar, however, though this old Tyrolean mintage is a symbolic forerunner of the thaler, a permanent name had not yet been awarded to this new type of coin.

At the beginning of the 15th century Central Europe was facing a shortage of precious metals. The historic sources of gold and silver appeared to have been exhausted and the economic life of this area of the "Old Continent" was experiencing a period of profound stagnation also accompanied by an administrative crisis.

Since the period of the Middle Ages the Holy Roman Empire had existed in this region as an independent supranational body. It had been established with reference to the ancient tradition of the vanquished Western Roman Empire and the Empire of Charlemagne (800-814) at the end of the second third of the 10th century, following the Imperial Coronation of Otto I (962-973.). De jure the Holy Roman Empire remained in existence until the year 1806, although its internal structure changed significantly during the individual centuries, as also did its size and the status of its ruler. He was called the "King of Rome" and after the Imperial Coronation (in medieval times this was conducted by the Pope as the Head of the Catholic Church) he enjoyed the resounding title of "Roman Emperor."

None of the Roman Emperors during the High Middle Ages, nor in modern times, in fact reigned over the entire empire. The effective rulers were the secular and ecclesiastical administrators of smaller government units; dozens of margraviates, principalities, counties, bishoprics, abbeys and other territorial entities, differing in their size and importance, and collectively referred to as "territorial principalities." Also directly subject to the Emperor were several dozens of independent cities, known as "Free Imperial Towns" (the most important of which were Augsburg and Nuremberg).

The real power of the Roman Kings and Emperors during this period was also diminished by the fact that they did not reign over the Holy Roman Empire as hereditary rulers but were elected. If the Imperial Throne became vacant for some reason, frequently several candidates fought a battle for it which was formally resolved in accordance with a decision by the Electoral College. Already in the 13th century, the number of Electors was established as seven; four were secular rulers (the rulers of Bohemia, Brandenburg, Saxony and the Palatinate) and three were members of the clergy (the Archbishops of Mainz, Cologne and Trier). The real power of the individual Electors and of the other Princes belonging to the Holy Roman Empire had often been greater than the capacities of the Emperor himself. Only a few rulers of the Holy Roman Empire during the Middle Ages and in early modern times attempted to cut through the vicious cycle of the vested interests of the territorial princes and to re-form this empire as a centrally controlled state. None of them, however, in fact succeeded.

Let us expand even further this brief excursus into the constitutional situation in late medieval Central Europe. Without this basic information it will be difficult to understand what certain 16th century rulers were actually seeking for in regard to the production of silver thalers and why, nowadays, collectors specializing in "German thalers" of the 16th–19th century have to use special catalogs because of their exceptional quantity, while the entire thaler mintage from all the other parts of Europe fits into one book.

If you consider the map of Europe today, the Holy Roman Empire in the early 15th century formally brought together in one entity what is now Germany, the western part of Poland, the Czech Republic, Austria, Slovenia, the northern and northwestern area of Italy, Switzerland, Liechtenstein, the Netherlands, Belgium, Luxembourg and the eastern part of France. To the east it was bordered by the Kingdoms of Poland, Hungary and Croatia; in the south by the Papal State (Rome itself was now no longer a part of the Holy Roman Empire) and the wealthy Venetian Republic; to the west by the Kingdom of France and to the north by the Kingdom of Denmark. The fundamental legal document, on which the Empire was based and known as the Golden Bull, was issued by Emperor Charles IV Luxembourg in 1356, who was the King of Bohemia (from 1346) prior to his election to the Imperial Throne. The expansion of the power of the Luxembourgs was directly related to this fact, as Bohemia, from the 13th century onwards, was one of Europe's leading silver mining areas and, after 1300 (when production of the Prague groschen commenced in the town of Kutná Hora), the significance of this increased. In fact, in the late 14th century Charles' son and successor to the Czech and Roman thrones, King Wenceslas IV. Luxembourg, attempted to introduce a Czech silver coin (the Prague groschen) as the common currency of the Holy Roman Empire. Thanks to the enormous export potential of the Czech silver mines this initiative was successful, at least in the southwestern part of the Empire, but the political instability and the religious wars of the early 15th century played havoc with this development. The failure of the supply of Czech silver to the European market had brought about serious complications for the entire Central European money market[4] and this became one of the reasons for the rapid increase in the prices of precious metals, because it was not possible to pay for either the gold or for the luxury goods imported from Asia and Africa into late-medieval Europe.

In addition to the wars in the Czech Kingdom in the early 15th century the lack of monetary gold and silver in circulation in Europe was also caused by the depletion of most of the other previously known domestic European sources of precious metals[5] and subsequently also by changes associated with dynamic shifts in power in North Africa and in the Balkans. The Ottoman Empire was then experiencing a period of vast territorial expansion. Early in the 15th century its troops occupied Egypt and gained control of Cairo, the main commercial center of North Africa. This made traditional European trading with African gold impossible. The conquest of Constantinople (today's Istanbul) in 1453 not only caused the final collapse of the Byzantine Empire, but also severed a major artery of trade between Europe and the Eastern region and disturbed for centuries the established system of maritime commerce in the Mediterranean. Additional Ottoman expansion continued deeper into the heart of the Balkans and manifested as an ongoing power-threat to Central Europe. The rapid advance of the Turks towards the north prevented the supply of precious metals from the Bosnian and Serbian mountains to Venice and also started to threaten what was then Europe's most important deposit of gold, mined in Upper Hungary (now in Slovakia) and Transylvania (in today's Rumania). From there came the famous Hungarian ducats; gold coins of high quality, which during periods of inflation of the lesser currencies in the 15th century, for many years became the principal stable currency of Central Europe, which enabled the concluding of long-term business contracts even during the collapse of the provincial financial systems.[6]

Disastrous experience, based on inflation, with the small-sized silver coins[7] produced an increased demand for precious metals in the world of trade. The maritime powers of Western Europe sought to resolve this through their expansion into southern Africa and by seeking new business connections with India and the fabulous Eastern regions, especially those abundant in gold. The Central European Monarchy did not have any such option and therefore the local rulers tried to make the best use of their domestic resources by intensively seeking new deposits. Apart from the traditional Hungarian mines, at the beginning of the early modern period the mining of gold ore in significant quantities commenced in Salzburg (in today's Austria), which at that time was an independent Imperial Archbishopric, and in several principalities in Silesia (today part of Poland), then belonging to the union of the Countries of the Czech Crown. Also the stabilization of the political situation in Hungary, where the native monarch Matthias Corvinus (1458-1490) brought the crown home, contributed to the resumption of the availability of large quantities of gold Hungarian ducats on the European money market.

During the last third of the 15th century there was also a recovery in the profitability of silver mining in Central Europe. This silver first appeared on the money market in the form of traditional medieval groschens. Understood at that time as a groschen was a larger coin made from silver plate with a diameter of cca. 2.7 cm and weighing about 3 grams. The specific payment strength of silver groschens minted by various issuers, differed significantly, however, and was based on the actual precious metal content.

In the late Middle Ages, however, silver was only mined in Europe in significant quantities in Saxony, Bohemia and the Tyrol.[8] Therefore, for the Central European financial market during the second half of the 15th century, silver coins from the mintage, put into circulation by those rulers who had a sufficiently large source of newly mined metallurgical silver,[9] were crucial. It was some time however, before the restoration took place of the monetary systems that had been shaken by inflation. In Saxony, a fundamental reform of the currency was implemented in the year 1465; in Bohemia and Austria this occurred four years later (1469). At this stage this still only concerned the stabilization of the national silver currencies of the Central European Monarchies and finding a new basis for responding to the ever-fluctuating ratio between the prices of gold and silver. Which is to say that the price-ratio between gold and silver varied in different parts of Europe. During the 15th century, the ratio between the price of gold and silver on the "Old Continent" moved within the wide range of 1:8.9 and 1:13, with significant regional and temporal variations; the average value hovered at around 1:10. Typically it was possible to purchase gold most inexpensively in the Italian trading centers, while it was more expensive in the north of Europe.

The Northern Italian trading centers found a means towards the more efficient utilization of Central European silver on the world market, by the inception in the 1470's of the issuance of heavy silver coins, containing much more precious metal than the common groschen. Unlike the conventional European groschen coins, in which the content of silver usually barely reached 50%, the newly introduced Italian coinage was made from high quality metal (usually averaging 93% of Ag) with the designation "lira" (Venice, 1472, the Doge Nicolo Tron coins, containing 6.29 grams of pure silver) or "teston" (Milan, 1474, the Galeazzo Maria Sforza coins, containing 9.29 grams of pure silver). Italian merchants first responded to changes in the market for precious metals and tried to ensure a sufficient quantity of silver coins that would have a higher content of pure silver and therefore higher payment strength, comparable with the traditional gold coins traded. These new silver means of payment, metrologically usually derived from the Venice lira or the Milan teston, from the late 15th century started to spread rapidly to the areas to the north of their inception: to the Savoie, in today's Switzerland, and to southern Germany (see **Tab. III/1**).

The first impetus for the introduction of this large silver coinage did not therefore arise in those areas where there was a sufficiency of mined silver (Saxony, Bohemia, the Tyrol). On the contrary, the merchants who started its production were those who exported silver from Europe out into the world and needed to have it available in the highest guaranteed purity and quality. Central European groschens, however, were not so suitable for this because they lacked stable metrological parameters (mainly their purity was inconsistent). The silver coins also did not have any unifying metrological characteristics, according to which the payment strength of coins could be assessed. In the case of gold this role was fulfilled by ducats and Rhenish guldens: for any gold coin it was possible, after the conversion of its weight and purity to determine its payment strength in relation to ducats or Rhenish guldens. However, this possibility did not exist for the silver groschen coins. Prague groschens, which, in the 14th century were the most important silver trading coins in Central and Eastern Europe, by the end of the Middle Ages no longer fulfilled this function due to their inconsistent silver content. This function was not fulfilled either by the groschen-type coins of other monetary systems (shillings, plapparts, Polish half-groschens etc.). Those interested in the supply of silver in the realm of the long-distance exchange of goods demanded this metal in a more credible form than a variegated mixture of groschens, the actual quality (i.e. the silver content) of which was very difficult to verify. Therefore, apparently illogically, these new silver coins of high purity started to be produced in places where silver was not mined at all – in northern Italian trading towns. Deliveries of groschen coins from Central Europe were melted-down there, refined to a higher purity and again monetized in the form of a new type of trading coin.

The impetus for the start-up of production of a large silver mintage of nearly pure metal was thus not primarily based on an imminent shortage of gold, as is often suggested in the older literature (the volume of gold mining was even significantly rising in Central Europe in the late 15th century) nor on the need to rapidly monetize newly discovered reserves of silver, but rather on the commercial interests of Italian exporters of silver to the African and Asian markets.[10]

The exchange rates of gold and silver represented important business information in the Middle Ages which was then routinely calculated by the bankers. Trading was carried out using coins and also precious metal bullion.[11] Minted coins held the advantage that their manufacturer already guaranteed their specific purity, while in the case of gold or silver bullion it was necessary to verify the quality of the metal. The most practical item for dealers in precious metals was therefore the precious metal coinage with the highest unit-weight. The problem, however, was the technical implementation of products of this kind, therefore in the Middle Ages gold or silver coins of a higher weight were not yet minted; the gold ducats and silver groschens weighed only about three grams.[12]

The European mints had a wealth of experience in the production of small coins and groschen mintage and slight technical advances of the second half of the 15th century also brought about some improvements that accelerated and made cheaper the manual production of groschen coins from thinner silver plate (with a thickness of about 0.3-0.5 mm). At the end of the Middle Ages the limiting technical factor in regard to the production of silver coins of a greater weight was the ratio between the diameter of the coin and the thickness of its blanks. Thinner metal coins could not have a very wide diameter because they could easily be damaged. The production of coins from thicker blanks was technically more difficult and time consuming, therefore for the monetarization of large quantities of mined silver it was still not worthwhile. Individual issuers gradually tried to produce coins of an even greater weight, using the purest silver. The pure silver was not suitable for coin production because it was too soft and the coins would have been quickly worn-down in the course of their circulation; with a higher proportion of copper the alloy was harder and therefore handmade manufacture using a thicker blank was more difficult. The most profitable silver coinage during the last quarter of the 15th century was that demonstrating a high level purity, in the range of cca. 93% Ag, and with a weight of between 6 and 10 grams.

This situation did not change fundamentally until the end of the 15th century. It is true that during the latter part of the 15th century larger silver coins, weighing up to about 30 grams, were also being minted in several places in Central Europe. These, however, similarly to the minted or cast Renaissance medals of the period usually had only a commemorative or decorative nature and were not intended for general circulation. Even the first mass-produced large silver coins of the thaler type, which received their first exposure in the 1480's in the Tyrolean Alps, were not actually exceptions to this practice.

A necessary condition for the appearance of new types of coins was undoubtedly a sufficiency of the requisite raw material, i.e. metallurgical silver. The newly discovered deposits of silver ore around the Tyrolean town of Schwaz (now in Austria), the mining of which had developed in the second half of the 15th century, amply fulfilled this condition.[13]

The ruler of the County of Tyrol at that time was Sigismund von Habsburg,[14] a cousin of Emperor Frederick III. He took advantage of these newly discovered sources of precious metal by setting up a new government mint in the vicinity, i.e. where today stands the town of Hall in Tirol (see **Tab. I**). Due to the close contacts between the Alpine region and northern Italy, the Archduke Sigismund was also quick to adapt to this new trend and the enormous quantity of silver from the Schwaz mines was processed into the form of large-sized silver coins.

Sigismund von Habsburg carried out a reform of the monetary system in the Tyrol through a new regulation in 1482, by which large coins, similar to the Venetian lira (93.8% Ag, weight of 6.366 g), came into circulation. They were also named in the same manner, although in the German variant they were called "pfundner" because they contained the same amount of silver as one pound (in Italian "lira," in German "Pfund") of older pfennigs. A Tyrolean pfundner had a value of 12 kreutzers and were equivalent in value to a fifth of one "Rhenish gulden," the gold coinage issued in the Rhineland and in the southern areas of the Holy Roman Empire by several secular and ecclesiastical princes.[15]

Rhenish guldens circulated in Central Europe in parallel with other gold coinage, though ducats (in Central Europe especially Hungarian ducats) were more popular in the sphere of international transactions because of their consistent metrological parameters and their higher gold content. Rhenish guldens contained a significantly lesser amount of gold and, specifically (unlike the stable ducats), over time, their purity had been gradually decreasing.[16] It was this lower content of gold, however, that was apparently the reason why this coin was eventually chosen as the benchmark value for the production of silver equivalents – because the silver coins (called guldiner) did not then have to be so large.

After the introduction in 1482 of the pfundner (valued at 1/5 of a Rhenish gulden) further experiments continued in rapid succession in the Tyrol with increasing silver content. Soon the Mint in Hall in Tirol began to produce coins weighing 15.9 grams (bearing the date 1484)[17] from the same quality alloy (93.8% Ag), which in their value corresponded to half that of the Rhenish gulden. The management of the Hall in Tirol Mint was at this time apparently experimenting and trying-out various methods for efficiently transforming extracted precious metals into mass-produced coins of proprietary highest payment strength. The most complicated phase of the production process was the preparation of the blank, i.e. a regular metal disc of the prescribed weight and purity. The coinage metal was hammered and shaped into a form in different ways. At the outset of the minting of half-guldiners and guldiners during the 1480's at the Hall in Tirol Mint the production of blanks for large coins was tried using casting, evidence of which is provided both from written sources and by microscopic testing of the structure of the metal of some preserved specimens. Cast blanks were more suitable for coinage, because the metal was softer and more pliable. This procedure did not prove successful, however, apparently because it was not technically possible to cast such a large number of blanks at the same time and additionally their secondary treatment (the removal of the risers and traces emanating from the casting gutter, etc.) was too labor-intensive and therefore costly.

In parallel with the half-guldiners coins of twice the weight were also minted from the same dies, though from a significantly thicker blank. These coins, described in the current German literature as "Dick-guldiners," already represented a direct equivalent of the Rhenish gulden in silver. Their external form, however (a thicker silver disk with a relatively small diameter) was impractical both in terms of their production and circulation.

Through the testing of different variants and technological processes at the Mint, eventually, after about two years they achieved a definite form for the coin that also contained the requisite amount of pure silver (i.e. the prescribed standard of 31.832 g). The diameter of the blank was expanded to approximately 41 mm and its thickness adjusted to cca. 2 mm. In this format, which (even after the lowering of the total silver content) was then generally respected by all the early modern coinage of the thaler type, the Hall in Tirol guldiners were minted bearing the date 1486 (see **Tab. II**).[18]

The reverse side, with the image of a rider and a heraldic decoration (which varies slightly in different versions) was retained even after the change of the era and the magnification of the coin image. For the issuer, the external appearance of the coins must have been extremely important, because this form was given preference over any technically simpler solution. The obverse side clearly represented the personality of the issuer. He was portrayed, with his name and title also engraved around the perimeter: "SIGISMVNDVS ARChIDVX AVSTRIE," i.e. Sigismund, Archduke of Austria. But this was an ancestral title (all the Habsburgs were Archdukes) and not related to any country that Sigismund ruled – even the actual Tyrol was "only" a dukedom. The reverse side was designed even more universally "Habsburgian," thereby effectively engendering anonymity. Coins with this reverse side could actually be minted by any of the current Habsburgs, because it included all the major symbols of the Habsburg hereditary provinces and of certain other possessions, whether it was Duke Sigismund of Tyrol or his cousin, Emperor Frederick III who ruled them (whether in reality or only theoretically). Therefore, in my opinion, Sigismund's guldiners can be considered as the first Habsburg coins, with their exterior design that would identify their universal validity within a wider territory (in this case throughout the Habsburg lands).[19] The Habsburgs later supported the same principle in regard to a universal Imperial currency. The imperial coins would also have one side identical (the universal imperial design) with the other side reserved for the specific issuer.

The obverse side underwent a significant change in the year 1486 with the transition to the minting of guldiners from thick blanks. A standing representation of the ruler was placed there and also on gold coins of the same payment strength. The same artistic composition of the obverse sides of both the gold and silver coins was designed to reflect the same payment strength as during the period of their issuance (60 kreutzers) and that regardless of their differences in size and weight and in the metal used for their production, they should be perceived to be of equal value as a means of payment. This is how the monetary accounting unit, "Rhine-gulden = 60 kreutzers," was designed to be used for both gold and silver coins.

This feature was intended to serve for the short-term coverage of a larger demand (if the debtor has agreed with the creditor "concerning the payment of" installments in silver instead of gold); however as a permanent principle for the production of legitimate trading coins, for which the payment strength would usually be indicated by the content of precious metal, it was unrealistic. During the late Middle Ages the ratio between the prices of gold and silver was also changing relatively rapidly and even though information then was transmitted infinitely more slowly than it is today, it was not possible to sustain the exchange rate of both types of coins at mutual parity. To be clear which kind of coin was meant the "Rhenish gulden," minted from gold, started to be known as the "Goldgulden" and its silver equivalent as the "Guldengroschen," later also abbreviated as the "Guldiner." In Latin texts the term "Uncialis" was also used for guldiners since they contained approximately one ounce of pure silver. This term did not catch on generally, however.[20]

The existence of two different versions of the coins described above, with an identical silver content (but a different diameter and dating) has become a reason for applying different datation to the oldest direct ancestor of the thaler coin. In earlier studies the year 1484 appears; subsequent Austrian and German literature tends rather towards the year 1486. Questions are still raised, however, not only in regard to the determination of the oldest Tyrolean thalers, but also concerning their real economic significance. Extensive minting of these silver trading coins in the Tyrol at the end of the 15th century is currently assumed only by the Austrian literature.[21] Most economic historians incline rather to the symbolic minting of these coins as a type of medal. Considered as a turning point in the production of coins of the thaler type is the development of their production in Saxony and in Bohemia in the early 16th century.[22]

In my opinion, the Tyrolean guldiners from the late 15th century truly had only a minimal impact on money circulation in Europe. The most important opinion that must be taken into account concerning this matter is that expressed by Karl Moeser and Fritz Dworschak in the first half of the 20th century, based on an analysis of the actual accounts of the Mint in Hall in Tirol. After considering all the available sources and comparing the preserved specimens in regard to the Tyrolean guldiners from the year 1486, they reached the conclusion: "...Ihre Verwendung ist daher in der Folge die ausgesprochener Ehr- und Verehrpfennige...."[23]

Ultimately this is logical. Although the silver wealth from the Tyrolean mountains was bringing in a fortune, Archduke Sigismund of Habsburg was facing huge financial problems and was even thinking about selling the entire Tyrol to the rulers of neighboring Bavaria. The actual operation of the mines and the production of the coins were effectively controlled by someone else. In 1482 Archduke Sigismund had leased the trade in the silver from the Alpine mines to the Augsburg company belonging to the Paumgartner brothers.[24] The marketing of Schwaz silver however was soon undertaken with a partner with stronger capitalization[25] and from the year 1488 the management of the mine and the mint were under the control of the Fuggers' Banking House in Augsburg.[26] They were the largest creditors of the old Count of Tyrol, who became famous for his debauchery (though with no male heir of the marriage bed, he apparently left behind dozens of illegitimate children) and his inclination to spend. Already in the year 1490, Count Sigismund (†1496) was forced by the Tyrolean nobility who were dissatisfied with his manner of ruling, and by his Habsburg relatives who feared the loss of an important area, to hand over the rule of the Tyrol to his great-nephew Maximilian, the future Emperor.

Count Sigismund's silver Tyrol guldiners were produced for only four years, however we do not know how many of them were actually made and how many of them went into circulation. Preserved specimens of these now very rare coins show that a relatively large number of dies were used in their production. This fact in itself does not imply that a large quantity of coins were produced. Sigismund's guldiners were conceived as a representative coinage with very fine detail in the rendering of the Emperor's features and with a provincial insignia shown on the reverse side. Such compositions were not suited to the large-scale production of conventional means of payment because the small relief produced by the handcrafted iron dies quickly became clogged and worn out, which increased the production costs. In the period of standard production by larger mints of the thaler coinage in the second half of the 16th century several dozen dies were commonly worn-out (the upper ones, which the minter hammered directly, wore-out more quickly). Relatively high costs involved in the production of the actual dies (together with those for other raw materials), are documented, for example, in the accounting documents from Augsburg. According to the accounts from the year 1533, the cost for the monetization of one talent of pure silver was calculated "...für eysen schneiden, müntzlon, eyssen, stachel, weinstein, salz, khupfer und abgang..." in the amount of 24 kreutzers.[27]

Technically much simpler, faster and less expensive was the production of the coins with lesser values, pfundners (1/5 of a guldiner = 12 kreutzers) and sechsers (1/10 of a guldiner = 6 kreutzers). These Tyrolean coins were introduced into financial circulation primarily in the Austrian lands and their vicinity, because the Hall in Tirol Mint, under the administration of the Augsburg banking house, was required to produce the maximum possible profit. The large silver guldiners were apparently produced only in limited quantities, primarily as commemorative coinage for Count Sigismund. Their purpose was to give an impression of the wealth and power of the issuer, not to serve the purposes of the circulation of money. A similar function was probably also performed by a similar coinage that appeared in the Alpine region during the same period and which in its exterior design and metrological parameters was undeniably influenced by the Tyrolean guldiners. These were the coins of the Dukes of Lorraine, minted in the area of present-day Switzerland. None of these coins, that were apparently produced only in a limited number, reached the international money market however nor did they influence it in any way. We definitely do not encounter them anymore after the early 16th century in the then commonplace "valuations," through which large companies, for their own purposes, assayed the fair value of the precious metals in those coins, which were most frequently traded in exchange for goods.[28] Sigismund's coins from the years 1484 and 1486 do not appear in any printed reports concerning European thalers until the mid-16th century, and then with inaccurate information concerning their silver content. Unlike for the standard trading coins of that period (i.e. genuine thalers, whether Czech, German or Austrian) in the case of this Tyrolean coinage from the 1480's verification of the actual silver content was not required because these coins were not used for commercial purposes – however they were well known because they were found in most courtly "cabinets of coins." Pictures of the Tyrolean "guldiners" were then without verification based on the real coins included by publishers of similar reports until the early 17th century.[29]

The above explanation of the overwhelmingly representative function of Sigismund's guldiners from the years 1486-1490 is also substantiated by the fact that immediately following the transfer of the rulership of the country to Maximilian von Habsburg in 1490 the production of Tyrolean guldiners was discontinued. Archduke Maximilian (a titular Holy Roman Emperor since 1486 and the designated successor to his father, Emperor Frederick III) nevertheless had considerable experience with the manufacture of larger-size silver coins. Due to his favorable marriage with the daughter of the Duke of Burgundy, Charles the Bold († 1477), as the representative of the latter's minor son, Philip, de facto he ruled the rich provinces of the Netherlands and Burgundy. On the occasion of that marriage, in the year 1477, barring which the Habsburgs would hardly have asserted themselves on the European political scene during the late Middle Ages, Maximilian of Habsburg had already commanded the minting of a magnificent Renaissance Medal, metrologically very similar to the later Tyrolean guldiners. This mintage is sometimes even described as the direct precursor of the guldiners and as a coin that was the inspiration for Archduke Sigismund (who as a close relative of Maximilian was undoubtedly familiar with this medal) for the preparation of his own large silver coins.

The financial conditions in Archduke Maximilian's Western European possessions, obtained through marriage, were destabilized in the 1480's by a long Habsburg – French conflict over the inheritance following the death of Charles the Bold and by two major uprisings in the Dutch provinces. In order to ensure a sufficient supply of funds for the mercenary troops from the year 1487 King Maximilian ordered the production of larger silver coinage. Maximilian's coin reforms in the Netherlands however had an inflationary aspect; the large silver coins that he issued contained less silver than they should have to correspond with their nominal value. Nevertheless Maximilian did not order the production of even larger coins, approaching in weight the guldiners of his great-uncle Sigismund – the production of large silver coins was then still too difficult technically and therefore uneconomical, even with the reduction of the silver content in periods of inflation. Though King Maximilian paid his Swiss and German mercenaries using silver coins with inflated values, the domestic Dutch traders and the nobility refused to accept them. By 1489 the monarch was already obliged to halt the production of these denominations and to return to minting smaller fully-valued coins of the groschen type.[30]

This is probably the main reason why King Maximilian, after the year 1490, did not give strong support to the expansion of the production of Tyrolean guldiners. He himself had an excellent appreciation of contemporary metallurgy and metalworking and was intensely interested in the activities of the metal smelters in his Capital City of Innsbruck and its surroundings (where the Schwaz mines and the Mint in Hall in Tirol were also located). In the final decade of the 15th century he also required large sums of money for his military and political projects and therefore he gave priority to the mass production of the coin denominations that were the most advantageous economically from the production point of view, while being already accepted with confidence in the world of European trade – especially the Tyrolean pfundners and sechsers.

For the purpose of creating a positive impression during the early years of King Maximilian's rule over the Austrian lands, guldiners were also produced from time to time by the Tyrolean mint. The only known type of Tyrolean guldiner of King Maximilian that was definitely still being produced in the late 15th century is dated with the year 1495. In its type it is similar to the coinage of his predecessor Sigismund. Instead of a knight on horseback on the reverse side of this guldiner there appears a single-headed imperial eagle, since Maximilian of Habsburg did not became the de jure reigning King of Rome until after the death of his father, Emperor Frederick III (†1493). The complex heraldic decoration of the reverse side was retained. Even this coin was probably not intended for mass production, but only as representational.

The fact that guldiners were not produced regularly and in large quantities in the late 15th century in Tyrol is also evident from the correspondence that has been preserved from the year 1501 between King Maximilian I and the medal-maker Benedict Burkhart. The monarch had repeatedly ordered the reprocessing of some newly acquired dies, because he was not satisfied with the image presented of his person. From the context it is evident that even this new upcoming production of guldiners should have had primarily a representational character. The master of the mint should also use the dies approved by the monarch for private individuals who have supplied their own silver to the mint. After paying the production costs, guldiners should be produced for them from the accepted metal.[31]

Extensive use of the Tyrolean guldiners of Emperor Maximilian I did not occur until later, early in the 16th century. At that time, however, the situation in the money market had changed dramatically, after the structure of the European currency system had been significantly affected by the then second leading producer of metallurgical silver, namely Saxony (now a part of Germany).

Since the 12th century the Dukes of the House of Wettin had ruled the Meissen Margraviate. Their sphere of government was extended following the extinction of the House of Ascania in the first half of the 15th century to also include the neighboring Duchy of Saxony, with which they also obtained an electoral role. The considerable influence of the Saxon Wettins was based primarily on their large reserves of silver ore, which had been extensively mined since the Middle Ages in the northern areas of the Ore Mountains (in Czech: Krušné hory; in German: Erzgebirge). During the last quarter of the 15th century, the discovery of new rich ore veins occurred and the mining areas in the Saxon part of the Ore Mountains became an equivalent competitor in the production of silver with the Tyrolean town Schwaz and Kutná Hora (Kuttenberg) in Bohemia. Apparently a great stir was created in the St. George mine near Saxon Schneeberg in 1477 by the discovery of a huge piece of silver ore with a very high metal content. The Saxon Duke Albrecht was allegedly so profoundly interested in this discovery that on the 23rd April 1477 he descended personally into the depths of the mine and had a symbolic snack on the silver ore boulder, measuring cca. 4 m^3 as if on a "silver table."[32]

The rumors about silver treasure in the Saxon mountains were not exaggerated, however. Thanks to their decisive advantage in the production of metallurgical silver across North Eastern Germany the Saxon Dukes were making decisions not only about the form of their coins, but also on the basis of a much broader perspective. In the mid-15th century the Saxon monetary system was not substantially affected by inflation, as had occurred in southern Germany, Austria and the Czech lands. The problems there seem to have been caused rather by the disunity between the newly minted coins and those still in circulation that had been issued during the 15th century by various representatives of the ruling family. The new Saxon groschen, introduced in a regulation of the 4th April 1465, contained only 1.49 grams of silver of 50% purity and one such groschen was meant to be equivalent to 1/20th of a Rhenish gulden or 1/25th of a Hungarian ducat.

While in the 15th century, during the seventies and eighties, the production of Saxon coins was affected by several government regulations, it essentially retained its medieval form. In the amendment of the year 1474 Saxony also made a temporary decision to produce silver coins of a higher quality (93.75% of Ag). However, the highest denomination minted was a groschen with a payment strength of 1/20th of a Rhenish gulden (or later 1/21st of a Rhenish gulden). As a result of multi-fold rapid and consecutive changes in metrological parameters, special names were adopted in Saxony for different types of groschen coins, derived from the images present on the coin, "Horngrosch," "Kreuzgrosch" and "Roselergrosch," or based on the mining area from which the precious metal, used for coinage of the relevant nominal denomination originated, e.g. "Schneeberger."[33]

A fundamental change in the attitude of the Saxon Dukes to the production of silver coins of a greater weight, did not occur until the discovery of new rich deposits of silver ore in the vicinity of Schreckenberg. Thanks to the lively mining activity and the influx of new residents a new mining town was founded and named Annaberg. First minted in 1496 from the local silver were Saxon silver coins of a greater weight. Their value was equivalent to that of three of the groschens minted during the same period from Schneeberg silver (called Schneebergers) and to 1/7th of that of a Rhenish gulden. Their purity reached 86.1% of Ag and they contained 3.92 grams of pure silver. They were named "Schreckenbergers" after the mining area or "Annabergers" in accordance with the mint. I am deliberately emphasizing the practice in the Saxon environment, at the turn of the 15th and 16th centuries, of naming specific coins according to their place of origin, because this circumstance was to play a crucial role later in the use of the term "taler."

The real turning point in the production of large silver coinage occurred in May of 1500, when the Saxon Princes concluded an agreement in Leipzig called the Leipzig Money Convention ("Leipziger Münzordnung") on a new Saxon currency. According to this agreement, the circulation of all foreign coinage in the country should cease (with the exception of Prague groschen, minted at that time in Bohemia, in Kutná Hora); the payment strength of the older coins was restored to the rate of 1 Rhenish gulden = 7 Schreckenbergers = 21 groschens (Schneebergers) = 42 half-groschens. Primarily, however, the Leipzig Money Convention introduced the minting of new large silver coins, described in the text of this mandate as "one Guldengroschen." Like the silver coins of Sigismund von Habsburg from the year 1486 this Saxon coinage was also intended to be of equivalent value in silver to the contemporaneous gold coins (the Rhenish gulden). With their real content of pure silver, however, these coins differed from the Tyrolean ones, because the ratio between the prices of gold and silver in the Tyrol in 1486 was different than it was to be in 1500 in Leipzig, Saxony. The quantity of silver in the first Saxon Guldengroschens (called later Guldiners) was derived from the ratio 1:10.8. The coins also had a high level of purity (93.77% of Ag), but, in comparison with the older Tyrolean coinage, a lower weight (29.23 g); therefore they contained only 27.41 grams of pure silver.

The Leipzig Money Convention in 1500 was established by an agreement between all three of the then leading representatives of the ruling House of Wettin. For this reason the oldest Saxon guldiners have an unusual appearance. That is to say that they depict three men: on one side is Duke Frederick III (as the representative of the main Ernestin line of the family the title of Imperial Prince Elector belonged to him) on the opposite side of the coin Frederick's younger brother Johan was portrayed and opposite him their Uncle Albert (see **Tab. III/2**). This format was then maintained on Saxon coins of this type for the next several decades (see **Tab. VIII/2**; **XVI/2,3**; **XVII/1,2**).

Also, from the year 1500, the oldest Saxon guldiners were produced, but only in small quantities. Their mass production did not develop until around the year 1507 and then continued. Only at the turn of the first and second decades of the 16th century, due to the Saxon coin production, did large silver coins become the object of long-distance wholesale trading. They were still impractical for normal cash transactions because they had too high a payment strength. They primarily functioned as a commodity that was in circulation for conducting business between different parts of the then known world. The main market center at which the Saxon silver coins were traditionally traded remained the town of Leipzig.

Even the discoveries of new ore veins did not contribute to the development of trading using large minted silver coins – the mineral wealth of the Tyrolean Alps, of Saxon Ore Mountains and of Bohemian Kutná Hora was utilized lavishly throughout the last third of the 15th century. A plenitude of new metallurgical silver was of course a necessary condition, but the mass production of silver guldiners came about through the technological advances of the early modern period.

The rapid development of metallurgy and the technical innovations introduced during the processing of metallurgical silver, primarily simplified the production of semi-finished coin blanks. Even large silver coins continued to be minted manually, as also were medieval groschens. The worker who struck the coin (the mint-master) did not influence the weight or the composition of the coin metal, he only embossed an obverse and a reverse relief onto a pre-prepared disc. However, in order that the mint-master by striking with a hammer could complete the last stage of the manufacturing process he had to have available pre-formed metal blanks of the prescribed weight and purity. While in the case of small and groschen coins minted from a thin metal it was possible to cover-up some inequality by striking the die, in the case of large guldiners this was not possible. Prior to minting their blanks required a totally regular shape, a smooth surface on both sides and regular edges. At the beginning of the 16th century, with the implementation of minor improvements and of the first mechanical machinery (used for the treatment of semi-products and for cutting discs from silver) this previously complicated and time-consuming phase of the production of coins was greatly accelerated. Technological progress brought with it a higher level of profitability and the minting of guldiners started to become more financially advantageous than the production of groschens or of other small coins.

During that period silver coins with the parameters of guldiners were not produced to any great extent outside the Saxon countries. Their mintage continued in small quantities for representational purposes for King (and since 1508 Emperor) Maximilian at the Mint in Hall in Tirol; at the end of his life (in 1518), Emperor Maximilian I († 1519) ordered the minting of representative guldiners in the Mint in St. Vitus in Carinthia. In 1507, exceptionally, large silver coins were also minted in Nuremberg, for the Saxon Elector Friedrich III as commemorative coinage to celebrate his appointment as Imperial Governor. During the first quarter of the 16th century (i.e. until 1524) the production of guldiner coins for several other issuers was undertaken; in most cases, however, these were only occasional representative mintages (most commonly with the character of a medal), which were never in circulation to any significant extent.[34]

The exception to this rule are the mintages for which the raw materials were provided by two new rich Central European sources of silver that, at the cusp of the second and third decades of the 16th century, had an influence on the European market for precious metals. One of these sources comprised the silver mines of the Princes of Mansfeld in the depths of the Harz Mountains, in the north-east of Saxony, where the minting of large silver coins was initiated in the year 1521. The second source was the ore mines of the Schlick Counts in north-west Bohemia. It was the extraordinary influx of Czech silver that was the impetus that after 1520 provided the new coins with their name – the thaler.

The derivation of this name (which is then, in various languages, referred to as the dollar, daalder, thaler, etc.) is both generally known[35] and quite simple. In Leipzig in Saxony, where, thanks to the long-term domestic production of silver the most important regular markets in precious metals took place, it was common to label different types of coins according to their place of origin (Schreckenberg groschen, Schneeberg groschen etc.). The sterling silver supplies were regularly subjected to metallurgical tests. Though the new Czech coins were produced exactly in accordance with the Saxon coin standards, to distinguish them in the records it was necessary to identify them by name. They were named simply in accordance with their place of origin "Guldengroschens from the Valley of Saint Joachim" (in German "St. Joachimstaler Guldengroschen"). However because in ordinary market parlance this name was too lengthy, the name was gradually shortened, first to "Joachimstalergroschen," then to "joachimstaler" and finally, "thaler" ("tolar" in Czech or "taler" in German).

Originally the term "taler" was therefore used to define the location of the origin of one specific type of guldengroschen (guldiner), i.e. a coin produced during the first half of the 1520's by four big issuers (according to the Saxon standards in the very Saxony, Bohemia and in Harz at the estate of the Counts of Mansfeld; with different metrological parameters by the Archduke Ferdinand in the Austrian lands) and also in less significant quantities by several other princely, urban or ecclesiastical mints, within the territory of the Holy Roman Empire. The Roman and Spanish King Charles V also initiated the mintage of large silver coins (with a nominal value of 8 reals) in Spain.

Within a relatively short period however (not longer than two decades), the meaning of the term "taler" changed completely and it started to be used in most of Europe for all large silver coins, regardless of their actual silver content. It became a general term, like the groschen = groat (a silver coin of a median value; called "groš" in Czech) or a pfennig = penny (small coins, called "peníz" in Czech). In the mid-16th century in Central Europe every large silver coin was called a thaler, albeit they had varying payment strengths and were issued as units of entirely different monetary systems. In the case of making payments it was necessary to be careful about how much which thaler is actually paying. To make matters even more complicated, the term "taler" also became a numerical monetary unit and the differences between the actual thalers (with various payment strengths) and "talers" as virtual numerical units had to be accurately differentiated. The complexities of the currency, that I will explain in the following chapters, however, were no longer related, however, to Jáchymov (Joachimstal) in Western Bohemian, although the production of thalers also continued there until the second half of the 17th century. The terms "taler," "daler," "daalder" or "dollar" have since then each lived their own independent lives.

But why is that this term became a part of history as one of the most important indicators of a particular type of coin? Older literature finds an explanation in the extremely high production level of the Jáchymov Mint during the second quarter of the 16th century. This is true; however the actual amount of monetized silver does not constitute a decisive argument. Indeed, in Saxony itself, at the time of the inception of the Jáchymov coinage, guldiners had already been produced for many years and also in a large number of copied versions.

The special features and the differences in the production and distribution of Jáchymov coins had other causes and therefore the commercial importance of Czech silver at the beginning of the early modern period temporarily eclipsed that of the other coins of similar types. That is to say that in the 1520's the "taler" was a term that identified a new commodity that began to appear in large quantities on the European money market. A simple, resonant word, one that everybody could remember easily.

Here we will pause for a moment. Why a "commodity"? It was money, after all. Why would they ship thalers from Bohemia to the market in Leipzig, when they represented the highest quality silver currency of that time? Why not use them for making payments directly in Bohemia or why not simply hold on to them? How much should someone pay in exchange for these high quality coins?

Thanks to these seemingly illogical conundrums we may have to explain just why the term "taler" became, in the 1520's a general designation for large silver coins. That is to say that at the beginning of their imaginary life the payment function of thalers was not its primary use. The vast majority of the earliest Jáchymov thalers were not produced in order to make direct payments, but in order to continue trading with them. They constituted a "trading silver" of guaranteed purity, intended for further use, either as a material for the mints of those rulers or towns who did not have their own resources of metallurgical silver available or for the production of silver jewelry and tableware. And actually, thalers were exported from Jáchymov to Leipzig not for sale, but mostly as shares in the mining of Czech silver for Saxon investors. Many Saxon businessmen and several contemporary Czech politicians became wealthy from this trading, but neither the actual King of Bohemia (to whom, de jure, the mineral wealth belonged) nor the indebted Royal Treasury (i.e. the state budget) benefitted very much during the period of the most extensive exploitation of the silver in the Ore Mountains.

The specific political situation in the Kingdom of Bohemia, which, until the end of the 15th century, as the renowned "land of heretics" was isolated from its surrounding European neighbors by an economic embargo, created an economic environment in which, inevitably, things happened differently than in the rest of Europe. It just so happens that when the most important Czech coin of the early modern period was issued in Jáchymov this was not by the King of Bohemia himself, but by descendants of the merchant families from the West Bohemian town of Cheb, whose ancestors had at one time made their living by trading in textiles.

Notes

1. Wolfgang Heß – Dietrich Klose, *Vom thaler zum Dollar 1486-1986* (München, 1986).
2. Carlton R. Scott, *The International Encyclopaedic Dictionary of Numismatics* (Iola, 1996), p. 281.
3. Erich Egg (Hg.), *Der Tiroler thaler: Die Prägungen der Münzstätte Hall in Tirol 1477-1809* (Innsbruck, 1972).
4. Henryk Samsonowicz, "European Economic Zones in the Middle Ages and Early Modern Times: An Attempt to Make a Comparative Analysis," in: Jerzy Kłoczowski (ed.), *East-Central Europe's Position within Europe: Between East and West – L'Europe du Centre-Est dans l'espace européen: Entre l'Est et l'Ouest* (Lublin, 2004): pp. 135-153.
5. Michael North, *Das Geld und seine Geschichte: Vom Mittelalter bis zur Gegenwart* (München, 1994), pp. 41-43 "Europäische Münzproduktion im Spätmittelalter (in kg)."

6. Artur Pohl, *Ungarische Goldgulden des Mittelalters* (Graz, 1974): pp. 21-33; István Dráskóczy, "Der ungarische Goldgulden und seine Bedeutung im ungarischen Außenhandel des 14. und 15. Jahrhunderts," in: Rudolf Tasser – Ekkehard Westermann (Hgg.), *Der Tiroler Bergbau und die Depression der europäischen Montanwirtschaft im 14. und 15. Jahrhundert,* Veröffentlichungen des Südtiroler Landesarchivs Bd. 16 – Pubblicazioni dell'Archivio Provinzionale di Bolzano, Vol. 16 (Innsbruck, 2004): pp. 61-77.
7. Richard Gaettens, *Geschichte der Inflationen: Vom Altertum bis zur Gegenwart* (München, 1982), pp. 40-52; Carlo M. Cipolla, "Currency Depreciation in Medieval Europe," *Economic History Review* 15 (1962-1963): pp. 413–422.
8. John H. Munro, "The Central European Silver Mining Boom, Mint Outputs and Prices in the Low Countries and England 1450-1550," in: E. Cauwenberghe (ed.), *Money, Coins and Commerce* (Leuven, 1991): pp. 119-183; Edwin P. Hunt – James M. Murray, *A History of Business in Medieval Europe 1200-1550* (Cambridge, 1999), pp. 130-131 ("Trading, Tourism and Silver-mining Centers of Late Medieval Western Europe") and pp. 172-174.
9. John U. Nef, "Silver Production in Central Europe 1450-1618," *Journal of Political Economy* 49 (1941): pp. 575-591; reprinted in Dennis O. Flynn – Arturo Giráldez (eds.), *Metals and Monies in an Emerging Global Economy (An Expanding World – The European Impact on World History 1450-1800)* (Aldershot, 1997), pp. 1-17.
10. Petr Vorel, *Stříbro v evropském peněžním oběhu 16. – 17. století (1472-1717)* [Silver in the European monetary circulation of the 16th and 17th centuries (1472-1717)] (Praha, 2009), pp. 69-78.
11. North, *Das Geld*, pp. 52, tab. "Gold – Silber – Relation 1401-1500."
12. Arthur Suhle, *Geld, Münze und Medaille: Führer durch die Schausammlung des Münzkabinetts* (Berlin, 1957), Karte 4: "Die Verbreitung der Sterlinge, Turnosen, Prager- und Meißner Groschen in Deutschland (1250-1500)."
13. Karl Moeser – Fritz Dworschak, *Die große Münzreform unter Erzherzog Sigismund von Tirol (Die ersten großen Silber- und deutschen Buildnismünzen aus der Münzstätte Hall im Inntal), Oesterreichisches Münz- und Geldwesen im Mittelalter VII.* (Wien, 1936), pp. 26-34; North, *Das Geld*, pp. 71, Tab. "Silberproduktion der Reviere Erzgebirge, Schwaz und Joachimstal (in t pro Jahr)."
14. Alfred Nagl, "Das Tiroler Geldwesen unter Erzherzog Sigmund und die Entstehung des Silberguldens," *Numismatische Zeitschrift* 38 (1906, Wien 1907), s. 45 -168.

15. Wolfgang Hess, "The Monetary Union of the Electors of the Rhine," in: Jacques Deraeve – Jean-Marie Duvosquel (eds.), *One Money for Europe – XIth International Numismatic Congress* (Brussels, 1991): pp. 79-82.
16. Walter Haupt, *Sächsische Münzkunde* (Berlin, 1974), tab. "Ausbringen des rheinischen Goldguldens," pp. 77; Bernd Sprenger, *Das Geld der Deutschen: Geldgeschichte Deutschlands* (Paderborn, 1995), pp. 86, tab. "Silberäquivalente des Rheinischen Goldgulden."
17. Rudolf Voglhuber, *Taler und Schautaler des Erzhauses Habsburg von Erzherzog Sigismund v. Tirol 1484 bis Kaiser Franz Josef I. 1896* (Frankfurt am Main, 1971), Nr. 1, pp. 29-30; Elvira Clain-Stefanelli – Vladimir Clain-Stefanelli, *The Beauty and Lore of Coins Currency and Medals* (New York, 1974), p. 115.
18. Moeser – Dworschak, *Die große Münzreform*, pp. 32 i tab. XII/61; Voglhuber, *Thaler und Schautaler*, pp. 29-31, 88-100, tab. XIV-XVI; Egg (Hg.), *Der Tiroler thaler*, pp. 32-33 i tab. 2/38.
19. Charlotte Becher – Ortwin Gamber (Hgg.), *Die Wappenbücher Herzog Albrechts VI. von Österreich (Ingeram-Codex der ehem. Bibliothek Cotta)* (Wien, 1986).
20. Helmut Kahnt – Bernd Knorr, *Alte Maße, Münzen und Gewichte (BI-LEXIKON)* (Leipzig, 1986), p. 330.
21. Egg, *Der Tiroler thaler*, pp. 16; Günther Probst, *Österreichische Münz- und Geldgeschichte: Von den Anfängen bis 1918* (Wien, 1973), pp. 276; "Das silberne Zeitalter (Wie Tirol zum Mittelpunkt Europas wurde)," *ECHO Spezial*, Nr. 5 (Juli 2002), pp. 8-14, 40-42.
22. Arthur Suhle, "Die Neugestaltung des deutschen Münzwesen im 16. Jahrhundert," *Urania – Monatschrift über Natur und Gesellschaft* 18 (1955): pp. 312-315; Gerhard Krug, "Die ersten ab 1500 auf innerdeutschem Boden als Währungsgeld geschlagene thalergepräge," *Hamburger Beiträge zur Numismatik*, Neue Folge, Heft 22/23, 1968/69, Band VII (Hamburg, 1972): pp. 491-506; Bernd Sprenger, *Das Geld der Deutschen: Geldgeschichte Deutschlands* (Paderborn , 1995), pp. 102-103; Carlo M. Cipolla, *Die Odyssee des spanischen Silbers: Conquistadoeres, Piraten, Kaufleute* (Berlin, 1996), pp. 64-65; Michael North, *Kommunikation, Handel, Geld und Banken in der Frühen Neuzeit (Enzyklopädie deutscher Geschichte, Bd. 59)* (München, 2000), p. 27.
23. Moeser – Dworschak, *Die große Münzreform*, p. 34.
24. Karl Otto Müller, *Quellen zur Handelsgeschichte der Paumgartner von Augsburg, 1480-1570* (Wiesbaden, 1955); Moeser – Dworschak, *Die große Münzreform*, p. 119.
25. Joachim Schüttenhelm, "Zur Münzprägung und Silberversorgung süddeutscher Münzstätten im frühen 16. Jahrhundert," in: Werner Kroker – Ekkehard Westermann (Hgg.), *Montanwirtschaft Mitteleuropas von 12.*

bis 17. Jahrhundert – Forschungsprobleme (Stand, Wege und Aufgaben der Forschung), Der Anschnitt – Zeitschrift für Kunst und Kultur im Bergbau, Beiheft 2 (Bochum, 1984), p. 164, Tab. 2: "Der Silberabfluß aus Tirol 1480-1491/1492-1519".

26. Richard Ehrenberger, *Das Zeitalter der Fugger – Geldkapital und Creditverkehr im 16. Jahrhundert I-II* (Jena, 1896); Stephen Zarlenga, *Der Mythos von Geld – die Geschichte der Macht: Vom Tauschhandel zum Euro: eine Geschichte des Geldes und der Währungen* (Zürich, 1999), pp. 116-118.
27. Moeser – Dworschak, *Die große Münzreform*, pp. 154-159 "Tabellen über den Haller Münzbetrieb 1477-1495"; Müller, *Quellen zur Handelsgeschichte der Paumgartner*, p.310.
28. H. Enno van Gelder, "Münzvalvation in Deventer und Dortmund 1488/89," in: Peter Berghaus – Gert Hatz (Hgg.), *DONA NVMISMATICA: Walter Hävernick zum 23. Januar 1965 dargebracht* (Hamburg, 1965), pp. 281-300; Hans J. Vogtherr (Hg.), "Die Lübecker Pfundzollbücher 1492-1496," *Quellen und Darstellungen zur Hansischen Geschichte*, Bd. 41, 1996; Henryk Samsonowicz, "Stosunki monetarne w Gdańsku na przełomie XV/XVI wieku," in: Stefan K. Kuczyński – Stanisław Suchodolski (red.), *Nummus et historia: Pieniądz Europy średniowiecznej* (Warszawa, 1985), pp. 297-302.
29. Wolf Stürmer, *Verzeichnis und Gepräge der groben und kleinen Münzsorten, welche die Kurfürsten, Fürsten und Stände des Oberen Sächsischen Kreis vermöge des Heiliges Reichs Münzordnung auf den Kreis- und Probations tagenvergleichen haben* (Leipzig, 1572; reprint Berlin 1979, ed. Jürgen Gottschalk); Petr Vorel, "Landesfinanzen und Währung in Böhmen (Finanz- und Münzpolitik im Spannungsfeld von Ständen und Königtum während der Regierung Ferdinands I. und Maximilians II.)," in: *Finanzen und Herrschaft (Zu den materiellen Grundlagen fürstlicher Politik in den habsburgischen Ländern und im Heiligen Römischer Reich im 16. Jahrhundert)* [Hgg. von Friedrich Edelmayer – Maximilian Lanzinner – Peter Rauscher], Veröffentlichungen des Instituts für österreichische Geschichtsforschung, Band 38 (München, 2003), pp. 186–214.
30. Gottfried Pusch, *Staatliche Münz- und Geldpolitik in der Niederlanden unter den burgundischen und habsburgischen Herrschern besonders unter Karl V.* (München, 1932); Erich Egg, *Die Münzen Kaisers Maximilians I.* (Innsbruck, undated [cca 1970]), pp. 41, 208-220; Peter Spufford, "Münzverschlechterung und Inflation im spätmittealterlichen und frühmodernen Europa," in: Michael North (Hg.), *Geldumlauf, Währungssysteme und Zahlungsverkehr in Nordwesteuropa 1300-1800* (Köln, 1989), pp. 109-126.
31. Egg, *Die Münzen Kaisers Maximilians I.*, p. 19.

32. Günter Ludwig – Günter Wermusch, *Silber: Aus der Geschichte einer Edelmetalls* (Berlin, 1986), pp. 80.
33. Gerhard Krug, *Die meissnisch-sächsischen Groschen, 1338 bis 1500* (Berlin, 1974,) pp. 91-110; Haupt, *Sächsische Münzkunde*, pp. 67-70.
34. Egg, *Die Münzen Kaisers Maximilians I.*, pp. 196-197; Walter Haupt, *Sächsische Münzkunde*, p. 205, tab. 54/1-5; Otto Tornau, *Münzwesen und Münzen der Grafschaft Mansfeld* (Praha, 1937); John S. Davenport, *German thalers 1500-1600* (Frankfurt am Main, 1979).
35. J. Earl Massey, *America's Money: The Story of Our Coins and Currency* (New York, 1968), p. 38; "Origin of the Word 'Dollar'" in Burton Hobson – Robert Obojski, *Illustrated Encyclopedia of World Coins: A complete reference work of coins and coin collecting with over 2500 photographs* (New York ,1970), pp. 125-126; Clara Semple, *A Silver Legend: The Story of the Maria Theresa Thaler* (Manchester, 2006), p. 8.

2

The First Appearance of the Thaler in Jáchymov

The town of Jáchymov lies in the north-west of the Czech Republic, on the southern side of the Ore Mountains, close the world-famous spa Karlovy Vary (Carlsbad). Jáchymov also enjoyed the renown of being a spa town, due to the therapeutic effects of the local radioactive water. It also attracted extraordinary attention from the world superpowers of the latter part of the 20th century, because it was there, deep beneath the surface of the earth, that the most significant sources of uranium ore in that region of the planet had been discovered that had become subject to the political control of faraway Moscow.

Five hundred years previously, however, not even an alchemist with the wildest fantasy could have imagined for what a range of diverse purposes a raw material like this might one day be utilized. Experienced prospectors had sought in the eponymous Ore Mountains for completely different ores. The results of their efforts were also of interest to the Great Powers of the early modern world, especially if new sources of precious metals were to be found.

However, from the discovery of a substantial ore vein to a newly minted shiny coin was a very long path. The mining industry required a huge capital input and this activity was also generally regarded as a very uncertain investment. In addition to financial resources it also required many industrial experts, knowledgeable concerning the subjects of mining and metallurgy; it required sound contacts in the business world and an experienced management team, able to organize complex work processes and to protect all this against grasping hands with sticky fingers. Whenever any of the Princes and Nobles at the end of the Middle Ages and during the early modern period discovered samples of gold or silver ore on their estates (and this is what almost everybody in Europe was attempting, in the hope of getting rich quickly), they were still far from achieving success, whether for technical reasons (from finding recoverable ore to the production of precious metal bullion was a long path) or for legal reasons.

For example, in the whole of Bohemia all the precious metals hidden in the depths of the earth belong exclusively to the King. This had been provided for by King Wenceslas II in the year 1300 through the famous law entitled "Ius regale montanorum," instituted during the period in which the Kingdom of Bohemia, due to the very rich ore deposits located around and beneath the City of Kutná Hora, was the largest producer of silver in the world known by European geographers and traders.[1] In Kutná Hora the minting had been initiated of a new silver coin of unusually high purity and weight that was called the Prague groschen, which rapidly became accepted as legal tender across a wide swathe of Central Europe, while as a trading silver it was exported far beyond the national borders. By centering the production of these coins in just one Royal Mint, the Czech rulers were able to ensure effective quality control over the output of their coins, as they were reproduced in their multimillions. The immediately recognizable appearance of the Prague groschen, its unvarying appearance (only the names of the Rulers were changing), its large weight in comparison with the other silver coinage in Central Europe at that time, and the reliable quality of the precious metal made this coin the most important form of legal tender in Central Europe during the 14th century. Based on the Czech model the minting of similar coins was later initiated in the Kingdoms of Poland and Hungary and in particular, in 1338, in the Margraviate of Meissen, on the northern (German) side of the Ore Mountains.[2] The Ore mountains ore mines centered around Freiberg in Saxony had earlier begun to gradually yield their silver treasure, but no one had realized that the same treasures were hidden on the southern (Czech) side of the same mountains.

At the cusp of the 14th century the silver wealth of Bohemian Kutná Hora was attracting not only Florentine financiers and Flanders merchants but also European politicians. They were so strongly attracted that the Roman King (and later Emperor) Henry VII, after the Czech Přemyslid Royal House died out in 1306, did not hesitate to give his eldest son, John of Luxembourg, in marriage to the daughter of King Wenceslas II and to then enforce his demands to rule Bohemia – both militarily and based on his Imperial Authority.

Under Luxembourg rule, the political picture in Central Europe changed completely. Significant internal reforms of the Holy Roman Empire jointly enacted by the Roman Emperor and the Czech King Charles IV by the Golden Bull of 1356 brought about stabilization of the situation. Understandably, the Luxembourgs took particular care of their own family interests (as did all their predecessors and successors) and thereby in terms of the Empire they established an exclusive status for their own ancestral domains, uniting them with a supranational formation, called the Lands of the Bohemian Crown. This comprised not only most of the territorial principalities in Silesia (created in the Middle Ages from territory that had originally been Polish as land to be made available for a side branch of the royal Piasts), but also remote Luxembourg. For a number of decades the principal political center of the Holy Roman Empire moved to the imperial seat of Prague.

One hundred years later, by the second half of the 15th century, everything had changed. The deep political crisis in the Empire during the early part of the 15th century, that was also accompanied by a decline in the authority of the Church, resulted in Bohemia in a religious reform movement that then escalated into a long-standing military conflict – the Hussite Wars. During the years 1419-1436 and again from 1439 to 1453 the Kingdom of Bohemia did not have a king and the members of the newly established domestic power elite, i.e. the real winners of the Hussite Wars, had to find ways in which to manage their land even without a Royal Court. A situation such as this was entirely favorable for the Czech nobility and the Royal Cities. They became used to deciding on land issues by themselves.

It was in this manner that over many decades a special form of political organization, known as "Estates Monarchy" came into being in Bohemia. This was a system through which not only could the kingdom function without a King, but that demonstrated a remarkable degree of vitality even during the years of religiously motivated national isolation and of an economic blockade. But therefore, when the Royal Power was later restored, the Czech King's monarchical rights were significantly restricted. The most significant decision was that the consent of the Estates Assembly, known as the Land Diet, would be required. In Bohemia this comprised three formally equivalent estates, in which sat the representatives of the higher nobility (the lordly estate), of the lesser nobility (the knight estate) and of the free royal town (the burgher estate). Theoretically any nobleman could attend the negotiations of the Land Diet; though practical politic was created only by major magnates to power influence of which a broader group of lower-ranking nobles was usually in some way subordinated.

In terms of monetary developments, following the great inflation at the end of the 1450's,[3] the Czech economy did not become stabilized until the generous monetary reform carried out in 1469 by King George I (a member of the noble house of the Lords of Poděbrady). Based on the restarting of extensive silver mining in Kutná Hora, he reintroduced the minting of Prague groschens that was interrupted at the beginning of the Hussite Wars. The newly minted "George's groschens" had the same exterior design (except of course the name of the sovereign) and the same silver content as the groschens of King Wenceslas IV from the early 15th century. In accordance with agreements with neighboring Saxony (the Saxon Duke Albert married the daughter of King George of Poděbrady) Saxon groschens could circulate freely in the Czech lands and vice versa.

Although the Czech King George I achieved great successes in the field of European diplomacy and demonstrated the prowess of a skilled warrior, under pressure from Matthias Corvinus and his domestic supporters he was obliged to seek for a powerful ally. He gave up the Right of Succession of his sons, to whom the Emperor Frederick III had granted the title of Münsterberg Prince together with extensive estates in Eastern Bohemia and Silesia. This agreement concerning the succession to the Czech throne was even concluded with the Polish King Casimir II Jagiello during the lifetime of King George I. The future King of Bohemia was to be Casimir's eldest son Vladislav, whose mother (Casimir's wife) came from the Czech Royal Family (she was the older sister of King Ladislaus the Posthumous, who died in 1457 at a young age and without any offspring).

The Polish Prince Vladislav actually did become King of Bohemia after the death of King George I in 1471, but he took over the throne at a very difficult moment. Not only did he have to struggle with the Hungarian King Matthias Corvinus for the Czech crown, but his royal powers had been significantly constrained by the Czech Estates. This also involved the minting of royal coins. In regard to the exercise of this sovereign right, the King was bound by the decision of the Provincial Diet, which was reaffirmed by an agreement between the King and Czech

Estates in 1485. By this agreement the King undertook that he would not alter the metrological parameters of the domestic coinage without the consent of the Czech Estates. On the part of the Estates, this demand was a defense against the gradual reduction of the weight and purity of Czech coins. In addition, of course, the Czech nobility were taking effective care of their income from the Kutná Hora Mint, which, in the late 15th century represented the only significant source of revenue for the Royal Treasury.[4] Strictly speaking it could have continued to be a source, had the King not been totally in debt.

The King actually owned almost nothing in Bohemia. His former chamber assets (i.e. the estate belonging directly to the King and managed by his office, the Court Chamber) had already been pawned long ago, in addition to the possessions of many former monasteries and religious institutions. The Royal Towns were in fact emancipated from the direct influence of the sovereign and had become an important part of the domestic political scene. The King, in order to obtain money, was borrowing from the domestic magnates who demanded as repayment either the assignment of additional assets of the sovereign (such as the property rights to former Church possessions) or a direct share of the proceeds of the Kutná Hora Mint. An accounting of the coins produced took place in Kutná Hora every week. And every week messengers from the Czech aristocratic castles arrived in Kutná Hora to fetch the appropriate amount for their masters. From the silver wealth of Kutná Hora came weekly to the Royal Treasury at best some tens of three-scores of groschens and sometimes nothing at all.

Czech King Vladislav II. Jagiello was known for his poverty; as a poor king who ruled a rich country, in which the real power and wealth were shared between a few noble ancestral families. However, this situation was not only the privilege of the Czech Estates. In Hungary, where King Vladislav Jagiello ruled from 1490, the situation was similar. In Hungary too the country was ruled by several families of magnates. The trade in precious and non-ferrous metals that were mined primarily in what is now Slovakia was dominated by a powerful group headed by the Thurzó de Bethlenfalva family (see **Tab. III/3**), originally burghers from Krakow in Poland.

During the late Middle Ages the mining was a profitable business. Frenzied prospecting activity had brought success through the discovery of new deposits of iron, copper, tin and other metals. Those who were even luckier also found in their domains ore veins containing precious metals.[5] Following a surprise discovery in the second decade of the 16th century of silver ore with a high content of the precious metal, for some time the Czech Ore Mountains became one of the most important production areas of silver in the world then known to Europeans, since silver had not yet been mined in significant quantities in the Spanish overseas colonies. Of the precious metals imported from overseas to Europe gold was the most significant and its vast supply during the first third of the 16th century caused a relative increase in the market price of silver. Those who controlled the lucrative silver mines in Europe were still profiting from the economic trends: on one hand the South German banking houses that could thereby fund the expansive policies of the Habsburgs with loans, on the other hand the Saxon Dukes, who succeeded in resisting these expansive policies in Central Europe by taking advantage of the economic and political consequences of the Lutheran Reformation.

Both the older and the most recent numismatic literature quite naturally associate the mining of Erzgebirge silver and the minting of the new large silver coins with the Schlik family. But who were exactly the Schliks? You will not find them amongst the old houses of the domestic Czech aristocracy. How did it come about that this family, almost half a millennium after the inception of their production of coins, is still associated with the name thaler that they used, which today is represented by the most common monetary unit in the world, the dollar?

The basics elements of the extraordinary role played by this family were initiated by Kaspar Schlik, a son of the Cheb burgher Heinrich Schlik, who in the late 14th century traded in Cheb in cloth and was engaged in the credit business. The young Kaspar Schlik, who with his origins as the son of a burgher patrician did not enjoy any aristocratic privileges, sometime in the early 15th century began a promising clerical career at the Court of the King, and later Emperor, Sigismund of Luxembourg.[6] We have no additional detailed reports about Kaspar Schlik however, until 1416, when he was accepted as a Secretary in the office of the Supreme Chancellor. In connection with this appointment he apparently obtained a deed from King Sigismund, confirming the right of the Schlik family (namely Kaspar, his father Heinrich and Kaspar's brothers) to use the emblem and the predicate "of Lažany." The promotion of commoner officials to the nobility was not uncommon in the Middle Ages, when they had advanced sufficiently high on the career ladder. By 1428 Kaspar Schlik already held the function of prothonotary while two years later he was a deputy chancellor. At the time that King Sigismund managed to obtain the title of Emperor (in 1433), he assigned the office of Imperial Chancellor, i.e. the Head of the Imperial Diplomatic Office, to Kaspar Schlik of Lažany (on May 31, 1433). The custody of the Emperor's seals, by which the legitimacy of Royal Documents was confirmed, also belonged under his direct authority.

Apart from the imperial functions described above Kaspar Schlik of Lažany also worked as the Czech Chancellor, who was in charge of official correspondence and the issuance of Royal Documents, relating to the Czech Kingdom. Thereby he also acted on behalf of the Emperor as a principal diplomat familiar with the Czech conditions and well versed in the Czech language, who in the mid-thirties of the 15th century negotiated with the Czech Estates concerning the conditions for the acceptance of Sigismund to the Czech throne.

Emperor Sigismund of Luxembourg was the younger brother of the Czech King Wenceslas IV (†1419) and in accordance with dynastic principles he was to accede to the throne in Bohemia in 1419. The Czech Land Diet, however, in 1420 refused to accept him as the King, amongst other reasons because he was blamed for the death of the famous Czech reformer and politician, Jan Hus. Emperor Sigismund was the initiator for convening the Church Council in the city of Constance (1414-1419). The Emperor also invited Master Jan Hus to this Council, and he guaranteed him in writing, ex-imperium, freedom to stay at the Council, freedom of speech for his opinions and his safe return to Bohemia. Master Jan Hus was imprisoned in Constance, however, and in 1415 he was burned at the stake as a heretic for his opinions and criticizing the Catholic Church. Hus's martyrdom became not only a reason to reject the succession of Sigismund of Luxembourg to the Czech throne, but also the stimulus for a wide-reaching reform movement that, in Bohemia, led to the emergence of our own Utraquist Church. As the Emperor and Potentate of the entire Holy Roman Empire Sigismund of Luxembourg attempted in vain to dominate the Kingdom of Bohemia militarily, including through several crusades that he organized personally with the Pope for the suppression of the Czech "heretics." The Czech reform movement, however, had never been defeated militarily and Emperor

Sigismund and also the Papal Court were obliged to accept this peculiar Czech evolution. An agreement (called the Compactata) was concluded in 1434 with the Roman Curia concerning the recognition of the Czech Utraquist Church and the Emperor Sigismund initiated negotiations with the local nobility, concerning the conditions under which (as the last male member of the Czech Royal Family of Luxembourg) he could be accepted as King of Bohemia.

It was the active intervention of Chancellor Kaspar Schlik of Lažany at the Czech Provincial Diet in 1435 that opened the way for a political agreement and for Emperor Sigismund to rule in Bohemia. Kaspar Schlik, with his thorough familiarity with the Czech environment and the Czech language, also took significant personal credit for the acceptance of Albrecht von Habsburg (the husband of Sigismund's only daughter) as the successor to the Czech throne following the death of Sigismund (†1437) and he remained a fiduciary of the new Czech King Albrecht von Habsburg (†1439).

Imperial Chancellor Kaspar Schlik of Lažany (†1449) was at the peak of his career during the short period of the postwar stabilization of the situation in the Czech Kingdom. He demonstrated exceptional abilities and he was able to take advantage very successfully of the patronage of Emperor Sigismund and his son-in-law Albrecht von Habsburg both for his own benefit and for that of his relatives. He had no heirs, but he was able to obtain for his brothers and their offspring magnificent aristocratic titles and vast estates in various parts of Europe which were at that time at least partially under the Emperor's influence. These also included the property rights to some estates in northwest Bohemia, issued by the Royal Office. Although many of Schlik's legal documents dated prior to 1437 already, shortly after the death of Albrecht von Habsburg, provoked astonishment and skepticism regarding their legitimacy, they served Schlik's "family business" extremely well, as was proven several decades later.

When Emperor Sigismund died in early December 1437, his chancellor Kaspar Schlik ordered the issuance of a witness list confirming that he had officially destroyed the Emperor's seal, in order that it could not be used later to produce false antedated Imperial Documents. He obviously knew very well that a forgery of this nature, created by using original office equipment and the seals of the Monarch, would be unrecognizable from the original for his peers and therefore their legality would be difficult to question. During his time in Office there had been ample time to prepare for such an eventuality and probably he had already made for himself several forgeries of this kind in respect to the family, the nobility and the property rights of the Schliks or prepared everything necessary for the possibility of their production later.[7] Technically documents of such a nature could probably not be proved to have been falsified because they would match all the formal requirements and characteristic that such Imperial Documents should have. Therefore it remained doubtful for a long time which of the Schlik documents Emperor Sigismund had actually issued himself, and which had been produced by his Chancellor. Kaspar Schlik later tried to confirm the validity of certain documents by entering their regesta into the Imperial Register (where there were recorded summaries of all the documents that had emanated from the Royal Office), some of them were not registered there at all.

The lien instruments on the West Bohemian estates in the Ore Mountains (primarily a lien in Loket District) were probably real. However disputes had already flared up concerning this property during Kaspar's lifetime in the period of the power struggle following the death of King Albrecht von Habsburg. Standing on the side of the Imperial Chancellor and his relatives was Duke Frederick of Saxony, who also held property rights in northwestern Bohemia. In the period following the deaths of Emperor Sigismund and his son-in-law Albrecht von Habsburg during which the Imperial Power declined considerably, Kaspar Schlik sought for a new political ally, and found him in the person of the Saxon Prince-Elector. The power orientation of the Schliks towards Saxony already had deep roots and their contacts with the Saxon Court were not only the consequence of the discovery of silver ore in the second decade of the 16th century.

The former Imperial Chancellor Kaspar Schlik died heirless in 1449, and he transferred all of his real or perceived rights to his brothers and nephews. Instead of using the historic name "Schlik of Lažany" they then used the title "Count Schlik of Pasoun and Holíč" (or in the German version "Graf von Bassano und Weiskirchen") and looked on themselves as Imperial Counts. These titles were formally associated with a northern Italian estate, Bassano del Grappa that had belonged to the Venetian Republic since the early 15th century. Nobody in Italy, not even in Bassano, was aware of or knew about the formal elevation of this estate to the status of an imperial county. It was just, in its manner, a formal act by which Sigismund of Luxembourg took advantage of a bygone and largely disputed claim of his father, Emperor Charles IV to the estate of Bassano del Grappa, in order to create a new Earldom for his Chancellor Schlik.

In Bohemia, however, it was generally known that Chancellor Kaspar Schlik and his brothers had been born into a burgher family, not a noble one. Even during Kaspar's life, however, through a gradual increase in their apparent nobility theoretically advanced from being a burghers family to the level of Imperial Counts. Such a fundamental change in Estate affiliation was not common even amongst the most important officials and fiduciaries of the Imperial Court. Therefore the associated privileges, based on which Kaspar Schlik and his brothers enjoyed their Earldom, already aroused suspicion during Kaspar's life and their authenticity was questioned.

Following the death of Kaspar Schlik, his younger brother, Matthias Schlik of Passaun, became the main representative of the family. This educated nobleman (a graduate of the University of Bologna) already during his brother's lifetime, in 1443 became a courtier of the new Roman King, Frederick III Habsburg and during the 1450's he acted as a mediator in negotiations between the Saxon Court and the Czech Land Administrator (later to become the King) George of Poděbrady. Most of the property rights obtained by Chancellor Kaspar Schlik, based on which claims to the Jáchymov silver mines resulted, eventually accrued to Matthias Schlik. These were primarily the Castle and the town of Loket with a relatively large area located in Loket District on the Czech-Saxony border (estates in Sokolov and in Ostrov nad Ohří and more). Matthias Schlik even expanded this territorially relatively compact unit with some mortgaged assets acquired from the Czech King George I. The most important of these, however, was Loket District itself, which from the very beginning of its Schlik tenure became an "apple of discord."

Loket (as an entire district) had already been given to Kaspar Schlik and his relatives by the Emperor Sigismund as a pledge. This collateral had been formulated as a temporary measure, nevertheless Matthias Schlik (in fact like other land magnates in Bohemia) sought to consolidate his legal right to his acquired estates. At the beginning of the 1470's this land of Matthias' was mortgaged and the King was not entitled to repay this debt until after the death of Matthias himself and of all his sons. The Schliks had thereby theoretically guaranteed their ownership of this territory for many years, and they began to behave accordingly towards their vassals. Although other Czech and Moravian lords sometimes proceeded in the same manner, only in the case of the Schliks were there dramatic and bloody conflicts, during which the burghers were willing to take up arms against their masters. Other local magnates on the other hand supported the towns under their dominion and provided them with all kinds of advantages, as the economic development of their vassal towns was bringing them considerable benefits during that period. The Loket burghers, however, refused to recognize Matthias Schlik and his sons as their direct landlords, referring to their historic privileges, granted in the 14th and 15th centuries by the Luxembourgs. Indeed, even though Matthias Schlik now boasted the title of Imperial Count, during that period he still lived as did his peers and friends from childhood, who all remembered clearly that he had grown up as burgher's son in nearby Cheb. Similarly, the minor nobility in Loket County did not accept the Schliks as their feudal lords and refused to pay the taxes to them that were due to the sovereign. Every poor knight considered himself as "more noble" than the first generation of wealthy merchants promoted to a peerage.

Disputes about Loket District, abounding in bloody clashes and "domestic wars" between the local ancestral nobility, the Loket burghers and their lien masters, then lingered on through local history until the early 16th century. The rulers of neighboring Saxony also interfered in the struggles over this border region, who had a considerable interest themselves in taking over the Schliks' dominant position in the Ore Mountains. In 1471 they initiated direct negotiations with Matthias Schlik concerning the sale of Loket District to neighboring Saxony, which, however, the Czech King George I categorically rejected. The recurring disagreements between the Loket burghers and the Schliks eventually resulted in the destruction of the town in 1476. Matthias Schlik and his sons burnt down the town, then conquered it and forced the surviving burghers, under threat of violence, to swear allegiance to them as their hereditary nobility. Such a procedure was contrary to the laws of the Czech lands and caused a tidal wave of dissent. This entire controversy also had an international impact, since Loket District was one of the few areas of "heretical" Bohemia, in which the majority of the population adhered to the Catholic faith. For their injustice towards the citizens of Loket a religious oath was imposed against the Loket Schliks not only by the Bishop of Wroclaw but also by the Pope himself.

Matthias Schlik defended his actions against the inhabitants of Loket District on the basis of imperial privilege, the content of which was deemed to be suspect by the lawyers of the day, but that in formal terms showed indications of being genuine imperial documents. This dispute was finally resolved by a decision of the Czech Land Court of 10th March 1486, stating: Claims concerning Property Rights and any other claims by the Schliks and/or their heirs shall be deemed invalid if they are in conflict with the general laws and regulations in force in the Kingdom of Bohemia.

This resolution was later incorporated into a newly instituted provincial law as an extremely significant legal precedent for dealing with any similar disputes in the future. It was also one of the important milestones in the gradual exclusion of the Kingdom of Bohemia from the political union of the countries of the Holy Roman Empire, a process that was concluded in the year 1495. From that time (until the early 18th century) the Czech lands were no longer a part of the Roman-German Empire[8] that was later re-established with new frontiers, which in connection with the subsequent mintage of silver thalers is rather an important circumstance. However, in 1486, any historic legal privileges, issued by the Roman Kings and Emperors were already losing their validity in the territory of the Kingdom of Bohemia, if they were incompatible with Bohemian law.

When Matthias Schlik died of old age in 1487, his property was divided between his three sons. In this manner three main branches of the Schlik family were created, identified in accordance with the principal domiciles of the three brothers: Loket, acquired by Jerome Schlik (†1491); Falknov (today called Sokolov) acquired by Nicholas Schlik (†1522) and Ostrov nad Ohří, acquired by Kaspar Schlik († before 1516). Some property rights remained common to all the brothers; this ultimately also concerned the silver mining. Therefore, the Schliks acted together in negotiations concerning the minting of thalers at the cusp between the second and third decades of the 16th century, not as an entire family (this issue did not concern the second cousins, i.e. the grandsons of the Nicholas Schlik who had died in 1444), but as an extended family, claiming historic property rights, inherited from their father (or grandfather) Matthias Schlik (+1487).

Due to the extensive land and property obtained by the Schlik family during the era of Imperial Chancellor Kaspar Schlik, at the beginning of the early modern period the Schliks belonged amongst the richest nobility in Bohemia. However during the second half of the 15th century they did not integrate with the Czech aristocracy, by whom they were still perceived to some extent as a foreign element. Their social background was under-privileged in terms of local norms, they professed the Catholic faith (in generally Utraquist Bohemia), and they differed in their language from most of the local nobility. The native tongue of the Schliks, who have been more connected socially with the Saxon Court, remained German. The aristocratic class in the Kingdom of Bohemia favored the Czech language which at the end of the 15th century also became the official language in which the minutes of the meetings of the Land Court and the Land Diet were kept and also all the records of land property (Latin was previously used for these purposes in Bohemia during the Middle Ages). These circumstance, and also the ongoing disputes in Loket District referred to above, are probably the reasons why, since the era of Kaspar Schlik (who served as Supreme Chancellor of the Kingdom of Bohemia in the years 1429-1439) no significant office has been assigned in the Czech Kingdom to any member of the Schlik family, even though in terms of their property ownership and social position they appeared to be predestined to it.

The "Schlik Case," however, had not been definitively closed even by the resolution of the Land Diet of 1486. Sebastian Schlik, a third generation member of the family, at the turn of the 15th and 16th centuries once again unleashed a controversy with the Loket burghers. For his argument he again used the old papers of his great-uncle Kaspar Schlik and demanded the obedience of Loket citizens as if they were his hereditary vassals. The Land Court agreed with the burghers, who entered into a defensive military alliance with the minor nobility of Loket District. In early 1504 a war began between the parties, because Sebastian Schlik refused to acquiesce in the decision of the Land Court. He claimed that, as an Imperial Count, he does not have to respect the court decision, because the Czech Lords who sit in the Land Diet are not equal to him in terms of their nobility. He demanded of King Vladislav Jagiello that the Saxon Duke as Imperial Elector should adjudicate this dispute in the role of a mediator.

This solution was absolutely inadmissible for the Czech lords, because it discounted the authority of the Land Court as the highest legal authority of the Estate Monarchy. It would also be very dangerous for the domestic nobility as a legal precedent, if preference were given to the formal imperial earldom (awarded to the burghers family) over the rights of the old ancestral nobility. The Czech aristocracy fundamentally rejected the argument of the "higher nobility" of the Schliks, because the Estates system in Bohemia did not recognize any imperial titles. The domestic nobility in the early 16th century was divided in terms of nobility into just two groups, the Lords Estate (the Lords and the Higher Nobility) and the Knights Estate (the Knights and the Lower Nobility). If the King were to comply with the demand of Sebastian Schlik, Imperial Princes who became members of the Land community would in the future be superior in terms of nobility to the old ancestral aristocracy. For this reason the Czech aristocracy was willing to intervene in the early 16th century in the protracted dispute over Loket District substantially more assertively than it ever had previously.[9]

Sebastian Schlik was declared by the Land Court in 1504 to be an enemy of the land, deprived of honor, all his property and estate privileges and sentenced to death. The Kingdom of Bohemia deployed its land troops, amounting to 3,500 foot soldiers, 150 horsemen and 200 chariots to besiege the Schliks' residence at Loket Castle. Faced by this superior strength, after a while the Schliks capitulated; however they managed to negotiate the annulment of the previous decision relating to Sebastian Schlik. In an extensive agreement dating from 1506 they made a commitment to continue to respect the rights of the Loket burghers and the other legal practices of the Kingdom of Bohemia, including the local principles that define the nobility. Consistently used therefore in the relevant documents is the manner of addressing: "*...Lord Sebastian of Lažany...*," because, even as Imperial Counts, the Schliks were prohibited to claim a higher position than that belonging to other members of the Lords Estate.

I have deliberately described in greater detail the older conflicts between the Schlik family and the Czech Estates community as a whole (not just with individual nobles), referred to above because these connections are essential for understanding the negotiations that followed after the discovery of silver ore in the Schlik domains soon after Loket Castle was besieged by troops of the Czech Estates.

The discovery of silver ore in this area in the middle of the second decade of the 16th century was not particularly surprising. The presence of metal ores (tin, copper and silver) in the Ore Mountains was generally known. By the end of the 15th century, after the new discovery of large deposits near the border on the Saxon side, groups of prospectors were heading into the depths of the Czech forests, surveying for new ore veins. Occasionally they found some ore there, but if the rock was not sufficiently metalliferous, it was not worthwhile to extract it. Why break up piles of stones, interlaced with veinlets of silver ore, when nowhere nearby are there smelters that could effectively process the ore? And to carry it over the mountains into Saxony? That would work out pretty expensive and, in addition, it was officially forbidden. However, information about Czech silver in the Ore Mountains was probably already known previously. That is perhaps why in the second half of the 15th century the Dukes of Saxony were showing such interest in many areas on the Czech side of the Ore Mountains, and especially in the Schlik domains in Loket District. The experience of mining in the nearby Saxon mines gave the idea that the discovery of even a small vein on the surface could lead to a nice lump of silver hidden inside the rock massif.[10]

Even around Jáchymov trial mining was already taking place in the 15th century. Though in the year 1512 in the vicinity of the Konradsgrün settlements no one knew any longer who was digging where and with what result. The old abandoned adit on the hill named Schrottenberg however attracted the interest of prospectors, who were perhaps more fortunate or better experienced than their predecessors. Two miners called Bach and Öser at the northeastern edge of the Schliks' Ostrov estate, close to the Saxon border, found a highly metalliferous deposit of silver ore, quite close to the surface. Mining specialists from neighboring Saxony, Kaspar Margenthal and Ägidius Bäuerlein were invited to an assessment of the potential profitability of future mining. They assessed this prospected source of ore as being extensive and of exceptional quality and recommended its extraction also based on the suitable natural conditions.

The Schliks themselves, however, did not have sufficient initial capital to start mining and processing silver. I'm referring to "the Schliks" specifically because the issues concerning the silver mines did not involve just one individual, as has been explained above. It therefore became common practice in Bohemia to talk about the "Lord Schliks," always in the plural. For that matter this was legitimate, since most of their property rights in the West Bohemia territory were formulated as a family pledge, not tied to individuals, but to entire generations of a family. The division of the property in 1487 into three parts (Loket, Sokolov and Ostrov) was only an internal agreement within the family and in the event of the extinction of one of the branches of the family, the liens would have fallen to other relatives. Therefore, even though a fabulous wealth of silver was found in the territory over which, in accordance with the prior division, the sons of Kaspar Schlik of Ostrov († before 1516) ruled, the descendants of Kaspar's older brethren from the Loket and the Sokolov branches also had a legitimate claim to it. And that is to say that negotiations between relatives concerning property (especially if there is indeed great wealth) are not always simple.

But before it came to the division of the proceeds, it was necessary to ensure the ongoing mining and to conclude contracts with the investors. Already, since 1516, when these negotiations were first documented in detail, it is Stephan Schlik of Passaun, the eldest son of the already deceased Kaspar Schlik (i.e. a grandson of Matthias Schlik and the grandnephew of the Imperial Chancellor, Kaspar Schlik) appears in the forefront.[11] He was a young man, less than thirty years old, when he became the principal representative of the Schlik family in regard to all subsequent negotiations and financial transactions. During that time the older Schliks were still alive, to whom, in accordance with the principle of ancestral hierarchy, the rights of the "head of the household" belonged (the contemporary social standards respected old age as a prerogative), but the family council, apparently rationally, mandated the ambitious and capable Stephan with a difficult task of this nature. The formal "elder of the family," Stephan's uncle Nicholas Schlik (born after 1450, †1522) was already too old to be traveling back and forth across the Ore Mountains between Annaberg and the Prague Diets and Stephan's cousin, Sebastian Schlik of Loket (born about 1470, †1527) based on his earlier excesses in the times of "Loket War" (1504-1506) was a "persona non grata" for Czech aristocratic society. The Ostrov branch of the Schliks was also more closely linked by their family ties to the Czech nobility: Stephan's mother came from amongst the Lords of Gutstein and Stephan's brother in law was Kristofer Pflug of Rabstein (it was within the Rabstein family that Stephan had found his wife in

1521). Family ties within the local aristocracy also played a vital role at that time in the negotiations regarding the Schlik silver mines.

The actual extraction and the processing of the silver ore in the newly commissioned smelters commenced in 1516, when, in the course of a few summer months, in a deep and steep forest valley a new mining settlement, was built numbering several hundreds of temporary dwellings (see **Tab. IV/1**). In the mining environment it was customary to give the names of saints to new mining districts. In this case, the choice fell on St. Joachim, apparently due to the fact that some of the mining personnel had come directly from Saxon Annaberg (according to the Christian doctrine St. Joachim and St. Anna were the parents of the Virgin Mary, i.e. the grandparents of Jesus Christ). The argentiferous valley was therefore named "the Valley of Saint Joachim" (in German the Latin-German version of "Sanctus Joachims Thal" was used). Two years after the commencement of mining (in 1518) it had already been necessary to adjudicate the relationship-problems created within the diverse mining community by the arrivals from different parts of Europe, by the issuance of a special mining order, adopted from the Saxon Annaberg.

Neither Stephan Schlik nor his relatives were particularly involved with the actual organization of the mining operations. For ensuring the extraction of the silver ore and of its processing in smelters Schliks took advantage of the experience of the Saxon miners and also of the "kverks," that is to say the investors who were financing the mining and who would receive an agreed share of the profits. We do not have records of the actual identities of these investors, however in 1516 a wealthy Annaberg burgher named Hans Thumshirn was already participating in negotiations concerning the future financing of the Jáchymov mines. It can therefore be assumed that already during the early years of the mining in Jáchymov a substantial portion of the local silver found its market in Saxony and in the other financial centers of business life in Central Europe. A clearer impression of the possible nature of these business relationships emerges from the contract that the Schliks concluded in 1518 with the Nuremberg bankers Hans Nützel and Jacob Welser. The Nurembergers offered the Schliks a loan of 34,000 Rhine-guldens, which was to be repaid in Erzgebirge silver: One pound of pure silver supplied (approx. 234 grams) was valued at 8¼ Rhine-guldens, which was slightly less than the standard price of silver on the Leipzig market.[12] From this amount, however, the kverks should receive their 8 Rhine-guldens in full as the reimbursement of mining costs and a share of the proceeds; only ¼ of a Rhine-gulden (i.e. 15 kreutzers) would be allocated towards the repayment of the Schlik's debt.

Thirty-four thousand guldiners represented a very large sum of money at that time for which, in 1518, the Schliks would be able to buy an estate together with the entire acreage of Loket District and including several towns and castles. It is very unlikely that they would have invested this entire amount in the construction of a new castle called Freudenstein, as is often referred to in the literature. No castle or chateau in Bohemia (albeit the most highly-priced) could have cost so much. The Schliks were supposed to repay the debt of 34,000 Rhine-gulden referred to above within three years. Under the given conditions this would have meant supplying to the market a total quantity of 136 thousand pounds of pure silver (cca. 31.8 tons), in the form of bullion or as minted coins. In the contract no differentiation was made between these two forms of supply; minted silver coins were also considered simply as a commodity, just like silver in the market. The contract with the Nuremberg bankers was very disadvantageous for Schlik and meant a de facto Nuremberg monopoly of the supplies of Jáchymov silver. Based on subsequent developments, however, it is evident that the contract with the Nurembergers was not implemented on the scale planned and that the Schliks apparently only partially utilized this credit during the year 1518.[13]

The problem arose not only in regard to the actual ability to repay the money borrowed, but also the manner in which the installments would be delivered. In the Czech Kingdom the export of metallurgical silver abroad was prohibited, and this circumstance could easily become a weapon to be used by any of the Schliks' enemies in Bohemia – and there were still enough of these who had "old accounts" to settle with them. By 1519, however, the illegal trade in Czech silver had a significant protector in the person of Emperor Maximilian I. The Emperor Maximilian was the primary guardian of the minor Czech King Louis Jagiello (born in 1506), who formally acceded to the throne following the death of his father Vladislav II in the year 1516. Emperor Maximilian I naturally protected the interests of the southern German bankers, to whom, in accordance with the agreement from the year 1518, the majority of precious metal extracted was to be delivered, because he personally was their major creditor. Following Maximilian's death in the early part of 1519, the power constellation, however, was substantially altered and the Schliks had to restart negotiations concerning the conditions under which it would be possible to export the mined silver.[14]

The King of Bohemia at that time was the very young Louis Jagiello, who had not yet attained adulthood. He was represented by a group of trustees, amongst whom, following Maximilian's death, George Hohenzollern of the House of the Brandenburg Margraves played a crucial role. The Schliks had the significant support of the Saxon court, which right at the end of the second decade of the 16th century in connection with the rapid expansion of Lutheran reformation was becoming a significant political counterweight to the Habsburgs. Major investments were arriving from nearby Saxony, based on which mining also was initiated in Jáchymov. It was therefore logical that the Saxon party would wish to ensure through the supply of silver both the return of their investment and their own business profit.

Ultimately, however, the decision was made on the Czech side. Representatives of the local nobility agreed to the export abroad of mined silver, but only with the proviso that the precious metal would take the form of minted coins, which was intended to facilitate control of the total amount of silver exported. Thereby a system was created, through which the rights of the minor King could be guaranteed for a share of the mined silver. This share, however, was not to be levied by the Royal Treasury, but applied towards the repayment of the King's debts (and likewise in regard to the proceeds from the mines and the Mint in Kutná Hora): from every monetarized pound of silver the Schliks were required to pay seven Czech groschens (i.e. 4% of the price of the metal); this royal share was to be divided between the three royal creditors from amongst the most important domestic politicians: i.e. Zdenek Lev of Rožmitál, Ladislav of Sternberg and Johannes Pflug of Rabstein. This agreement was concluded during the year 1519, when the first test samples of oldest Jáchymov thalers and double-talers bearing the year "1520" were also created. These were made as sample specimens for a meeting of the Czech Lands Diet, which was supposed to give its opinion concerning the production of new coins in Jáchymov.

The Czech Lands Diet in its resolution of 9th January 1520 ordered Lords Schliks to establish a new Mint where both the standard Czech Land coins i.e. the Prague groschens, following the Kutná Hora model (using one third of the coinage metal) and also the new coins, the "guldengroschens" and their fractions in accordance with the Saxon metrology (using the other two thirds of the coinage metal) should be minted. By this order of the Land Diet the exports of Jáchymov silver in the form of these new coins were at least partially legalized, even though in Schliks did not yet have the consent of the King himself, who was then still a minor. King Louis Jagiello, however, confirmed the agreement described above shortly afterwards in 1523 when he had assumed governing.

From 1520 extensive coining of large silver coins commenced on a regular basis at the newly established Jáchymov Mint, in accordance with the Saxon model. The actual production of the coins was directed by Saxon experts and the preparatory work was undertaken with the knowledge and consent of the Duke of Saxony. Therefore in accordance with the preliminary agreements the new Schlik coins (unlike the Czech government coins, the Prague groschens), had completely free access to the Saxon market and could be imported in unlimited quantities as merchandise. The traditional strong contact between the Schlik family and the Saxon Court was also demonstrated by the rapid spreading of the Lutheran Reformation from Saxony to the Czech side of the Ore Mountains. Luther's teachings were followed by most of the current members of the Schlik House.

The main export destination point for the Jáchymov products was then the precious metal market in Leipzig. Based on the surviving documentation, which contains information concerning the quantity of silver subjected to quality tests, we have a fairly accurate picture of how much of the metal was exported from Jáchymov to Leipzig during the period from 1520 to 1528.[15]

The operation of the entire Mint depended on this exporting that ensured the highest profits. Lower denominations (i.e. the Prague groschen) were not produced at that time in Jáchymov to any great extent, so for the Jáchymov Mint, and for the local silver mines, smaller coins were bought abroad in exchange for quality thalers to ensure the payments for the employees. This was both easier and cheaper.

This apparent paradox, in my opinion, conceals the "secret" of the extraordinary expansion of the use of these specific "guldiner groschens from Jáchymov" (Joachimstalers = thalers) on the European money market. The Saxon mines in Erzgebirge in addition to the Tyrolean mines in

Schwaz at that time produced more silver than did Jáchymov. However, these were both sovereign enterprises and their managers (regents) had to provide coins in their countries for regular circulation. Much of the silver mined had to be monetarized in the form of lower denominations, e.g. Saxon groschens or kreutzers or Tyrolean pfundners (see **Tab. VI/3**). Ferdinand of Habsburg or the Dukes of Saxony might also use silver bullion for their trading in precious metals because it was cheaper (with no cost for minting coins) and because no one could prevent it.[16]

In the case of the Schliks it was a completely different story. They did not have to worry about the production of standard current coins; a sufficiency of these was provided for monetary circulation by the Royal Mint in Kutná Hora. Although the Diet resolution of the year 1520 obliged them to use a third of monetized metal for minting Prague groschens, it was really difficult to control this activity. The production costs for the minting of coinage of lower denominations from silver of a lower quality were, in the final balance, higher than that for producing thalers; in addition the Prague groschen could not be exported to the Saxon market. Therefore, in Jáchymov, it was thalers that were coined first and foremost. And because at the same time the Schliks were not permitted to export metallurgical silver bullion outside the country, the vast majority of the silver mined in Jáchymov was processed into large trading coins – thalers. In 1520's for these reasons they dominated the market for precious metals, because there was a surplus of them available in comparison with the silver trading coins of the thaler-type minted by the other issuers.[17]

The immense popularity of the Jáchymov thalers was not based solely on their high silver content (without their stable weight and the purity of the metal they would not have survived in the market), but also on their quality workmanship and their impressive appearance, which were to some extent influenced by the resolution of the Diet in 1520 referred to above, prescribing the appearance of coins that were to be minted in Jáchymov. The large silver coins, i.e. the guldengroschens, did not have any domestic tradition however, therefore when designing their outer appearance the Schliks were not bound to any specific pattern, only by the generalized condition that one side of the coin should be "royal" (with the name of the Sovereign) and that on the other side the coat of arms of the Lords Schliks should be placed.

The external design of the Schlik thalers, while strictly respecting the resolution of the Diet, still offered sufficient space for adequate ancestral representation, which certainly provoked the envy of many princes, both domestic and foreign. The obverse side was conceived traditionally, with the image of the heraldry of the Kingdom of Bohemia (a double-tailed crowned lion), placed freely in the middle of the coin field, without a shield; with a peripheral inscription in Latin bearing the name and the title of the ruler ("LVDOWICVS: PRIM: D: GRACIA: RE: BO," i.e. Louis I., by the Grace of God King of Bohemia). The reverse side, however, is completely atypical. On the large silver coin appears the figure of a saint, but not the patron saint of a country (such as St. Wenceslas in Bohemia or St. Ladislav on the Hungarian ducat), but simply Saint Joachim as the protector of a specific mining area that was named after him ("Valley of St. Joachim," Sanctus Joachims Thal). This saint is also symbolized by the letters "S" and "I" on his right and left sides. Another new element is the noble ancestral coat of arms in a distinctive form, located at the Saint's feet on the axis of the coin. Until then no private aristocratic coat of arms had appeared in such a form on any European coinage; the heraldic decoration of coins was a common practice, but this consisted almost exclusively of land insignia or of the family crests of the Royal Dynasties. The Diet resolution, however, expressly permitted the Schliks to use their coat of arms as an image on coins, an opportunity that they took advantage of. The text of the Diet resolution, however, does not say anything that indicates that the Schliks should minted new coins using their name, i.e. that on the coins (next to the name of the King on the reverse side) there should also be the name of the issuer from the Schlik family (on the opposite, obverse side). Stephan Schlik and his brothers did not make any mistake even in regard to this fine detail. The resolution of the Czech Provincial Diet states that coins can be minted in Jáchymov by Stephan Schlik and his brothers. Therefore, on the periphery of the reverse side are written (in several slightly differing versions of acronyms) these letters: "AR: DOM: SLI: STE: ET. FRA: COM: D: B," which in a full transcript meant "ARMA DOMINORUM SLICORUM STEFANI ET FRATRES COMITUM DE BASSANO," i.e. "the coat of arms (crest) of the Lords Schliks, Stephan and his brothers, the Earls of Passaun" (see **Tab. IV/2; V/2**).[18]

Apart from the Saxon investors, also participating in the revenue from the Jáchymov Mint, after the year 1520, were not only numerous members of the Schlik House, but also other Czech nobles, who were involved in the project by their ownership of shares in it. Therefore King Louis Jagiello during his brief and lackluster reign was not able to achieve any substantive changes. He himself as the King of Bohemia had never obtained any direct benefit from the wealth of Jáchymov. The Royal Treasury, however, was supported financially, though indirectly, by large loans from the Czech Lord Zdenek Lev of Rožmitál, who was one of the "silent" participants in the Schlik minting, from the proceeds of which Lord Zdenek received installments towards the payment of the King's debts. The Schliks were well aware that the future of their minting in Jáchymov was directly dependent on the Czech King. If the King were a powerful monarch, who had sufficient funds, in the future he would be able, without facing any major legal challenges, to enforce the repayment of the lien on the Schlik estates. The younger Schliks, who prior to the year 1520 had been significantly engaged in negotiations concerning the establishment of the private mint, therefore attempted to gain the trust of the young King. They also embarked with him on a fateful campaign against the Turks. The troops of the Czech and Hungarian King Louis Jagiello clashed tragically with the Turks in the unequal battle of Mohacs in the year 1526. The young King died during the retreat from the battlefield; Stephan Schlik also failed to return from the battlefield. His body was never found; however after some time he was declared dead. In order to say farewell to him his brothers made a spectacular renaissance "death" thaler in the Jáchymov Mint, on the periphery of which it is stated that Stephan Schlik sacrificed his life for his country in the fight against the Turks (see **Tab. VI/1**).

The Schliks' minting in Jáchymov continued, however, even after 1526, because, in essence, it was not dependent on any individual member of the Schlik family. Mining, manufacturing and the sale of coins, these were all in the hands of professionals (including miners and financiers) who simply levied the relevant shares for the Schliks' treasury. The actual deaths of Stephan Schlik and King Louis in 1526 therefore did not directly create much change in Jáchymov. Only the name of the Czech King on the reverse side was replaced with: "FERDINANDVS PRIMVS" (see **Tab. VI/2**).

The new Czech King Ferdinand I of Habsburg was well aware of the importance to the Treasury of the Jáchymov mines and of the mint and within a few months he enforced a major change. In the year 1528 the Czech Provincial Diet decided that the production of coins in Jáchymov under the direction of the Schliks was to the detriment of the rights of the "Bohemian Crown" and annulled the Diet decision of the year 1520. In accordance with the option contract the profits from the mining business and the short-term symbolic fees derived from the volume of silver monetarized were retained for the Schliks for several years, but in comparison with the income that was engendered by the activities of the Mint, these were really symbolic amounts.

In 1528 the Jáchymov Mint was transferred to direct royal administration and already in the following year (1529) a new form of thaler started to be issued, bearing pictures of the Czech King and the Czech and Hungarian heraldries (see **Tab. VII/1**). Somewhat paradoxically, the new Ferdinand Jáchymov thalers continued to be minted (until 1547) in accordance with the original metrological standards derived from the Saxon guldiner, although Ferdinand himself had a different concept of the monetary system, that I shall describe in greater detail in the following chapter. Without the consent of the Czech Land Diet, however, he was not able, based on his own will, to alter this situation. The final decision that the Land Diet adopted concerning the metrological parameters of the Jáchymov coinage, was from the year 1520 – in which it is clearly stated that coins should be produced there, corresponding to the Saxon guldiners, not to the Tyrolean coins.

At the time that the Czech King Ferdinand I took over the Jáchymov Mint, the term "taler" had already started to be used in Central Europe as a generic name for the large silver coins but it was not linked only to Jáchymov products. The oldest known record, in which the term "taler" is already used in its broader sense (while at the same time still distinguishing it from the "real thaler," i.e. the coin from Jáchymov) is in an accounting document from Augsburg in Southern Germany dating from the year 1533;[19] in the 1540's, in the hereditary inventories of the Port of Hamburg "talers" are spoken about without the necessity for specifying the meaning of this already well known and widely used term.[20]

Notes

1. Karel Castelin, *Grossus Pragensis: Der Prager Groschen und seine Teilstücke 1300-1547* (Braunschweig, 1973); Petr Vorel, *Od pražského groše ke koruně české 1300-2000: Průvodce dějinami peněz v českých zemích* (Praha, 2004).
2. Gerhard Krug, *Die meissnisch-sächsischen Groschen, 1338 bis 1500* (Berlin, 1974); Henryk Samsonowicz, "European Economic Zones in the Middle Ages and Early Modern Times: An Attempt to Make a Comparative Analysis," in: Jerzy Kłoczowski, ed., *East-Central Europe's Position within Europe: Between East and West – L'Europe du Centre-Est dans l'espace européen: Entre l'Est et l'Ouest* (Lublin,) 2004), pp. 135-153.
3. Richard Gaettens, *Geschichte der Inflationen: Vom Altertum bis zur Gegenwart* (München, 1982), pp. 40-51; Peter Spufford, "Münzverschlechterung und Inflation im spätmittelalterlichen und frühmodernen Europa," in: Michale North (Hg.), *Geldumlauf, Währungssysteme und Zahlungsverkehr in Nordwesteuropa 1300-1800* (Köln, 1989), pp. 109-126.
4. Jarmila Hásková, *Die Währungs- und Münzentwicklung unter den Jagellonen in Böhmen 1471-1526 (Sborník Národního muzea v Praze, řada A, č.1/2)* (Praha, 1969); Petr Vorel, " 'Groše české' a 'groše míšeňské' jako peněžní početní jednotky 15. až 18. století," in: Eduard Šimek (red.), *Dokumentace a prezentace dějin české mince a měny grošové doby v našich muzeích* (Praha, 2002), pp. 57-68.
5. Dennis O. Flynn, "Spanish-American silver and world markets in the sixteenth century," *Economic Forum* 10, no. 2 (Salt Lake City, Utah, 1979-1980): pp. 46-72; Stanley J. and Barbara H. Stein, *Silver, Trade and War: Spain and America in the Making of Early Modern Europe* (Baltimore – London, 2000), pp. 106-146.
6. Heinrich Gradl, *Die ältesten Geschichte der Schlick*, Adler 16, 1886; Artur Zechel, *Studie über Kaspar Schlick* (Praha, 1939).
7. Max Dvořák, "Die Fälschungen des Reichskanzklers Kaspar Schlick," *Mitteilungen des Instituts für Österreichische Geschichtsforschung* 22 (1901): pp. 51-107; Albrecht Pennrich, *Die Urkundenfälschungen des Reichskanzlers Kaspar Schlick neben Beiträgen zur seinen Leben* (Gotha, 1901).
8. Vorel Petr, "Die Länder der böhmischen Krone und das Heilige Römische Reich in der Frühen Neuzeit [The Czech Lands and the Holy Roman Empire in the Early Modern Age]," in: Jiří Pešek – Petr Vorel [Hgg.], *Neue tschechische Interpretationen der Fragen des tschechisch-deutschen Zusammenlebens* (47. Deutscher Historikertag / Dresden 2008 – Die Vorträge der tschechischen Gastsection) (Magdeburg, 2011): pp. 21-32.
9. Josef Petráň, "Stavovské království a jeho kultura v Čechách (1471-1526)," in: *Pozdně gotické umění v Čechách (1471-1526)* (Praha 1984):

pp. 14-72; Josef Macek, *Jagellonský věk v českých zemích (1471-1526), 3. Města* (Praha, 1998): pp. 323-376.

10. Lubomír Nemeškal, *Jáchymovská mincovna v 1. polovině 16. století (1519/1520-1561) – Význam ražby tolaru* (Praha, 1964); Eduard Šimek, "Tolarové období," in: *Peníze v českých zemích do roku 1919* (Praha, 1996); pp. 63-75; Lubomír Nemeškal, *Počátek ražby českého tolaru a konec ražby pražského groše (1469-1561) – Peněžně – historická studie* (Praha, 1997).
11. Nemeškal, *Jáchymovská mincovna v 1. polovině 16. století*, pp. 21-28.
12. Walter Haupt, *Sächsische Münzkunde* (Berlin, 1974), pp. 94-103.
13. Josef Janáček, "Die Fugger und Joachimstal," *Historica* 6 (1963): pp. 109-144.
14. Petr Vorel, "History of the Jáchymov Mint and catalogue of coinage from the years 1519/1520-1619," in: Lubomír Nemeškal – Petr Vorel, *Dějiny jáchymovské mincovny a katalog ražeb I. 1519/1520 – 1619* (Pardubice, 2010): pp. 261-268.
15. Lubomír Nemeškal – Petr Vorel, *Dějiny jáchymovské mincovny a katalog ražeb I. 1519/1520 – 1619* (Pardubice, 2010), p. 39, Tab. 3 "Celkový přehled jakostních testů jáchymovských tolarů v Lipsku" and Tab. 4 "Celkový počet tolarů testovaných v Lipsku."
16. Michael North (Hg.), *Von Aktie bis Zoll: Ein historisches Lexikon des Geldes* (München, 1995), pp. 362-363.
17. Petr Vorel, "Czech Roots of the American Dollar," *Kosmas* (Texas A&M University) 23, Number 2 (2010): pp. 32-42.
18. Heinrich Miltner – Josef Neumann, *Beschreibung der bisher bekannten böhmischen Privatmünzen und Medaillen* (Praha, 1852), pp. 492-527.
19. Karl Otto Müller, *Quellen zur Handelsgeschichte der Paumgartner von Augsburg (1480-1570)* (Wiesbaden, 1955), Nr. 39, pp. 309-312; Gerhard Krug, "Die ersten ab 1500 auf innerdeutschem Boden als Währungsgeld geschlagene thalergepräge," *Hamburger Beiträge zur Numismatik,* Neue Folge, Heft 22/23, 1968/69, Band VII (Hamburg, 1972), p. 505; North, *Von Aktie bis Zoll,* p. 389.
20. Konrad Schneider, "Bargeld in Hamburgischen Nachlass- und Gürerinventaren des 16. bis 18. Jahrhunderts," *Hamburger Beiträge zur Numismatik*, Neue Folge, Heft 30/32, 1976/78 (Hamburg, 1985): pp. 99-147.

3

The Struggle over the Thaler in Central Europe in the 16th Century

By the cusp of the second and third decades of the 16th century the silver thaler had already earned its place in the sun in Europe and was becoming an increasingly popular form of monetized silver. At that time, however, the future destiny of the thaler was far from decided and it was another half-century before the thaler became the main silver tender of Europe. In the early 16th century it was already well established in the function of a trading coin but its historical development was to be influenced by many factors. The establishment of a silver pan-European currency was significantly influenced by political interests and therefore the progress of the thaler during the early decades of its life was quite complicated. It was specifically influenced primarily by the attempts to rationalize the currency situation within the Holy Roman Empire that took place during the first two thirds of the 16th century.[1]

Although it had a titular Monarch, during the late Middle Ages the Holy Roman Empire was, de facto, a conglomeration of independent state entities that utilized diverse monetary systems. It is very important for the integrity of every state to have a unified monetary policy, but even Maximilian I who was the Holy Roman Emperor from 1493-1519 and who, to some extent, restored the authority of the Imperial Throne, failed in this area to proceed any further than having ambitious plans. As a result of the Emperor's death in 1519, unification of the currency, which he had promised at the General Assembly in the previous year (1518), did not take place even within his own Austrian lands.

Although the differences in the silver content of the various types of coins did not pose any insoluble problems, for commercial reasons it would have been preferable had there been some unification of the metrological parameters of silver coins over a wider territory. For gold, which was utilized for wholesale transactions, such a consensus had already existed for a considerable period. High-quality ducats, minted from gold of a high purity and Rhenish guldens (minted from gold of a lower quality), held the status of more or less metrologically standard coins, whoever they were issued by. Inevitably, in the case of gold coins too, some minting lords attempted to gain more by making their coins "thin." There was, however, a generally binding consensus about what a "standard" ducat or a Rhenish gulden should look like and possible variations in fineness or in weight could be compared against such models. In the case of minted silver, standards similar to these did not exist; the individual issuers simply coined "their" groschens, batzens, shillings, hellers or pfennigs and also altered their metrological parameters as needed and in accordance with their own subjective considerations.

However, not only the Emperor, but also the other rulers who were involved in the trade in precious metals realized the additional advantages that would also result in regard to silver minting from the creation of a single currency area. Also strongly supporting the creation of a uniform silver currency throughout the territory of the Holy Roman Empire were the financially powerful Banking Houses in the southern Germany cities (Augsburg, Nuremberg), which, for that matter, also belonged amongst the Emperor's major creditors. It would also have been advantageous because the holders of all key European areas of silver mining of that period, which were located in the Ore Mountains, the argentiferous Harz Mountains in Lower Saxony, Saxony-Anhalt and Thuringia and in the Tyrolean Schwaz, gradually became involved in the mass production of large silver coins in the early 1520's.

When, in 1521, the eighteen-year-old Archduke Ferdinand of Habsburg, the grandson of the deceased Emperor, took over as ruler of the Austrian hereditary lands, there was no longer any dispute about whether to produce large silver coins or not. The issue was whether it would be possible to agree on their validity throughout the Holy Roman Empire and to thereby facilitate their circulation. No one had any objections to this. More complicated, however, was the second question; i.e. what exactly the new coins should look like and how their production should be organized.

For one simple reason, it was the largest producers of metallurgical silver who were deciding about what form the newly introduced coins would have. They could afford to comply with the prescribed silver content since they acquired the precious metal from their mines at a significantly lower cost than its usual price in the market for precious metals. This difference easily covered the production cost of the minting of the coins and thereby brought additional profit. The coins minted by these producers were trusted and were accepted without hesitation in the world of high commerce. The other minting lords, who were purchasing silver for their mints, would also need to adapt to the established standard, but if they complied with the prescribed quantity of precious metal their profit would be minimized. Therefore, at the outset of the negotiations concerning a possible common Imperial currency there were fundamental differences between those sovereigns who had a plenitude of silver from their own mines and those who were obtaining it in another manner.[2]

Unacceptable for the "miners" faction, for example, was the proposal to establish an official government mint in each of the Imperial countries, to which every mining operator would be obliged to surrender all the silver mined at a fixed purchase price.

For Central Europe the cusp of the second and third decades of the 16th century represented a time of chaos and the destabilization of traditional values. The dramatic circumstances surrounding the controversy sparked by the opinions of Martin Luther whose criticism in 1517 of the then Catholic Church constituted the prelude of a rapidly spreading European Reformation. Luther and his teachings (based on ideas similar to those of a prior Czech reformer Jan Hus, to which Martin Luther adhered) were met with condemnation by the Papal Court and the publication of an Imperial anathema. Martin Luther, however, found a powerful protector in the person of the Elector of Saxony. It was he, as the first amongst the Imperial Princes, who realized the possibilities that this new fledgling religious denomination offered, not only as the expression of the inner religious feelings of believers, but as an effective tool in the struggle against the ambitious plans of the Habsburgs. And additionally as a means of bolstering his own power and the government budget, since, thanks to the reformation of the Church, the nation had been freed of burdensome taxes to the Papal Court and, in addition, the sovereign had also taken over control of what was previously church property.

In this turbulent political situation, the Elector of Saxony undertook an extensive diplomatic offensive, the intended result of which was the imposition of the Saxon guldengroschen (guldiner) – i.e. the thaler as this coin had already started to be called, based on its Czech version from Jáchymov – as the principal currency of the Holy Roman Empire. This is to say that, in accordance with the Saxon metrological model, based on the Leipzig Minting Rules from the year 1500, the guldiners were minted not only in Saxony itself. Therefore, the largest quantity of silver appeared on the European market in the form of thalers, with an identical silver content, whether they were produced in the Schlik's Jáchymov, by the Saxon mints or in the county of Mansfeld.[3] It was therefore quite logical to adopt the most widespread metrological model and to establish this as the starting point for the creation of a new Imperial Currency. It was in this spirit that preliminary discussions were conducted in the early 1520's at which time the Habsburgs were not politically powerful enough to be able to withstand the Saxon pressure.

At that time the then teenage King Charles V of Habsburg (* 1500) was the Ruler of the Holy Roman Empire, who, in the early 1520's, was busy dealing with uprisings in Dutch and Spanish towns and also with complications with his younger brother Ferdinand (* 1503), who was demanding his share of the family heritage in the Austrian lands and was also struggling (similarly to other Princes in Central and Southern Germany) with a large popular uprising. Even during this difficult period, during which the Archduke Ferdinand of Habsburg was obliged to demonstrate his determination and his ability to govern, the young Ruler nevertheless kept the currency issue in his sights. At the beginning of the year 1524 he proceeded with substantive financial reforms, by means of which he stabilized, and above all unified the currency in the Austrian lands. The silver mines in the Tyrol and, in Upper Austria, provided a sufficient quantity of the precious metal so that Archduke Ferdinand could afford to manifest his own ideas about what a new silver currency in Central Europe should look like.

The basic principle of the new pan-Austrian silver currency established in 1524 was based on the model previously introduced by Archduke Sigismund of Tyrol. The basic unit was to be the guldiner as the silver equivalent of the Rhenish gulden (Goldgulden). The guldiner was additionally divided into sixty kreutzers. However, with this the similarity to Sigismund's monetary system ended because, during the forty years that had elapsed since Sigismund's time, the ratio between the values of gold and silver had changed. Ferdinand's guldiners, minted in accordance with the Directive of 1524, had a significantly lower silver content than that of Sigismund's coins of 1486.

This fact, in itself, was not to create any interference with anything; even in the actual Austrian lands it did not cause any confusion because, in any case, the old silver guldiners from the year 1486 were no longer in monetary circulation. Ferdinand's monetary reform, however, prepared as a second alternative for the meeting of the Imperial Assembly, actually prevented an agreement on the single pan-Imperial silver currency. Ferdinand's guldiners, made in accordance with the Austrian standard, dating from the year 1524, should also have had a lesser silver content than the Saxon and the Jáchymov thalers, minted in accordance with the Leipzig Minting Rules from the year 1500.

Finally, however, following long diplomatic negotiations, a common pan-Imperial currency was agreed by the Imperial Council, but in such a form that, for various reasons, it did not match the expectations of any of the major producers of silver. In Saxony, where the rapidly spreading Religious Reformation had become the principal rival to the power of the Habsburgs, the introduction of the pan-Imperial currency, in accordance with the Saxon model, was pushed through the Imperial Assembly. At the end of 1524 the Imperial Princes adopted the Coin Decree of Esslingen, in accordance with which the coins of all the issuers within the Holy Roman Empire were supposed to be minted. The principal silver units (the guldiner and the groschen) were required to be virtually identical to the coins minted in Saxony (the thaler and the Saxon groschen, representing 1/21 of a thaler). A concession to the Habsburg Party, whose principal representatives pointedly failed to participate in these negotiations, was an agreement on the design of the currency. On one side of the new Imperial coins the Imperial Emblem and an inscription with the name and title of the Ruler of the entire Empire (at that time the Holy Roman Emperor Charles V) were to placed, while the other side was allocated to the issuer, who was entitled to design the image and the inscription area, in accordance with his own discretion.[4]

In the end, however, not one of the major producers of silver minted Imperial coins in this design. The new thalers, with their "common" side bearing the Imperial symbols and the name of Charles V of Habsburg, were produced only briefly by the Palatine Elector Ludwig V (dated with the year 1525), by one branch of the Hohenzollern of Brandenburg for the Bayreuth-Ansbach principality and by the Imperial town of Lübeck (dated with the year 1528). All the major producers of large silver coins continued minting their own coins after 1524, as if the Imperial rule did not exist. However, the metrological parameters of thalers prescribed by the Coin Decree of Esslingen, was basically attained (albeit with a slight reduction in the purity of metal) both by the counts of Mansfeld (see **Tab. VIII/3**) in Saxony and by the Western-Bohemian Schliks and later also by Duke Henri Brunschwig, whose name appeared on a large number of the new thaler coins minted from the year 1531. Indeed, enforcement of the Imperial guldiner (taler), in accordance with the Saxon model of 1524, represented an important diplomatic victory for the then already Lutheran Saxon Court. None of the major producers of metallurgical silver respected the regulations, according to which one side of thalers should be designed as "Imperial," i.e. bearing the heraldic symbol of the entire Empire and the name of the Roman king (or emperor; see **Tab. IX/2,3; X/1-3**).[5]

However, neither did Archduke Ferdinand of Habsburg respect the Coin Decree of Esslingen, since the new Austrian coins, minted in accordance with Ferdinand's own monetary reform of early 1524, were not compatible with the new Imperial standard.

The Austrian (guldiner) and the Saxon or Czech (taler) models of the silver currency had gradually begun to differ in one aspect that existed at their inception; this was their relationship to gold currency. Ferdinand's monetary reform in 1524 was based more on the traditional concept concerning the possible maintenance of a constant ratio between the prices of gold and silver (1 goldgulden = 1 silver guldiner), while simultaneously maintaining the silver content of the smaller coins. Twenty Austrian three-kreutzers (= 60 kreutzers) should contain the same amount of silver as one guldiner (= 60 kreutzers). In contrast, at that time, silver thalers of the Saxon type were not directly linked to the price of gold and did not even have their own independent hierarchy of smaller coins (only one based on fractions, the smallest of which was 1/4 of thaler). Their payment strength was simply expressed in the units of account of the country where they circulated and that was their big advantage. In contrast, Austrian guldiners were established with a fixed payment strength of 60 kreutzers and this direct link to a smaller nominal sum complicated their use in monetary circulation.

As the brother of King Charles V, Archduke Ferdinand was unable to let a new Imperial law pass by in silence and he made a protest that the newly adopted standard was inconsistent with the previous privileges held by the Habsburg dynasty. Therefore, on March 10, 1525, Charles V issued in Madrid, based on the Royal Prerogative, a special privilege for himself, for his brother and all their descendants, by which the Habsburg countries were expressly excluded from the purview of this Imperial coinage law. This privilege, that permitted the production of coins of the thaler type with a slightly reduced silver content than that prescribed by the Imperial Minting Ordinance, was taken advantage of by the Habsburgs until the mid-18th century.[6]

From the year 1525, therefore, within the Holy Roman Empire, theoretically two main types of large silver coins could be produced: the Habsburg guldiners, minted in the Austrian lands (produced in this form, in fact, only from 1528), and guldengroschens of the Saxon type, called thalers, whose metrological parameters essentially corresponded to those of the "Imperial" guldiner, as defined by the Coin Decree of Esslingen in the year 1524. In Austrian accounting sources dating from the first half of the 16th century, domestic guldiners were distinguished from foreign thalers, because they had a different content of silver and thereby also a different payment strength. Only since the later decades of the 16th century, had the term "taler" been used for any large silver coins and when the Austrian guldiners from the 1520 to 1540 were re-named thalers (to distinguish them from the Imperial guldiners that equaled 60-kreutzers, introduced in 1559), but not during the time when they were actually minted.

By the year 1524 a long struggle had commenced in regard to the appearance of the silver coins in the territory of the Holy Roman Empire. This struggle lasted until the cusp of the 1560's and the 1570's, when, following the death of Emperor Ferdinand I († 1564), through certain provisions of the Chamber of Deputies, the production of thalers as a pan-Imperial coin (never completely terminated; see **Tab. VIII/2,3; IX/1**), was officially re-instituted. While this struggle was seemingly taking place in the background of the more significant religious conflicts of the first decade of the Reformation, it was of greater significance. The endeavor of the Imperial Princes (and particularly of the Saxon dukes) to maintain their individual monetary policy, independent of the Imperial power, was a manifestation of strong separatist tendencies in the area. The minting of silver thalers had become a means of manifesting political (and religious) independence from the Imperial Center, which was ultimately also applicable in Jáchymov itself.

In the Central European arena of power the political situation changed dramatically in favor of the Habsburgs after the year 1526. In that year, in a battle with the Ottoman Turks who were penetrating ever more deeply into the heart of Europe, the Czech and Hungarian King Louis Jagiello died – the last male representative of the Czech branch of the Jagiello dynasty. On the basis of the family alliance contracts Archduke Ferdinand of Habsburg, as the husband of only Louis' sister, Anna Jagiello, claimed entitlement to a royal position The Czech Estates community did not recognize these Habsburg hereditary claims and insisted on a free election of a new king. However, Archduke Ferdinand, as objectively the best candidate for the Czech throne, won this election and took over the reign of all the lands constituting the Bohemian Crown. In Hungary though, his position was far from secure and a long war had to be fought for the Jagellonian heritage with John Zápolya, a local magnate who claimed the right to the Hungarian throne.

Thanks to his acquisition of the Czech Royal Crown, King Ferdinand, in addition to his resources of Tyrolean and Austrian silver, gained control over the silver wealth of the Czech Ore Mountains. Immediately at the outset of his reign, Jáchymov Mint was at the center of his interest and by 1528 he had already succeeded (through a parliamentary decision) in legally cancelling the right of the Schliks to mint coins (they retained only a share in the mining of silver). From 1528 the Jáchymov Mint functioned as the Royal Mint, producing coins with the image of King Ferdinand I. Minted there, however, were not guldiners of the Austrian type, but the coining continued of thalers, in accordance with the Saxon model. This is to say that King Ferdinand, even as the King of Bohemia, was unable to change the metrological parameters of the Czech coinage, since this required the consent of the Provincial Diet. Despite persistent efforts to adjust the Czech monetary system in accordance with the Austrian model, King Ferdinand did not achieve this goal during the first twenty years of his reign. He succeeded in this only temporarily, in connection with the Schmalkaldic War during the years 1546-1547, the first major religiously motivated war that became a test of the strength and cohesion of the anti-Emperor camp.[7]

Following the Coronation of Emperor Charles V (1530) King Ferdinand I was elected by the Imperial Assembly as the Roman King (1531). In this new position, he also served as the representative of his brother in Imperial matters at those times when Charles V was not present in the Imperial territories. And because Charles V, as King of Spain and the ruler of large nations, frequently traveled to Western Europe and to North Africa, his younger brother's importance in respect of Central European policy began to increase. This was soon reflected in the achievements of the young Roman King in terms of monetary policy.

Ferdinand I did not wish to abandon his model of a 60-kreutzer guldiner. In 1534, he managed to conclude an agreement through which the currency was unified over a large area belonging to southern Germany. This consisted mostly of countries whose rulers did not accept the Reformation and sought (often unsuccessfully, as in the case of Ferdinand Habsburg himself) to prevent its spread amongst the population. In the northern regions, where the Reformation prevailed, even at the level of its rulers, Imperial princes and towns introduced the minting of thalers in accordance with Saxon model. The polarization of the political forces was thereby, to a large extent, mirrored in the monetary developments, as most issuers of silver thalers in the northern area of Germany in the 1540's were associated with the Schmalkaldic Unity, founded in 1530, as an expression of disagreement with the power politics of the Habsburgs. The Anabaptist community also used large silver thalers in 1534 to represent their religious beliefs when they created a temporary commune in the Westphalian city of Münster.[8] Already in the 1530's the monarchs of the Danish Kingdom and the Kingdom of Sweden, who adopted the Calvinist Reformation, initiated the extensive production of thalers.[9]

The Holy Roman Emperor Charles V had successfully expanded the power of the Habsburg family and the Catholic Church by fire and sword on both sides of the globe. He created a tremendous empire with previously unimagined resources, above which, as it was then described, "the sun never sets." Meaning: throughout the entire 24 hours there was daylight in at least some parts of the world controlled by the Spanish Habsburgs. However in Central Europe itself, where the roots were of the Habsburg expansion into world-rule, Emperor Charles V and his political agenda were not so successful. In the early years of the rapid spread of the Reformation both the Habsburgs and the opposing Imperial Rulers sought for the diplomatic resolution of disputes, which outwardly appeared as an attempt to legalize or to suppress religious reformation. The Habsburg brothers, however, were linked by other severe conflicts and were able to take effective action against the opposing princes in the Empire: Charles V fought a struggle for influence in northern Italy and vied with France, Ferdinand I tried to defend his claims to the Hungarian Royal Crown militarily and, in particular, to organize the defense of Central Europe against the Ottoman Empire. On this battleground the situation became really critical and in 1529 the Turkish troops even besieged Vienna. Rumors spread through Europe about the invincible strength of the Islamic armies, which the rival Christian Princes of the Holy Roman Empire are not capable of withstanding. How was the Emperor Charles V to defend the Holy Roman Empire over which he reigned when the Empire itself was on the verge of an internal schism?[10]

The center of the opposition in the Empire, however, was to be found far to the north, in Saxony, while Turkish expansion threatened the southeast, where the Emperor's brother, King Ferdinand reigned. In order to be able to mobilize the forces of Christian Europe the Habsburgs could not intervene against the Reformation by force because they themselves needed military and especially financial aid on the Austrian and Hungarian borders. The military successes of the Turkish Sultan Suleiman II and the penetration of Islam into the heart of Europe were interpreted in the contemporary political propaganda as God's punishment for Christian disunity but the Protestant opposition was well aware that even without these power-political circumstances the Habsburg efforts to strengthen the Imperial powers would face only difficulties.

The situation did not change until the early 1540's when the Emperor Charles V concluded a peace treaty with France (1544) and with the Roman Curia, which commenced the preparation of a religious council in Trent in the South Tyrol. The Council was supposed to define the opinion of the Catholic Church concerning the European Reformation. The Balkan border with the Turkish Empire still remained unresolved, but with the division, in 1541, of the historically Hungarian countries into three spheres of influence (Habsburg, Transylvania and Turkey) even here the situation stabilized. At the cost of making compromises, the hands of the Habsburgs were freed for a military intervention within the Empire. With cleverly thought-out diplomatic preparation, substantial investments and promises, through which alliances were achieved with some of the Protestant Princes, in April 1547 the Habsburg side finally defeated the forces of the opposing Imperial Princes in the Battle of Mühlberg and captured the Saxon Elector.

However, the Habsburgs were not able to solve the problems of the religious Reformation through victory in one battle. The war deepened the debt of the Habsburgs, especially to the Southern Germany Banking houses and it was also necessary to satisfy the requirements of those Protestant Princes who, in the struggle to strengthen Imperial Power, for various reasons, stood on the side of the Habsburgs. Although the Habsburg troops won on the battlefield in 1547, the Emperor Charles V and his brother Ferdinand I had to retreat in some respects during the subsequent negotiations to retain at least outwardly intact the semblance of the unity of the Holy Roman Empire.

One of the controversial points that was negotiated long before the Schmalkaldic war was the question, raised once again, of a common pan-Imperial currency. During the previous quarter century silver thalers had become the principle type of coin traded on the European market. The thaler remained the most common type of coinage, produced from newly-mined metallurgical silver, but the production from the historic Central European resources in the Tyrol, the Erzgebirge and the Harz had already, in the mid-16th century, gradually started to lose its previous attractiveness. Critical was not the actual volume of newly mined silver (which in later years sometimes even grew in spurts), but primarily the increase in the financial costs. The mining of Central European silver became ever more expensive. Even though the silver mines were still producing the same, or even greater, volumes of precious metals, they ceased to be profitable and viable. The quantity of coins that were produced from newly mined silver was barely sufficient to cover the costs of the extraction and processing of the raw material and its minting.

There were additional causes for the prolonged stagnation of Central European silver mining. The precious metal was mined from increasingly greater depths, which enormously increased the mining costs (in particular for pumping out the mine water and to power the water-mining facilities); meanwhile the metal content of the processed ore was dropping. Contributing more to the reduction in the profitability of the old mining areas of Europe, however, were a generalized reduction in the prices of precious metals and an increase in the costs of the other goods and raw materials needed for the operation of mines. These significant changes in price relationships, described as a "price revolution," were due to the huge and ever-increasing influx of gold and silver from overseas colonies, especially from the South American mines. This change was more pronounced in the case of silver than that of gold.

The large-scale importation of silver to Europe from overseas did not commence until the 1540's, but due to the richness of the South American silver deposits it soon exceeded the volume of the domestic European production. It immediately ceased to be important, whether this or that sovereign had silver mines in his or her own country because in Europe it became simpler to obtain silver for minting coin by purchasing it, rather than through risky and increasingly less profitable mining ventures. Coins of the thaler type also started to be minted in a large volume by the mints of countries that were not themselves producers of any precious metals of their own.[11] The negotiations at the beginning of the second half of the 16th century concerning a unified Imperial currency were therefore far more complex than previously, in the year 1524, when the importing of overseas metals had not yet become such a significant factor and when the important powerful European producers of silver (Ferdinand of Habsburg and the Saxon Duke) could promote their own interests. Eventually, nevertheless, a meeting of the Imperial Council reached a definitive conclusion, announced in the year 1551, in the form of a second Imperial Minting Ordinance for the Mints in the Holy Roman Empire.

This second Imperial Minting Ordinance of 1551 (see **Tab. XI**) was, however, to become a very short episode in the history of European currency. That is to say that it was based on a compromise that was intended to fulfill the requirements of many parties but, as such, it did not have very much support from any of them individually. The basis of the new Imperial currencies was to be the coin traditionally defined as the "Güldener." Its value, however, was not derived from its parity with gold coins (i.e. the Rhenish gulden), but was to be valued at the stable fixed equivalent of 72 kreutzers. This numeral was also to be stamped on the coins, which was, until then, anunheard of novelty; no major Central European coin, prior to that time, had its nominal numerical value directly imprinted on it.[12]

The denomination of 72 kreutzers for the new Imperial guldiners was evidently impractical, since it is clear at first glance that it is more difficult to calculate multiples and proportions of this amount. It could, however, have served as a first step towards the gradual unification of the monetary conditions within the Empire. In order for the common currency to function it also had to respect the previous monetary systems, since it was not technically feasible, within a brief period, to remint the tender in circulation. One consideration was for the old and the new coinage to run in parallel over the long-term, whereby they would be easily convertible in regard to their circulation within the individual countries. The smaller groschen coins no longer played a significant role in long distance trading (this trade was conducted almost exclusively with coinage of the thaler type), but in terms of ordinary daily practice this aspect was very important. Had the new Imperial guldiner became the common currency of all the areas of the Empire its nominal value of 72 kreutzers would not have been badly formulated. It was also compatible with the Spanish monetary system that was based on multiples of eight. With the increased influx of silver from the Spanish overseas colonies and due to his temporary political predominance within the Empire Charles V could permit consideration of a Spanish and Imperial monetary union.[13] The second Minting Ordinance therefore pointed not only towards the establishment of a new stable Imperial currency, but also indicated that this system was practicable for the more rapid distribution of Spanish colonial silver in the European markets. Had Charles V's plan succeeded everything might have been easier because in the entire area of Habsburg influence money could have been exchanged easily in accordance with the ratios 8 Spanish reals = 24 Saxon groschens = 72 Austrian kreutzers = 1 Imperial guldiner.

In accordance with the agreement of 1551 the new Imperial guldiner would have had basically the same content of silver as the Saxon thalers currently in circulation during that period, i.e. like the Imperial guldiner that featured in the Coin Decree of Esslingen of 1524, though it had a slightly lower purity and therefore a correspondingly higher weight. However, in order to unify the currency ratios within the Habsburg monarchy, the official payment strength of the older thaler coinage was determined as 68 kreutzers, based on the actual silver content. This naturally created confusion; for normal business purposes thalers were equivalent to 70 kreutzers (later their value continued to increase), while in respect to the collection of taxes or for other official purposes the thaler should have been accepted as only worth 68 kreutzers. These problems were also amongst the reasons that the Imperial monetary reform of the year 1551 did not materialize to a greater extent.

Only gradually, and with little appetite, did some Imperial towns and princes commence issuing the new 72 kreutzer thalers. In the mid-1550's King Ferdinand I also started implementing their coinage, but only in the Austrian lands (see **Tab. XII/1, 2**).[14] Old thalers continued to be produced in the Czech mints (see **Tab. XII/3**) with the newly established payment strength of 68 kreutzers, which, however, officials of the relevant institutions themselves were able to immediately convert at the higher rate. This situation was not to last for long however.

Political developments in Central Europe had taken a completely different direction than Emperor Charles V had anticipated. The opposition of the Protestant Imperial Princes was too strong and in 1552 they again instigated armed resistance against the Habsburgs. In 1555 the Emperor was forced to adopt a compromise deal that went down in history as The Peace of Augsburg. This established the basic principle of "whoever rules determines the religion" ("*cuius regio, eius et religio*"), i.e. that the individual rulers of the sub-principalities of the Holy Roman Empire would in the future have the right to decide whether their country would be Catholic or Lutheran. This treaty became the basis for a process, later defined as confessionalization, which divided Europe, in accordance with religious principles, into several mutually warring camps and was to eventually lead to a destructive and disastrous war in the first half of the 17th century.

Emperor Charles V perceived this religious peace as a great personal loss and decided to retire from public life. In 1556 he passed on the ruling of Spain to his son Philip II, resigned from the position of Holy Roman Emperor and retired to the seclusion of the monastery, where he died in late 1558. The Holy Roman Empire did not even mind that it had no Emperor. Following the abdication of Charles in 1556 his brother Ferdinand I, who had already been representing the Emperor since 1531, took over the fulfillment of his duties as ruler, if necessary, as a titular King of Rome. However Ferdinand I of Habsburg had to wait until the spring of the year 1558 for the Imperial Election of the College of Electors.

One of the first successes that Ferdinand I achieved as the Emperor was the acceptance of the Third Minting Ordinance in the year 1559. Emperor Ferdinand realized in this manner his own concept of how the ideal Imperial currency should look. In fact, he reasserted his own earlier model, introduced in the Austrian lands in 1524. The basic unit of currency was a guldiner of sixty kreutzers. However, the fair value of the kreutzer as a small coin had already been declining since 1524 and therefore the new guldiner required a significantly lower content of silver than did the homonymous Austrian coins minted according to the standard from 1524, which were commonly called thalers. The metrological parameters of the guldiner from the year 1559 onwards were not primarily derived from gold coins, but from tiny kreutzers, i.e. a 60-kreutzer coin (a guldiner) had a silver content that corresponded to 5/6 of that of an Imperial Guldiner (a 72-kreutzer coin) dating from 1551. Older kreutzer coins could therefore be incorporated into the new monetary system.[15]

The Emperor Ferdinand I began to carry out the minting of coins in accordance with the new Regulation first in his hereditary Austrian lands; from 1561 he also ordered the production of these coins in the Kingdom of Bohemia (see **Tab. XIII/1,2**),[16] while the new guldiners, paying sixty kreutzers, were also minted in some Imperial towns. The vast majority of the principalities of the Holy Roman Empire, however, ignored the Third Minting Ordinance, in addition to the two previous ordinances, and continued to produce coins in accordance with their own customs and laws (see Tab. **XIV/1**).

After the death of Holy Roman Emperor Ferdinand I († 1564), his eldest son, Maximilian II (1564-1576), became the Holy Roman Emperor (and King of Bohemia and King of Hungary), based on the previous election. However, based on the last will of Emperor Ferdinand I, the core possessions of the Habsburg in the Danube region were actually divided amongst his three sons in three parts. The oldest, Maximilian, obtained Upper and Lower Austria, together with Vienna, the younger Archduke Ferdinand became the ruler of the Tyrol while the youngest, Archduke Karl von Habsburg, established his new headquarters in Graz, from where he reigned the south-eastern portion of the family heritage. As a result of this division of the hereditary Habsburg Countries, the coins of two new rulers appeared on the European money market, but this fact was not in itself as important for the further development of the Central European currencies as was the change that occurred on the Roman throne.

The new Emperor Maximilian II basically resigned the all-Imperial power ambition of his father, both in the religious-political area (from his youth he was in favor of the Reformation, though for political reasons he formally professedthe Catholic Faith), and also in the monetary field. He accepted the requirements of the Imperial Princes, who pointed out the impracticality of the Austrian version of a 60-kreutzer guldiner (that was minted in larger quantities only by the Austrian and Czech mints) and in 1566 he agreed to an amendment to the Third Minting Ordinance. This legal regulation, valid in the territory of the Holy Roman Empire, once again legalized the production of the "good old" thalers. Their weight (29.23 g) corresponded to that of the currently minted Saxon thalers; their purity, however, was reduced to 88.9% and they payment strength would be 68 kreutzers.

The amendment of 1566 did not actually revoke the Third Minting Ordinance from 1559 (which is why it was defined as only an amendment, not as a new law, even though it had the content of the latter) and in the Holy Roman Empire, for some time, the synchronous coinage of "Imperial" thalers and "Imperial" guldiners, i.e. 60-kreutzers, continued (see Tab. **XIII/3, 4**). Their production, however, was inconvenient, because due to the slight but persistent inflation of the value of small coins, the nominal value of silver contained in them was already at that time greater than the "60 kreutzers" embossed on the coin. Eventually, the only area in which the Imperial guldiners continued to be minted regularly in large quantities was the south-eastern part of the Empire that was under the direct rule of the Habsburgs, i.e. the Czech Kingdom and all the three portions of the Habsburg ancestral possessions that were under the rule of Maximilian II and his two brothers.

However, under pressure from the Bohemian Estates, who had been seeking over long period for the carrying out of internal monetary reform, in 1573 the Emperor Maximilian II agreed to stop the minting by the Czech producers of the kreutzer denominations, whereupon the production of special provincial coins (white groschens) and "old-new" thalers was re-introduced (see **Tab. XIV/2**). These were determined to have a payment strength of 70 kreutzers (or 30 white groschens of the Czech monetary system).[17] In order, through the approval of currency reform in Bohemia, not to be in conflict with the Imperial legislation, in 1573 Maximilian II issued, by Imperial Prerogative, a regulation for himself to free the countries under Habsburg rule from the applicability of the Third Minting Ordinance. Soon afterwards the production of thalers also commenced in Hungary (in 1573) and in the Styrian area of the ancestral Habsburg domains (in 1574). The production of Imperial guldiners (60-kreutzers) in the Habsburg lands continued until the eventual death of Maximilian († 1576), not only at the mint in Vienna but also, though only to a limited extent (on behalf of Archduke Ferdinand of Tirol), at the Mint in Hall in Tirol.

The "struggle for the thaler" had therefore, in fact, run its course by 1573 and, with no formal restrictions existing, mass-produced Imperial thalers began to again carry out the function that they had fulfilled since their launch in the 1520's – that of a trading coin (the payment strength of which was determined by its content of precious metal) or, as it was then called a "hard coin."

An adjustment implemented in 1566 determined the optimal silver content of "Imperial" thalers, according to which, in the individual currency areas across the Holy Roman Empire the payment strength of the thaler coinage of the individual European issuers was defined.[18] The initial effort to establish a specific permanent face-value for the thaler (of 68 kreutzers), which was intended, to some extent, to match the Austrian monetary system, proved futile. In fact the thalers in monetary circulation performed a different function and it was their fluctuating and changing payment strength that was their biggest advantage, which made the thaler a stable means of payment during periods of steep wartime inflation, which central Europe was to encounter several decades later.

Based on the amendment of 1566, the "Imperial" taler, was a coin with a prescribed content of 25.987 grams of pure silver. Its specific payment strength in each individual country was determined in accordance with the local monetary system and was updated continuously (see **Tab. XIV/3; XV; XVI; XVII**). In this form and based on this function the "Imperial" talers remained in use over a substantial area of the Holy Roman Empire until the mid-18th century. Apart from this function, however, in some countries the term "taler" was also a designation defining the monetary unit; used also in respect of the copper credit coinage and paper notes. I shall elucidate these variants in more detail in the following chapter.

The thaler itself (i.e. the "real," completely silver coin) did not form the basis of a more complex monetary system; they could not be converted into "change" and nor were they divisible into any smaller units, except as fractions (usually half-talers and quarter-talers), which had the identical purity and the corresponding weight. So full-bodied thalers could circulate throughout Europe without any major restrictions and without the necessity of their metrological parameters having to be altered in respect of fluctuations in the prices of gold or silver, nor in regard to the deterioration in the quality of the small coins of this or that other country. The monetary circulation responded to such fluctuations through a change in the payment strength of thalers; that usually indicated its growth. Thereby, in Central Europe, for almost the next two centuries a two-level system of monetary circulation remained fixed:

The higher level was represented by full-bodied current ("gross") coins, the payment strength of which was primarily derived from their content of precious metal and these could therefore circulate, without any restrictions, over a wide area. This category included silver thalers and gold coins.

The lower level was represented by the "common coins," issued by individual Monarchs for internal circulation. At that time they were also usually made mostly of silver, but their payment strength was defined by an official regulation and was usually slightly higher than the amount that would correspond to the quantity of the precious metal. Therefore their circulation at face value was restricted to the territory in which the relevant issuer ruled; in other countries they were accepted either at a lower value (determined by their valuation in accordance with their actual silver content) or else their circulation was forbidden.

This system was not unique to Central Europe, since all the countries with a developed system of monetary exchange had already been struggling with similar systems. In centralized monarchies with a strong tradition of Royal rule, such as France, England or Spain, the situation was simpler because the Royal Court usually consistently controlled the consistent production of coins and any changes to their metrological parameters (including the inflation reduction of precious metals) could be centrally managed.

The Holy Roman Empire, however, was a conglomerate of many hundreds of more-or-less important state units, linked to a certain extent through traditional medieval feudal ties. Dozens of individuals and legal entities owned minting rights and no power existed that was able to undertake control over this confusion. Even the Imperial brothers, Charles V and Ferdinand I, were not able to achieve this -let alone their respective followers later, at the turn of the 16th and 17th centuries, when the Empire was awakening to the next massive military conflict.

Notes

1. Friedrich Schrötter, "Das Münzwesen des Deutschen Reichs von 1500 bis 1566," in: *Jahrbuch für Gesetzgebung, Verwaltung und Volkswirtschaft im Deutschen Reich* 35 (1911), pp. 129-172; 36 (1912), pp. 99-128; Herbert Rittmann, *Deutsche Geldgeschichte 1484-1914* (München, 1975); Bernd Sprenger, *Das Geld der Deutschen: Geldgeschichte Deutschlands* (Paderborn, 1995, 2. Aufl.), pp. 102-110; Michael North, *Kommunikation, Handel, Geld und Banken in der Frühen Neuzeit* (München: Enzyklopädie deutscher Geschichte, Bd. 59, 2000), p. 27.
2. Carlo M. Cipolla, *Die Odyssee des spanischen Silbers: Conquistadoeres, Piraten, Kaufleute* (Berlin, 1996), zvl. pp. 54, tab. „Import Spaniens vom Gold und Silber aus den amerikanischen Kolonien (in Tonnen)."
3. Otto Tornau, *Münzwesen und Münzen der Grafschaft Mansfeld* (Praha, 1937); Walter Haupt, *Sächsische Münzkunde* (Berlin, 1974).
4. Petr Vorel, *Monetary Circulation in Central Europe at the Beginning of the Early Modern Age – Attempts to Establish a Shared Currency as an Aspect of the Political Culture of the 16th Century (1524-1573)* (Pardubice, 2006), pp. 43-60.
5. Wolfgang Heß – Dietrich Klose, *Vom thaler zum Dollar 1486-1986* (München, 1986), pp. 38-39, Karte 2 "Reichsguldiner und Guldengroschen Münzstätten 1524-1535."
6. Carl Ernst, "Das österreichische Privilegium des Quentchens," *Numismatische Zeitschrift* 38 (1906), pp. 169-173; Günther Probst, *Österreichische Münz- und Geldgeschichte: Von den Anfängen bis 1918* (Wien, 1973), p. 396; Michael North (Hg.), *Von Aktie bis Zoll: Ein historisches Lexikon des Geldes* (München, 1995), p. 337.
7. Schrötter, "Das Münzwesen des Deutschen Reichs," p. 164; Heß – Klose, *Vom thaler zum Dollar*, p. 47; Horst Rabe, *Reich und Glaubensspaltung: Deutschland 1500-1600* (München, 1989), pp. 258-273; Vorel, *Monetary Circulation*, pp. 85-88.
8. Gerd Dethlefs, "Münzen und Medaillen auf die Wiedertäufer in Münster," in: *Die Wiedertäufer in Münster* (Stadtmuseum Münster - Katalog der Eröffnugsausstellung vom 1. Oktober 1982 bis 27. Februar 1983) (Münster, 1982), pp. 244-264.
9. Bertel Tingström, *Swedish Coins, 1521-1968: An Illustrated Reference Book of Swedish Numismatic* (Stockholm, 1969); Kersten Krüger, "Die Staatsfinanzen Dänemarks und Schwedens im 16. Jahrhundert (Eins Strukturvergleich)," in: Hermann Kellenbenz – Paolo Prodi (Hgg.), *Fiskus, Kirche und Staat im konfessionellen Zeitalter* [21. – 25. September 1987] (Berlin: Schriften des Italienisch–Deutschen Historischen Instituts in Trient, Bd. 7, 1994), pp. 187-208; John S. Davenport, *European Crowns 1484-1600* (Frankfurt am Main, 1985), pp. 76-77, 249-252.

10. Hermann Kellenbenz, "Das römisch-deutsche Reich im Rahmen der wirtschafts- und finanzpolitischen Erwägungen Karls V. im Spannungsfeld imperialer und dynastischer Interessen," in: H. Lutz (Hg.), *Das römisch-deutsche Reich im politischen System Karls V.* (München, 1982), pp. 35-54; Geoffrey Parker, "The Emergence of Modern Finance in Europe 1500-1730," in: Carlo M. Cipolla (ed.), *The Fontana Economic History of Europe II: The 16th and 17th Centuries* (London, 1974), pp. 527-594.
11. Gottfried Pusch, *Staatliche Münz- und Geldpolitik in der Niederlanden unter den burgundischen und habsburgischen Herrschern besonders unter Karl V.* (München, 1932).
12. Bernd Sprenger, *Das Geld der Deutschen: Geldgeschichte Deutschlands von der Anfängen bis zur Gegenwart* (Paderborn, 1995, 2nd ed.), pp. 104-105.
13. Petr Vorel, "Money in the Political Culture of 16th Century Central Europe," in: Halina Manikowska – Jaroslav Pánek (eds.), *Political Culture in Central Europe (10th–20th Century), Part I – Middle Ages and Early Modern Era* (Prague, 2005), pp. 179-201.
14. Heß – Klose, *Vom thaler zum Dollar*, pp. 62-65; Map „Reichsguldiner zu 72 Kreuzer und thaler Münzstätten 1551-1559" (p. 64).
15. Vorel, *Monetary Circulation*, pp. 88-95.
16. Petr Vorel, "Měnová politika Ferdinanda I. v Čechách a ukončení ražby pražských grošů [Monetary policy of King Ferdinand I of Habsburg in Bohemia and the termination of minting of the Prague groschen]," *Český časopis historický* [The Czech Historical Review] 100 (2002), pp. 265-292.
17. Petr Vorel, "Landesfinanzen und Währung in Böhmen unter Ferdinand I. und Maximilian II. (Finanz- und Münzpolitik im Spannungsfeld von Ständen und Königtum während der Regierungen Ferdinands I. und Maximilians II.)," in: Friedrich Edelmayer – Maximilian Lanzinner – Peter Rauscher (Hgg.), *Mitteleuropäische Finanzen im 16. Jahrhundert [= Das Heilige Römische Reich und Europa, Bd. 1]* (Oldenburg, 2002).
18. Geoffrey Parker, "The Emergence of Modern Finance…," pp. 527-594; Thomas Winkelbauer, " 'Das Geld ist sanguis corporis politici'. Notizen zu den Finanzen der Habsburger und zur Bedeutung des Geldes im 16. Und 17. Jahrhundert," in: Wolfgang Häusler (Hg.), *Geld. 800 Jahre Münzstätte Wien* (Wien, 1994), pp. 143-159.

4

Thalers and the European Wars during the 16th to the 18th Centuries

From the cusp of the 1560's and the 1570's whoever wished to do so was issuing his or her own thalers in Central Europe. In the smaller princely and municipal mints, scattered at that time in the area encompassing present-day Germany,[1] Switzerland[2] and the historical Silesia (see **Tab. XVIII/3**),[3] dozens of different thaler coinages were minted, frequently issued for ceremonial reasons, as commemorative or occasional coins, or as souvenir items (similar to today's silver and gold commemorative coins). The vast majority of these, at the time of their issuance, had no wider economic significance and their function can be compared to that of Renaissance medals. Perhaps for this reason, some Renaissance Medals made by persons who never had any minting rights appear in the catalog inventory of thaler coinage as if they were coins.

Not all issuers, however, adhered to the established metrological standards and the market was also infiltrated by thalers that had a deliberately reduced silver content. Such coins were minted by certain secular and ecclesiastical princes and towns for their own enrichment. In addition to these (essentially fraudulent) coins, however, due to the widespread exchange of goods, the coins of other monetary systems that were minted in accordance with different metrological standards also appeared in circulation. At first glance they looked like thalers and they were also commonly described as thalers, even though they had a different value.

Most countries were attempting in some manner to regulate and to control the quality of the foreign coins, pervading their territory on the basis of both trading and financial speculation. Special testing departments were established at the State Mints, headed by authorized officials, whose task it was to check on a regular basis the quality of the coins in circulation, especially the gold coins and the thalers, with which most of the "big" payments (including state loans) were implemented at that time. The same types of problems occurred even in the case of "normal" (i.e. low-denomination) coins, but at this lower level of monetary circulation it was possible to prohibit the acceptance of unreliable small foreign currencies even at the risk of loss to their holders.

However, the demand for "hard" coins (gold coinage and silver trading coins of the thaler type) was greater, as they represented a versatile tender and were particularly important both for wholesale business and for financial speculation. Therefore, even in the case of divergent metrological parameters, their circulation was not usually forbidden but their payment strength was officially determined, based on valuation. The real silver content of the relevant coinage was ascertained by testing offices and its payment strength was subsequently quoted in domestic currency. For the needs of merchants and of the officials of financial institutions identifying details of the European coins in circulation in particular countries, including their xylographic images, were published regularly.

The ruling mandates or Parliamentary decisions relating to the circulation of money, usually took the form of a large-scale sheet (poster) with printed illustrations of the coins that were the subject of the adjustment.[4] These decrees were posted on official notice boards, e.g. at Town Halls or on church doors in towns where annual markets were held. For regular use these valuations were subsequently published in print and sold on the book market. They actually became a type of forerunner of coin collectors' catalogs, even though their buyers were not so much interested in their value as collectibles (this category had not yet been identified at that time), but in the quantity of precious metal from which its payment strength was derived.

Apparently paradoxically, the first such printed catalogs of thalers were created as early as in the 16th century in the Netherlands,[5] i.e. an area of the business environment in which there had been a certain distrust of large silver coins since the period of inflation coinage during the early Regency of Maximilian I. At that time, however, the Dutch provinces constituted one of the most advanced commercial and manufacturing areas in Europe and silver thalers were arriving there from Central Europe for the highly-demanded goods from Flanders, Brabant and elsewhere. In order to simplify their own business, the Dutch at first started to not only monitor, but to also officially publish the quality of the thalers (or "Daalders" as the generalized Central European term "taler" was adopted in Flemish) that were coming into the hands of Dutch traders. Such catalogs had become an indispensable business tool, and therefore also a profitable business item for publishers.[6]

This practical novelty appeared in the more easterly-located areas of Central Europe a little later. In Saxony, a similar catalog of thalers and certain other coins was published in print for the first time in 1572 and later also in other countries.[7] The data from these valuation manuals as well as the pictures published of specific coins were mostly concerned with various other issues and with the conversion of the silver content into the domestic currency.[8] In the Holy Roman Empire there were several major currencies, from which it was quite simple to convert the payment strength of these coins into any other currency.[9]

Also specifically added to the newly issued valuation manuals, based on actual testing, were new coinages that individual issuers put into circulation.[10] So at the end of the 16th century the quantity of registered thalers and of coins similar to them reached impressive proportions. From this flood of hundreds of different types of thalers it is impossible, simply based on actual valuation manuals, to assess their actual significance in monetary circulation. Images and valuations of some thalers, minted only in a minimal number of examples for the purposes of a single individual, could reach valuation catalogs more or less by chance and this says nothing about their wider expansion in the European market.[11]

In the last quarter of the 16th century the range of European countries in which large silver trading coins were made under the name "taler," greatly expanded towards the east. In 1573, their coinage (interrupted in 1561 at the time of the introduction of guldiner currency) was restored in the Kingdom of Bohemia[12] and, at the same time, within the Habsburg monarchy, it was also extended to Hungary. Prior to the year 1573 the Hungarian Mints primarily produced gold ducats and, from silver, only small denarii.[13]

Following the conclusion of a Peace Treaty between the Habsburg Empire and the Ottoman Empire (in 1568) large-scale silver coinage became an important source of exports to the area of Southwest Asia. Although their exports within the Habsburg monarchy were strictly limited, ways were always found for its export because this trade brought large profits.[14] Therefore the rulers of all the European countries bordering directly on the Ottoman Empire, after the year 1568, commenced the regular production of thalers:[15] in addition to the Habsburgs in Hungary there were the princes in Transylvania (today's Romania), who possessed large stocks of gold and silver from their own mines.[16]

From the 1560's the production of Scandinavian thalers also significantly increased. One of the reasons for this was the one-off monetization of large stocks of silver from the Swedish mines, which King Gustav I Vasa (†1560) had amassed over the years as a "National Treasure" and that only his successor, Eric XIV, permitted to be processed into silver thalers. Swedish interest in increasing the production of coins of this type was also influenced by changes to the Customs Tariffs in the Sunda Straits. While previously the fee for passing through a certain number of vessels had been set in gold, after 1566 Denmark introduced a new tariff in accordance with which it demanded payment in silver thalers, in accordance with a specific tonnage. This measure generally increased the demand for silver thalers throughout Scandinavia[17] and also in Eastern Europe.[18]

The minting of new coins based on the "Imperial" thaler model was also introduced during the last quarter of the 16th century in the Polish-Lithuanian Union, which at that time not only vied with the Ottoman Empire in southeastern Europe, but also began to assert itself more strongly in the struggle for supremacy on the Baltic Sea, which served as a transport artery for profitable trading with Eastern Europe and Scandinavia. In the 16th century, Poland itself did not have its own significant resources of precious metals; this was why, typical for its coinage of that time, was the bulk production of small groschen coinage that penetrated in large quantities into the monetary circulation of the adjacent territories of the Habsburg monarchy. Therefore the production of Polish thalers had not started on a larger scale until the reign of the Polish King Stephen Bathory (1576-1586), who was also a Prince of Transylvania and could utilize the rich resources of precious metals from the Carpathian Mountains for the production of his coins.

In the last third of the 16th century a relatively large area was established in Europe in which the "Imperial" thaler (Reichstaler, Rijksdaaler) was produced and accepted as the principal silver coin with a more-or-less standard content of precious metal. Identified by this term were not only the coinages from the Mints within the territory of the

Holy Roman Empire, but also other coins of the thaler type produced in Bohemia and Silesia, in Scandinavia, Poland, in Hungary and in Transylvania, which met the relevant standard. Correlated then with the "Imperial" thaler were the variations in silver content of other coins of the thaler type circulating in the territory, whether this involved a coinage that was presented as an "Imperial" thaler but that contained less silver, or the coins of other monetary systems. These problems, however, mainly concerned large business companies and the Financial Chambers of Royal Courts or aristocratic magnates.[19] Throughout Central Europe the thaler was rarely found in common circulation; market and normal financial transactions were paid mainly using small coins from a variety of monetary systems.

The Religious Reformation and mandatory Confessionalization, which divided the territorial principalities and the Imperial towns of the Holy Roman Empire into several warring groups (1555), became a serious obstacle to the economic integration of this area. Together with the power-issues and the financial problems of the Spanish branch of the family (the abdication of Charles V in 1556 and the Spanish financial crisis of 1557) in association with the division of the Danubian monarchy amongst the various branches of the Austrian family-tree (1564) the gradual retreat of the South Germany banks from their position at the apex of the imaginary pyramid of the financial world of contemporary Europe commenced. Although the Southern German Imperial towns still maintained their importance in the world of "high" finance their reputation began to be overshadowed by other business centers, located in the north, on the coast of the North Sea and the Baltic Sea. Thanks to the favorable trading potential with Eastern Europe and Scandinavia some port towns quickly developed in these new conditions (Hamburg, Bremen, Gdansk amongst others). The most significant financial center in Europe, however, at the cusp of the 16th and 17th centuries became the northern Netherlands, together with its commercial capital, Amsterdam.[20]

The area then known as the Spanish Netherlands had already been part of the Habsburg Empire from the last quarter of the 15th century, when Maximilian I of Habsburg gained control of these countries through his advantageous marriage in 1477 within the dominions of Burgundy. This was a fairly complex conglomeration of seventeen territorial units in the areas of present-day Netherlands, Belgium, Luxembourg, north-eastern France and north-west Germany. In constitutional terms the Netherlands provinces had different statutes and also a different internal administrative structure; de jure they were actually a personnel union of separate individual countries under the sway of one ruler, who was also the King of Spain.

Even though the Dutch provinces and Spain had a common sovereign, in other ways they had developed quite differently. Spain by itself gradually stagnated economically, left behind by the rest of Europe and was unable to offer any significant domestic commodity in terms of the exchange of goods.The Spanish King and his grandees had sufficient gold and silver, but it quickly disappeared on astronomical spending for social representation and also for wars. The financial situation of the Spanish King (and Holy Roman Emperor) Charles of Habsburg at the end of his reign was extremely dismal, even though, at the beginning of the second half of the 16th century, the influx of silver from the Mexican, Peruvian and especially the Bolivian mines began to increase dramatically.

The King of Spain did not, however, own all the gold and silver that was mined in the colonies. Only one-fifth of it belonged to him, and even from that it was necessary to pay a lot of expenses, not counting the losses incurred during the transit to Europe. While tremendous quantities of precious metals were passing through Spain during the 16th century, there was an actual shortage of gold and silver for internal circulation on the Spanish mainland. From the year 1543 Charles of Habsburg was obliged to establish the minting of copper credit coins in Spain. When Charles of Habsburg, ominously in debt from the wars with France and with the German Protestant Princes, resigned from further governance in Spain in 1556, his son Philip II inherited an onerous burden. By 1557 he was already obliged to declare the state bankrupt and the devaluation of credit money.[21]

The main source for the revival of the Spanish Treasury was to become the Netherlands. Already during the days of Charles the Bold, Duke of Burgundy (†1477), the Dutch part of his empire belonged amongst the most economically developed regions of Europe. During the reign of the Habsburgs this area was also the source of their wealth as, thanks to the development of production and of trade the Netherlands brought substantial profits to the Habsburgs' Treasury. The importance of the Dutch part of the Habsburg Empire even increased, in connection with the importation of American gold and silver into Europe. That is to say that in the second half of the 16th century most of the precious metals from overseas were no longer directed to Spain, but instead to the commercial ports in the north of the Netherlands, which became a "gateway to Europe" for the importation of precious metals from the colonies. The Dutch ports had become major centers of commerce and this was where colonial gold and silver was processed into the form of coins that could be traded in the European market in large quantities.[22] The trade in silver was more advantageous than that in gold, because the exchange ratio between gold and silver was different than it was in Spain. In the late 15th century this ratio was already fixed at 1:16 in Spain, whereas further to the east silver was more expensive. Let me mention, for example, the 1:10.8 ratio that was established in Leipzig at the time of the commencement of the production of Saxony guldiners in 1500. During the first half of the 16th century the cost of silver also became less in relation to that of gold in Central Europe, but it was still was much more advantageous to utilize Spanish colonial silver in Central or Eastern Europe than in the Iberian Peninsula. One of the first measures introduced therefore by the Spanish King Philip II, in order to increase the profits of the Spanish Royal Treasury, was to initiate the minting of a new type of silver coin in his possessions lying further to the east; in Italy and particularly in the Netherlands.

The new silver coins were metrologically based on the old Spanish silver 8 reales coin and their payment strength in the Netherlands was adapted to this "octonary" system. From the Netherlands this coinage quickly reached areas of Germany where it was called in accordance with the name of the sovereign, Philip II, "Spanish Philip's thaler" ("spannisch Philips thaler") and, in the south of Italy abbreviated to "Filippo" (see **Tab. XIX/2,3**). These Philip's thalers had a higher silver content than the "Imperial" thalers, so they were accepted in the monetary circulation at a higher value. While a full-bodied "Imperial" thaler in 1572 in Saxony obtained 24 groschens, the value of a Philip's thaler was 25 groschens and 2 pfennigs.

Spanish colonial silver had provided a powerful impetus for the further rapid economic development of the Netherlands, since it was not spent there mainly for royal and noble social representation (as in Spain itself), but utilized effectively in business. In terms of business activities in the northern Dutch provinces an important role was also played by the fact that in these regions the Religious Reformation, specifically that of the Calvinist type, was spreading rapidly. For supporters of this path towards European Reformation, success in commercial business had not only a practical, but also in a sense a spiritual significance, because, according to the thinking of the period , it represented a manifestation of God's favor. Particularly in the case of the Calvinist doctrine, modesty, thrift and the effective and efficient use of funds belonged amongst the major socially accepted virtues.

The increasing tax demands of the Spanish Royal Court, in addition to the fundamental differences concerning religious issues, had been provoking open resistance to the Spanish Governor's rule since 1566. The Spanish King Philip II made a vain attempt to suppress opposition in the Dutch provinces with the use of force. In the year 1579 the country was effectively divided through the announcement of the Union of Arras in the south, in the Catholic provinces (comprising approximately the area of present-day Belgium and Luxembourg and oriented against the Habsburgs) and, later the same year, also of the Union of Utrecht in the predominantly Calvinist and Lutheran north (approximately the area constituting the present-day Netherlands). An attempt to completely dissociate the northern Dutch provinces from the Habsburg monarchy was initiated in the year 1581 through the proclamation of the independence of the United Provinces of the Netherlands, which elected as their sovereign William I of Orange (who retained the title of "Governor"). During the subsequent three decades the Spanish Court attempted, with scant success, to overcome the opposition in the Netherlands by military means. In addition to its considerable financial resources the independent northern Netherlands had significant allies, especially in England, Spain's principal maritime rivals.[23]

No change took place in the relationship between the Spanish and the independent northern part of the Netherlands until the cusp of the 16th and 17th centuries. At that time the Spanish King, Philip II Habsburg, ceded the rule of the Netherlands to his son-in-law, Albrecht of Habsburg. During that period marriages within the Habsburg family constituted a common manifestation of dynastic politics and therefore no one was particularly surprised that an uncle should marry his own niece (Philip II married the daughter of his sister Mary) or by marriages between cousins. Albrecht of Habsburg, the younger brother of then Emperor Rudolf II attracted attention, however, in a different manner. It was during the reign of this Habsburg that, through diplomatic means, the Dutch dispute was successfully resolved for a certain period of time and, in 1609, both sides agreed to a cease-fire, through which for the next twelve years the independence of the northern provinces was actually tolerated. This stabilization of the power relationship, in the same year (1609), enabled the establishment of an independent Amsterdam bank within the environment of the most important financial center of contemporary Europe, which, since the mid-16th century, the Amsterdam Financial Stock Exchange had increasingly become.[24]

The Amsterdam bank played an important role in the continuing development of the Northern Netherlands and of its financial system. Its credibility was guaranteed by the authority of the Town Council. Through the bank all financial transactions of a non-monetary character could be conducted, which greatly benefited the Dutch trading companies. The bank also verified the authenticity of foreign currencies and guaranteed the payment strength of those coins that it provided.[25]

This event symbolically launched a period of many decades during which the Dutch bankers and traders (both Christians and Jews) not only decisively supervised the flow of money between the Royal Courts, but also, through commercial companies and new approaches within the banking sector, controlled a significant proportion of the intercontinental shipping of goods.[26]

The changes in the power constellation of the Dutch provinces were also significantly reflected in the European coinage. The Dutch coinage, produced primarily from metal imported from the Americas, became the most commonly produced silver European tender, in the largest volume. The coins were minted in a relatively large range of different metrological types and were of varying fineness and weight. In the world of long-distance commerce, however, primarily three types of Dutch coinage of the thaler type were employed. In the northern provinces these were primarily the "rijksdaalders" (metrologically corresponding to "Imperial" thalers; see **Tab. XX/1; XXII/1-3**) and "lion thalers"; in the southern provinces it was mainly the "patagon." In the southern provinces from the cusp of the 16th and 17th centuries, on the one hand the production of Philip's thalers faded, but on the other hand significantly the production of a second type of coin developed, minted from American silver by Philip II. These were known as "Burgundy thalers," or sometimes "patacons" or "patagons" because these coins were made of silver imported from the silver mines in Patagonia, then one of the Spanish colonies in South America. Archduke Albrecht von Habsburg continued producing these patacons and from the year 1612 they were minted in large quantities. They contained only 24.65 grams of silver (considerably less than Philip's thalers and the "Imperial" thalers). To differentiate them from other coins of the thaler type they came to be known as "Albertustalers" though they also still retained their older names, "patagon" or "patacon" (see **Tab. XX/2,3; XXI/1-3**).

The minting of silver "lion" talers had already been initiated in the Mints of the northern provinces in the year 1575, i.e. even before the Declaration of Independence. This coinage, with a relatively low silver content (20.736 g), was originally intended as a coin for internal circulation within the provinces with a fixed payment strength of 48 stuivers (i.e. 8 shillings). In each province slightly different types of coins were produced and therefore the newly introduced coinage carried an identical design, as a symbol of the unity of a newly created state. The reverse side bore an expressive symbol of a lion (hence the name "lion" thaler), while on the face was the bust of a man-at-arms holding a shield with the emblem of the specific province, the name of which also appeared in the inscription (see **XXIII/1,2**).

The difference in the origins and the purposes for which this coinage was intended was clearly apparent at that time: the "Albertustalers" (patagons) were trade coins produced from direct supplies of Spanish colonial silver, similar to the older Philip's thalers (though with a reduced content of precious metal). Unchanged in their form, they were produced in Brabant and at other mints by the Spanish King Philip III, who regained the rule of the Spanish Netherlands following Albert's death in 1621, without a male heir.

The individual provinces of Northern Holland minted "rijksdaalders" as their trading coins that corresponded in their silver content to the "Imperial" thalers. The newly introduced "lion" thalers were originally intended as coins for internal circulation and in the Northern Netherlands had their fixed payment strength denominated in stuivers. Although the Northern Netherlands were not able to count in the same manner on the direct delivery of silver from the Spanish colonies, as from their southern "sibling" (where the reign of the Spanish Habsburgs was still in force), the northern provinces obtained a plenitude of precious metal from business activities and succeed in purchasing it themselves, both in Europe and overseas. At the end of the 16th century the Dutch East India Company took control over trading in the former Portuguese colonies in East Asia and established the basic elements of Dutch colonial rule in what is today Indonesia. With these business ties, established over the long-term and its experience in maritime transport, Northern Holland had an open door to advantageous trading with the Asian region.

During the first half of the 17th century he three Dutch coins of the thaler type, i.e. patagons, rijksdaalders and lion thalers, became the most important silver coins in circulation in Central and Eastern Europe. Not only because they maintained a relatively stable silver content, but primarily because they were available on the market for precious metals in large quantities. It can also be said that, to a considerable extent, it was this money that funded the troops of the opposing sides in the long conflict that came to be known in European history as the "Thirty Years' War" (1618-1648).

The war that symbolically commenced in 1618 with the armed resistance of the Czech aristocracy and of the Towns against the policy of the Viennese Courtand its Czech governors for reinstituting Catholicism, after the accession of the Styrian Archduke Ferdinand of Habsburg to the Imperial Throne (from 1619 as Emperor Ferdinand II) grew into a large-scale conflict in which the military leaders of all the European powers made good use of their many years of experience gained in the wars in the Netherlands and the Balkans. The main experience, however, on the basis of which both the Czech Estates troops and the Imperial forces engaged in conflict, was the awareness that it is not possible to win a war without having any money. On the battlefield, therefore, it was not the power of religious ideas or of patriotism that took a stand there, but paid mercenary troops, who, in principle did not care for which side they were risking shedding their blood.

A Great War conflict, spreading steadily throughout the entire region of Central Europe, created war-inflation throughout the vast territory of the Habsburg Monarchy and also a substantial area of the Holy Roman Empire during the years 1621-1623 that was known as the period of "kipr" – copper currency – or of the "long coin."[27]

In the first phase of the great European conflict called "The Bohemian War" (1618-1620), inflationary tendencies had already begun to appear in the monetary circulation of the warring parties within the

Habsburg monarchy in the form of the introduction of coins with higher denominations that contained less silver than would correspond to their value. In 1619 the Estates Government decided to finish minting coins in the Czech lands in the provincial currency (white groschens, small groschens), switched to a kreutzer system and also introduced the minting of higher denomination coins (of 12, 24 and later also 48 kreutzers). These coins had a far lower silver content than corresponded with the relevant kreutzer multiple, as required for the "Imperial currency" in accordance with the amendment of 1566, but this difference, at that time, was in the range of only a few percent.

The wave of inflation actually broke during later years in which Emperor Ferdinand II rented Royal Mints throughout most of the Habsburg Monarchy to the Minting Consortium, formed by a group of officers, politicians and financiers from different corners of Europe and professing various religions. The Emperor granted this group a monopoly on trading in silver, copper and charcoal and permitted the production of royal coins in unlimited quantities, in accordance with the specified parameters. For this privilege, the Consortium committed to paying a fixed annual fee to the Imperial Treasury. Thereby was initiated, in 1621, the mass production of high-denomination coins (up to 150-kreutzers), which had a relatively low content of silver (see **Tab. XXIV/1,2**). The Consortium took advantage of the ambiguity of the lease agreement, which did not clearly specify from which weight unit of silver the fineness of the coins produced was to be derived. Together with the expansion of the production volume, the quality of the silver in the newly minted war coins deteriorated. In a similar manner, there was a deterioration of the quality of coins in the other countries of Central Europe, especially in Saxony. Wartime inflation caused extreme price increases for all goods, reaching levels of up to ten times higher than those of the pre-war period.

These inflationary changes did not affect silver thalers, however. The "Imperial" thalers were also minted as trading coins (see **Tab. XXV/2**), in accordance with their original parameters, during the war by all the stakeholders. Inflation, almost copper, coins were only a provincial tender currency (i.e. multiples of kreutzers in the case of the Habsburg coinage or groschens in the case of the Saxon coins; see **Tab. XXIV/3**). No one would have described the inflationary Austrian or Czech 150-kreutzer as a thaler; even though it had a similar size and weight as the latter, because it was neither issued as a thaler nor did it have the respective purchasing power. The inflation coins that were in circulation were named in accordance with their nominal value, which was stamped directly on the coin: the 120-kreutzer was a double-Rhine-gulden (1 Rhine-gulden = 60 kreutzers), the 150-kreutzer was a double-and-half- Rhine-gulden. The concurrently coined (or older, pre-war) full-bodied silver thalers had a substantially higher and growing value among the inflationary currency, computed as many hundreds of kreutzers.

During the year 1623, bankruptcies were announced in various individual countries affected both by wartime inflation and, in addition, the drastic devaluation of credit tenders to a fraction of their nominal value.[28] In the Habsburg Monarchy State bankruptcy (called "Calada") was announced in December 1623. Although the war conflict was far from over, from 1623 the production of inflation tender ceased in the territory of the Holy Roman Empire and the individual Regents again restored, to a greater extent, the production of quality thalers in accordance with the pre-war metrological parameters (see **Tab. XXV/3**). The payment strength of the "Imperial" thalers was again defined as 90 Imperial kreutzers or 24 Saxon groschens (in effect, at this value, it gradually stabilized prior to the Thirty Years War).

During the war, however, full-bodied silver thalers were not minted for circulation but mainly to finance mercenary armies. During that period individual issuers begin to systematically introduce the mechanical minting of coins using rolling machines. This innovation enabled the achievement of finer and more detailed rendering of the image part of the coin. Seemingly paradoxically, during a devastating war during the first half of the 17th century that completely devastated large swathes of Northern Germany and the Czech lands, the thaler coinages of the Central European issuers were benefitting from an exceptionally high quality of design. The most important producers of quality thalers in wartime, in addition to the Habsburg Emperors Ferdinand II (1619-1637) and Ferdinand III (1637-1657), were the Austrian Archdukes of the Tyrol branch of the Habsburg family see **Tab. XXXI/2,3**), then the Salzburg archbishops (see **Tab. XXVII/3**), the Saxony Electors (see **Tab.XXVIII**), the Braunschweig-Lüneburg Dukes and certain Imperial towns, specifically Augsburg (see **Tab. XXIX**). Several wartime upstarts also began to mint their own coins, mostly from amongst the Habsburg Generals who had acquired large estates in Bohemia, confiscated from the Protestant Estates. Apart from the Imperial Generalissimo, Albrecht von Wallenstein, there was, for example, Jan Ulrich Eggenberg and also the Schliks (see **Tab. XXVI/1-3**).[29] Thereby, a hundred years after the nationalization of Jáchymov Mint, Schliks' thalers started to be produced again in Bohemia, though they no longer had any significance for monetary circulation. Like all the "private" princely and ecclesiastical thalers, produced in the territory of the Habsburg Monarchy they had only the character of representational and memorial coinage.

Even during the war, in the area of the Holy Roman Empire, the term "taler" remained restricted to silver trading coins, defining this coinage as uniquely different from the credit currency. Quite exceptional in Central Europe at this time (in contrast to Scandinavia: see below) are cases in which the term "taler" was used as a numerical unit of currency. Adherence to this development that had its inception in the Habsburg monarchy in the second half of the 16th century was interrupted by the consistent implementation of unit of account "1 Rhine-gulden = 60 kreutzers." Also a brief episode in the development of a European currency was the usage, in the case of the Silesian Evangelical Estates, of the term "taler" as a monetary unit. In 1621 they issued silver and gold coins of high (and in many cases curious) thaler values which, however, had nothing in common with the real "Imperial" thalers. The term "taler" was used in this case only as an equivalent for 72 kreutzers (see **Tab. XXV/1**).[30]

The prolonged wars in Central Europe, in which neighboring powers (primarily France, Denmark, Sweden, Poland and others) were also actively engaged militarily, on different sides, caused a total collapse of the monetary systems and disruption of the economy. Circulating in the fields-of-war were heterogeneous older and recently minted coins, which troops of the individual warring parties carried with them. In places which had been avoided for some time by war looters, and where there was something to trade, payment was made mainly in small coins. Prevalent amongst the silver coinages of the thaler type were the above-mentioned coins, minted in the Netherlands. Dutch coins also began to be significantly utilized in trade with Eastern Europe and the Caucasus region. In the mid-17th century, from amongst the trading silvers exported by European traders, Netherlands thaler coinages from such faraway lands as, for instance, Georgia were dominant.[31]

The wartime disruption of the currency monetary systems in the Holy Roman Empire had long-term consequences and it took many years before the individual countries approached the issue of currency consolidation of. For both political and technical reasons, it was unthinkable to consider any longer a pan-Imperial currency reform, analogous to that negotiated between the years 1551-1566. The power interests of the Imperial Court in Vienna were already focused in another direction. The currency reform carried out by the Emperor Leopold I of Habsburg in 1659 was therefore applied only to those countries in which Leopold I ruled, regardless of whether they were a part of the Empire (the Austrian hereditary lands) or not (the Czech lands, Hungary).

The essence of the monetary reform during the year 1659[32] was the significant devaluation (by 15 to 25%) of the foreign mintage circulating in the Habsburg lands. Through this adjustment, also called the "small Calada" (a reference to the State Bankruptcy of 1623), it was intended that foreign coinage should be removed from circulation and replaced by domestic currency. It also introduced the production of higher kreutzer denominations (15-kreutzers and later also 6-kreutzers) and their metrological parameters were united throughout the monarchy of Central European Habsburgs. The "Imperial" thaler continued to be produced in accordance with the former metrological standards, by which the Habsburg "Imperial" thalers could have a slightly lower silver content than the other "Imperial" thalers. In the business world, however, the Habsburg thalers from before 1659 and from later were accepted as equivalent to the other full-bodied "Imperial" thalers, because the difference defined was not considered significant. Factors additionally considered were some degree of manufacturing tolerance and the gradual reduction of the weight of coins in circulation due to wear and tear.

Considered significant, however, was the difference, since 1659, in silver content between the thalers and the smaller coins. At the time of the renewal of coins of "good grain" in 1623, thirty triple-kreutzers (the payment strength of which was identical to the thaler, i.e. 90 kreutzers) contained a total of 24.649 g of pure silver, which was only about 4% less than the standardized amount of precious metal in the "Imperial" thaler (25.679 g). After 1659, however, triple-kreutzers (groschens) were minted with a significantly reduced silver content (in the thirty items there was a total content of Ag of 21.623 g), therefore the differ-

less than the standardized amount of precious metal in the "Imperial" thaler (25.679 g). After 1659, however, triple-kreutzers (groschens) were minted with a significantly reduced silver content (in the thirty items there was a total content of Ag of 21.623 g), therefore the difference in the content of precious metal between the thaler and its official nominal value (90 kreutzers), paid in triple kreutzers, had increased significantly to 14.26%. The difference was the same even when paying with small kreutzers. The price of "wide thalers" (as goods for export, i.e. monetized silver) therefore also started to increase in the territory of the Habsburg monarchy, since export trading companies were willing to pay more kreutzers for full-bodied thalers than was their officially determined payment strength.

Other states of the Holy Roman Empire in which "Imperial" thalers were minted tried to take measures to prevent the influx of the less valuable small new Imperial coins (which were otherwise, prior to 1659, commonly accepted throughout the whole Empire). This measure was based on an agreement between the Brandenburg and Saxon Electors, concluded in 1667 at the Zinna Monastery (south of present-day Berlin). Through this agreement, the "Imperial" thaler, paying 90 kreutzers as a monetary calculation unit, was introduced in the area within which the power of both prince Electors extended. One coin with a nominal value of 10.5 thaler should be produced from one grzywna of pure metal. A year later (in 1668) another important producer of coins, the Duke of Braunschweig-Lüneburg, also acceded to this Agreement, thereby expanding the area of the new monetary system to the northwest edge of the Holy Roman Empire.[33]

In this manner, in the late 1660's, two areas were established in Central Europe in which, for many decades, thalers played a different role in monetary circulation:

1) In southern Germany and in the are of the Habsburg Monarchy (including the Czech lands and Hungary) the "Imperial" thaler continued to be coined as a trade coin with a fixed silver content and a variable purchasing power, expressed in the unit of account of Rhine-gulden = 60 kreutzers.

2) In the North German territorial principalities the term "Imperial" thaler represented only a unit of account (90 kreutzers). Coins were placed in circulation bearing an inscription defining fractions of these numerical "Imperial" thalers. The largest denomination produced was

a coin bearing the fraction "2/3," i.e. two-thirds of one unit of account of the "Imperial" thaler, which amounted to sixty kreutzers. Therefore, the coins carrying "2/3" were also known as guldiners, because in the older Imperial currency rules (dating back to 1559) it was the guldiner that represented the equivalent of sixty kreutzers. Smaller fractions were also paid analogously, i.e. 1/3 of an "Imperial" thaler = 30 kreutzers (see **Tab. XXXIX/1**), 1/6 = 15 kreutzers. In addition to these "Imperial" thalers (= 90 kreutzers), however, in some of these countries silver thalers were also minted for commercial purposes using the older standard. To prevent confusion the terms "Reichstaler in specie" or "Speciestaler" were used for these coins, as well as for the "wide thalers" from previous years and for the thaler coins produced in the southern region referred to above.

Soon other issuers began to imitate the North German monetary system. Thereby a large number of coins with face values of "1/3" and "2/3" of an Imperial thaler entered into circulation which did not, however, contain the prescribed amount of precious metal (i.e. the coins with a nominal value of 10.5 numerical "Imperial thalers" did not actually contain a grzywna of sterling silver). The largest issuers of these coins that were not full-bodied were the small German principalities of Eisleben, Coburg, Sonderhausen and others. In this manner their rulers helped themselves to a one-time significantly larger amount of money (in the case of newly minted coins it was difficult to identify a reduced content without carrying out metrological tests). Coins of this type were also minted in numerous counterfeiting workshops. The newly introduced system rapidly started to collapse and that period of the 1680's in northern Germany was later to become known as the second period of the "kipr" (copper) coin.[34]

As in 1667, the major issuers of silver coinage, i.e. the Electors of Saxony and Brandenburg and the Duke of Braunschweig-Lüneburg, who also possessed their own mining silver again attempted to rectify this situation. In 1690, in Saxon Leipzig, they concluded a new agreement through which a new thaler currency was introduced, whereby twelve one-taler coins contained a total of one mark of silver. This derivation of the nominal currency units in accordance with their unit weight of silver proved to be very practical and was in the future actually to become the manner in which it was possible to unite the dozens of different sub-monetary systems in Germany. In the area of northern Germany the "Imperial" thaler continued to define a numerical unit that was equivalent to ninety kreutzers or (in Saxony) twenty-four groschens. The designation "Taler Courant" was given to this monetary unit, which was abbreviated as "Rtlr." Still minted as the coin with the highest value was only the 2/3 Rtlr, which was equivalent to 16 Saxon groschens or 60 kreutzers. These, with their weight of 17.32 g and 75% Ag purity, contained 12.99 grams of pure silver and in practice could be accepted as equivalent in value to 1/2 of an old "Imperial" thaler, i.e. the Speciestaler. In the northern German monetary system full-bodied Imperial thalers (9 items were coined from one mark of silver) therefore had a value of 1 1/3 of a Rtlr, i.e. 32 Saxon groschens = 120 kreutzers.

In this way, de facto, these two monetary systems (the southern and the northern) started to converge with each other again, since, as a result of the further reduction of the silver content of the smaller coins of the Habsburg monarchy during the years 1680-1693 there followed a rapid rise in the price of the Habsburg thalers, that increased in value to 120 kreutzers. The payment strength of the minted silver "Imperial" thaler coin then oscillated at around this value until the mid-18th century.

The old "Imperial" thaler, essentially based on the Leipzig Minting Rules from 1500, despite the slight drop in the purity of the "wide thalers" or "speciestalers" (as minted silver thalers were actually distinguished from simple numerical monetary units) remained as an extra-territorial unifying element in accordance with which (regardless of the complex internal monetary systems and the onset of inflation) the national currencies of Central, Northern and Eastern Europe were defined.

This fact can be documented, for example, by the developments that took place in the Kingdom of Sweden, which adopted the silver thaler as its major trading coin as early as in 1534. Thaler credit currency first appeared in Europe in the 17th century in Sweden. The Swedish Royal Treasury already had prior experience with minting copper coins from during the war years, when, from 1624, large copper coins were produced (öre and their multiples and fractions). The coins normally issued there were Swedish marks, the "mark swenska" (8 öre = 1 mark, 4 marks = 1 thaler of Swedish currency), and their nominal value was not stamped on them. The copper coins of this system were initially not even actual credit coinage, but monetized non-ferrous metal (copper) with the corresponding values: e.g. a 1 öre copper coin weighed about 50 grams.

In addition to Swedish marks, silver thalers continued to be minted in accordance with the older metrological templates. During the first half of the 17th century the Swedish silver thaler maintained a stable content of precious metal (29.2523 grams of 87.5% Ag), corresponding to the "Imperial thalers" produced at that time in Central Europe. Therefore it was named the "riksdaler" or the "riksdaler species" in Swedish to distinguish it from the numerical monetary unit, the "daler." These coins were minted on a regular basis only until 1647 (then also subsequently later in 1653, 1654 and 1676).

From 1649 Queen Kristina (1632-1654) instituted the production of copper credit dalers (in denominations ranging between 1/2 and 10 dalers), which were to replace the scarce silver that was in circulation. The concurrence of copper and silver coins, however, soon created a significant difference between the payments strength of the two types. In Sweden therefore, already as early as in the second half of the 17th century, a distinction was made between the data concerning the credit copper coins ("daler kopparmynt," abbreviated to "K.M.") and that concerning the silver marks converted to dalers ("daler silvermynt," abbreviated to "S.M."). In the early 1660's paper credit- vouchers that were issued by the StockholmsBancoin currency units of copper and silver thalers entered the Swedish money circulation.[35] In the 18th century the ratio between the amounts defined in silver and copper currencies settled at the ratio of 1:3.

Thereby at the cusp of the 17th and 18th century, Sweden had three thalers, all differing significantly in their payment strength. The basic numerical monetary unit was the "taler of silver currency" ("daler silvermynt"), which represented simply a numerical unit of the Swedish coins that were denominated at that time in marks. The "taler of copper currency" ("daler kopparmynt") had a three-fold lesser payment strength. The applicable conversion therefore was 1 daler S.M. = 3 dalers K.M. = 4 marks = 32 öre. However the old Swedish and the foreign silver thalers (known as the "riksdaler species"), the payment strength of which was still variable during the second half of the 17th century, also remained in the Swedish money circulation. At the beginning of the 18th century these stabilized at the level of 3 dalers S.M., i.e. 96 öre.

For quite a long time this system worked well. Sweden was both a major exporter of copper in Europe (so that it could afford to issue small copper tender of extra weight, corresponding to the price of the metal) while the minting of "talers of copper currency" was not inflationary. The situation changed only with the losses by Sweden during the wars for naval supremacy in the Baltic in the early 18th century. In 1715, the Swedish King Charles XII (1697-1718) ordered the issuance of small copper credit coins that were to be the equivalent of the "taler of silver currency" (they bore the inscription "1 daler S.M."). The issuer of this tender showed great imagination in choosing the motifs on the reverse of the coin (where ancient deities are also depicted; see **Tab. XXXIX/2,3**), but the mass production of "talers" of this type, minted from 1715 to 1718, led to the rapid inflationary collapse of the Swedish currency.[36]

The weakening of Sweden and the acquisition of its eastern territory had become a prerequisite for the rapid growth of the power and influence of Tsarist Russia. Here, too, the silver thaler became the prototype for the new coins introduced by Peter I in the early 18th century in Tsarist Russia.[37]

The early modern coinage of the Russian Empire was not particularly complex. Although the monetary system had been centralized by the reform of the early 1530's, the principal coin that was minted, was a tiny silver kopek. Trade with Eastern Europe was passing through the Polish-Lithuanian Union and East Prussia. The Baltic countries started minting thalers for commercial purposes already in the 1550's, somewhat sooner than did Poland.[38]

However, prior to the Russian colonial expansion into Asia in the 18th century,[39] precious metals were very rare in Eastern Europe and by using Central European silver coins it was possible to buy goods more cheaply. Therefore the struggle for trade supremacy in these regions became the catalyst for many wars involving Denmark, Sweden, Poland and later also including Russia.

Medieval silver coins (mostly Prague groschens dating from the 14th century) were already being imported into Eastern Europe in large quantities. In the first third of the 16th century silver thalers from the Ore Mountains were already included in the exchange of goods with Eastern Europe. This is suggested by the name "yefimok" (written in Cyrillic "ефимок"), by which all the coins of the thaler type that appeared monetary circulation in Russia in the 16th and 17th centuries were known. This name came into being in accordance with the Jáchymov thaler of the years 1520-1528, on which Saint Joachim (called Yefim in Russian) was depicted. These were already distributed in large quantities in the eastern areas of Europe before the term “taler” became established as a generic term in European trading, i.e. already in the 1520’s and 1530’s. The merchants in Eastern Europe were not familiar with the origins of the Jáchymov coinage; hence the word “taler” meant nothing to them. They created a name for the new unknown coins that was derived from the figure of the Saint that they could see on the coin.

During the 16th century and the first half of the 17th century full-bodied “Imperial” thalers were exported in large quantities to Eastern Russia for commercial purposes. Their destination was not Russia itself, but to be a vehicle for business exchange; the majority of this trade silver travelled further east, to India and China, where silver had a much higher purchasing power in comparison with Europe. A portion of this trade silver, however, was also absorbed by the Russian monetary circulation. Since in the mid-17th century, in addition to the earlier Imperial thalers, the North Dutch lion thalers also started to be imported, which had a similar appearance but a lower silver content, the Russian Tsar Alexei Mikhailovich I (1645-1676) made an attempt to protect the domestic monetary circulation by an extensive and technically demanding operation by which full-bodied thalers were initially re-marked using Russian dies, then later simply provided with a plate mark with the symbol of a czarist eagle and dated “1655.”[40]

Silver “yefimoks” = thalers were used in Russia either for direct payments or as “pagament” for minting the tiny domestic silver kopeks. Larger silver coins were not minted there until the early 18th century. This change was brought about through the military successes of Tsar Peter I (1689-1725), who at the time of the Northern War (1700-1721) by the occupation of Estonia, Livonia and Karelia obtained from Sweden access to the Baltic Sea.

This ambitious Tsar, who was attempting the creation of a modern centrally controlled state, after winning the war introduced a new currency, the Russian ruble, that was minted from the beginning of the 18th century (not in larger quantities however until after the war in the 1720’s) in accordance with West-European metrological standards (see **Tab. XXXVII/3**). Together with the coinage of silver rubles he also introduced a decimal system, i.e. 1 ruble = 100 kopeks. An exception was represented by the Russian “talers” issued in 1757 for commercial purposes for the area of Livonia and Estonia. These coins, also defined as

Livonian coins, represented 96 kopeks, in a similar manner to the Swedish "rijksdaler in species," that paid 96 öre (see **Tab. XXXVIII/3**).[41]

The additional export of Central-European thalers into Eastern Europe, which was still plentiful at the beginning of the 17th century, was also not inhibited by either the economic reforms of the enlightened Russian Tsar nor by changes in the power constellation in the Baltic, but by the simple fact that in the early 18th century Central Europe suffered from a lack of silver.

Large domestic silver coins (the North-German "2/3 thaler" and the South-German and Habsburg "Imperial" thalers) at the cusp of the 17th and 18th century had not yet appeared in the monetary circulation. They were exported in large quantities as trade silver as part of the passive European trade balance to Southwest Asia and North Africa and further, to India and China.[42] On one hand Central Europe was covering its trade deficit for the importation of luxury goods from the Orient with its silver, while on the other hand there was less and less of this silver from domestic mining resources.

In the place of domestic Imperial thalers, from the early 18th century in Central Europe there were increasingly more large silver French coins that had a lower silver content than the Imperial thaler coinage, but there was a plenitude of them. It is worth mentioning that the design of the "French thaler" (the silver ecu) of the first quarter of the 18th century was directly imitated by the original Russian silver rubles.

The beginning of the 18th century had brought about significant changes in the political organization of Europe. After the Spanish branch of the Habsburgs died out (in 1700) a protracted war for the Spanish Succession was unleashed, since the Austrian Habsburgs claimed entitlement to the Spanish Royal Throne on the basis of old ancestral rights treaties. The second son of Emperor Leopold I (†1705), Archduke Charles, should have become the new King of Spain. During the first decade of the 18th century, by expending substantial funds, militarily enforcing the reign of Charles of Habsburg (as the Spanish King Charles III) actually proved successful. However, when after the death of his elder brother Joseph I (†1711), the last male representative of the Habsburg family became the ruler of the Central European Habsburg Monarchy and the Roman Emperor, the power constellation changed (see **Tab. XXXIV/1,2; Tab. XXXV/1-3**). The Habsburgs in Spain lost the support of their existing allies, especially England and the

Netherlands, and, in 1713, Charles III was forced to abandon his throne in Madrid. Through peace treaties, however, the Austrian Habsburgs acquired territory in Italy and in the southern Netherlands from the Spanish Succession. French Prince Felipe de Bourbon became the new King of Spain and France thereby gained access to supplies of Spanish colonial gold and silver. Due to the advantageous relationship between the prices of the two metals, French minted silver began to flow primarily into Central Europe.[43]

France itself commenced the production of large silver coins, called "ecu d'argent" in French or, by the monarch, also "louisd'argent" (they were a silver equivalent to the gold ecus or "luisdors"), very late, since it did not have available significant sources of this metal of its own. The first "French thalers," as the new silver ecus were commonly called in the thaler currency area, were minted on the orders of the King Louis XIII from the year 1641 (see **Tab. XXXII/1,2**). With the centralized production of coins, the French thaler coinage had a unified design and differed only in accordance with the mint mark. At the cusp of the 17th and 18th centuries, however, as a result of the monetary instability under Louis XIV, who would boost the Royal Treasury simply by re-minting older coins to create a tender of a higher denomination, they did not inspire great confidence (see **Tab. XXXVII/1,2**). Yet from the beginning of the 18th century French thaler coins (especially the full ecu and the half ecu) infiltrated into the monetary circulation in Germany, because they were the only large silver coins that were available in substantial quantities.[44] After the reform in 1726, when France was already the most important European producer of minted silver coins (it replaced in this role the previously dominant North Netherlands), the influx of this tender into the Central European countries significantly increased (see **Tab. XXXVIII/1,2**).

French silver ecus were accepted in the common money exchange in Central Europe as equivalent to the "Speciestolar," i.e. 32 Saxon groschens or 120 kreutzers, even if they contained less silver than did the actual full-bodied Imperial thalers. That is why they became such a profitable import commodity. The domestic large silver coinage practically did not circulate in the vast Imperial territory and the small coins represented a very variegated jumble of means of payment of many smaller principalities and insignificant mini-states with their own local currencies. "French thalers," in the first half of the 18th century, had become the most important silver currency in the German lands, that was accepted easily and with confidence in the business world. Although the rulers of the territorial principalities and also the Emperor Charles VI tried to limit the circulation of French coins (e.g. coinage from an enemy state) through various regulations and by an officially ordered reduction of their payment strength, since there was not a sufficiency of their own trusted Imperial silver coins of higher values available, such efforts had only minimal effect. The changes from this development brought with them significant news affecting the power and the political map of Central Europe, that led to the death of Emperor Charles VI († 1740), through whose person the male side of the Habsburg family died out.

Notes

1. John S. Davenport, *German thalers 1500-1600* (Frankfurt am Main, 1979).
2. Jean Paul Divo, *Die Thaler der Schweiz* (Zurich-Luzern, 1966); Daniela Braun (red.), *Von altem Schrot und Korn (Münze und Geld im 16. Jahrhundert: [Ausstellungskatalog], Schweizerisches Landesmuseum,* Heft Nr. 3 (Zürich, 1987), pp. 19 "Karte mit den 22 Münzherren und den 6 Währungsgebieten des 16. Jahrhunderts."
3. Józef Andrzej Szwagrzyk, *Pieniądz na ziemiach polskich X-XX w.* (Wrocław, 1973).
4. Enno van H. Gelder, *Gedrukte Muntplakkaten (Catalogus van gedrukte muntplakkaten vóór 1815 in de collecties van Rijksmuseum Het Koninklijk Penningkabinet te Leiden en Het Nederlands Muntmuseum te Utrecht* (Leiden, 1995), Nr. 1016-1017.
5. David Chilosi – Oliver Volckart, "The Knowledge Economy of the Renaissance: The Advent of Printing and Financial Integration in Central Europe," *Český časopis historický – The Czech Historical Review* 109 (2011), pp. 262-282.
6. *Ordonnantie statuyt, en de Permissie der K. M. van den gouden en silueren penninghen / cours en ganck hebbende ouer alle zÿne landen van herwaerts ouer Ghe publiceert int Jaer M. D. achtenueertich Den. xvÿ. Julÿ [17. 7. 1548]* (Amstelredam, 1557).
7. Volf Stürmer, *Verzeichnis und Gepräge der groben und kleinen Münzsorten, welche die Kurfürsten, Fürsten und Stände des Oberen Sächsischen Kreises vermöge des Heiligen Reiches Münzordnung auf den Kreis- und Propationstagen verglichen haben* (Leipzig, 1572; reprint Berlin, 1979).

8. Jarosław Dutkowski, "Uwagi o taryfach evaluacyjnych monet z XVI i XVII wieku" [The Considerations about the Valuation Manuals from the 16th and 17th Centuries], in: Шуст Роман - Крижанівський Андрий - Швець Володимир – Белопольский Сергій [red.], *Грошовий обіг і банківска справа в Україні - минуле та сучасність (Матеріали міжнародної конференції: "Грошовий обіг і банківска справа в Україні - минуле та сучасність", яка відбулася у Львові 14-15 травня 2004 року)* (Львів, 2005), pp. 166-198; Petr Vorel, "Peníze a peněžní početní jednotky v 16. století" [The Money and the Units of Account in the 16th Century], *Theatrum historiae* 6 (2010), pp. 219-233.
9. Petr Vorel, *Stříbro v evropském peněžním oběhu 16. - 17. století (1472-1717)* [Silver in the European monetary circulation of the 16th and 17th centuries (1472-1717)] (Praha, 2009), pp. 67-68, Tab. Nr. 4 „Hlavní peněžní početní jednotky užívané v Evropě v 16. – 17. století" [The main units of account used in the Europe during the 16th and 17th Centuries].
10. Ryszard Kiersnowski (red.), *Constitucie Piotrkowske Roku 1567 - Uniwersał króla Zygmunta Augusta z dnia 14 czerwca 1567 roku* (reprint Warszawa, 1967).
11. Adam Berg, *New Müntzbuech, darinnen allerley gross und kleine silberne und goldene Sorten* (München, 1597).
12. Petr Vorel, *The Money in Bohemia 1520-1620* (accompanying text to a permanent numismatic exhibition at the Pardubice Museum of Eastern Bohemia at Pardubice Castle, Pardubice, 2004).
13. Lajos Huszár, *Münzkatalog Ungarn von 1000 bis Heute* (Budapest, 1979), pp. 147-149.
14. Şevket Pamuk, *A Monetary History of the Ottoman Empire* (Cambridge, 2004) , p. 144, Tab. "The exchange rate of European coins expressed in akçes 1584-1731."
15. Andrzej Mikolajczyk, "Polish Factor in the Balkan Monetary Affairs of the late 16th and 17th Century," *Zeitschrift für Balkanologie* 22, 1986, pp. 61-75.
16. Adolf Resch, *Siebenbürgische Münzen und Medaillen von 1538 – 1898* (Hermannstadt, 1901), tab. 7-13; Anna-Maria Velter, *Katalog der Münzausgaben des Fürstentums Siebenbürgen (Der Sammlung "Ing. Constantin Orghidan")* (Bucharest, 1994), Nr. 114-146.
17. H. Hede, *Danmarks og Norges Monter 1541 – 1814 – 1963* (Copenhagen, 1964); Bjarne Ahlström, *Coins of the Swedish Possessions 1561-1878* (Stockholm, 1967); Kersten Krüger, "Die Staatsfinanzen Dänemarks und Schwedens im 16. Jahrhundert (Eins Strukturvergleich)," in: Hermann Kellenbenz – Paolo Prodi (Hgg.), *Fiskus, Kirche und Staat im konfesionellen Zeitalter* [21.–25. September 1987], Schriften des Italienisch–Deutschen Historischen Instituts in Trient, Bd. 7 (Berlin, 1994), pp. 187-208.

18. Федоров Дмитрий Яковлевич, *Монеты Прибалтики XIII - XVIII столетий (Определитель монет)* [Coins of the Baltic states during the 13th – 18th Centuries (Catalogue of Coinage)] (Таллин, 1966); Antoni Mączak, "Money and Society in Poland and in Lithuania in the 16th and 17th Centuries," in: Vera Bagnoli Barbagli (ed.), *La Moneta nell'economia Europea secoli XIII-XVIII* (Atti della "Settima Settimana di studio" 11-17 aprile 1975), Istituto Internazionale di storia economica "F. datini" Prato, Serie II - Atti delle "Settimane di Studi" e altri Convegni 7 (Firenze, 1981), pp. 579-613.
19. J.-F. Bergier, "From the 15th Century in Italy to the 16th Century in Germany: A New banking Concept?" in: *The Dawn of Modern Banking* (New Haven, 1974), pp. 105-129; Stephen Zarlenga, *Der Mythos von Geld – die Geschichte der Macht: Vom Tauschhandel zum Euro: eine Geschichte des Geldes und der Währungen* (Zürich, 1999), pp. 159.
20. Richard Ehrenberger, *Das Zeitalter der Fugger – Geldkapital und Creditverkehr im 16. Jahrhundert I-II* (Jena, 1896); Michael North, *Kommunikation, Handel, Geld und Banken in der Frühen Neuzeit* (Enzyklopädie deutscher Geschichte, Bd. 59) (München, 2000), pp. 38-39.
21. Richard Gaettens, *Geschichte der Inflationen: Vom Altertum bis zur Gegenwart* (München, 1982), pp. 52-73.
22. Herman Van der Wee, "World Production and Trade in Gold, Silver, and Cooper in the Low Countries, 1450-1700," in: Hermann Kellenbenz [red.], *Precious Metals in the Age of Expansion* (Papers of the XVIth International Congress of the Historical Sciences – Introduced and edited on behalf of the International Economic History Association), Beiträge zur Wirtschaftsgeschichte, Band 2 (Stuttgart, 1981), pp. 79-86
23. Geoffrey Parker, *Spain and the Netherlands 1559-1659* (Short Hills, 1979); Charles P. Kindleberger, *World Economic Primacy: 1500 to 1990* (New York, 1996), pp. 68-80.
24. Jürgen Schneider, "Zur Bedeutung von Börsen – Ein Forschungskonzept, dargestellt am Beispiel der Hamburger Börse (16. – 19. Jahrhundert)," in: Michael North (red.), *Nordwesteuropa in der Weltwirtschaft 1750-1950* [Northwestern Europe in the World Economy 1750-1950] (Stuttgart, 1993), pp. 245-256, Zarlenga, *Der Mythos von Geld*, pp. 164-181; North, *Kommunikation, Handel, Geld und Banken*, pp. 34-35.
25. John F. Chown, *A History of Money from AD 800* (London, 1995), pp. 130-132.
26. Jonathan I. Israel, *Dutch Primacy in World Trade 1585-1740* (Oxford, 1990); Michael North (Hg.), *Von Aktie bis Zoll: Ein historisches Lexikon des Geldes* (München, 1995), p. 96.
27. Gaettens, *Geschichte der Inflationen,* pp. 74-99; Thomas Winkelbauer, "Nervus Belli Bohemici (Die finanziellen Hintergründe des Scheiterns

des Ständeaufstands der Jahre 1618 bis 1620," *Folia historica Bohemica* 18 (1997), pp. 173-223; Hans Jürgen Gerhard, "Ursachen und Folgen der Wandlungen im Währungssystems des Deutschen Reiches 1500-1625: Eine Studie zu den Hintergründen der sogenannten Preisrevolution," in: Eckart Schremmer (Hg.), *Geld und Währung vom 16. Jh. bis zur Gegenwart* (Stuttgart, 1993), pp. 69-84.

28. Fritz Redlich, "Die deutsche Inflation des frühen 17. Jahrhunderts in der zeitgenössischen Literatur: Die Kipper und Wipper," *Forschungen zur Internationalen Sozial- und Wirtschaftsgeschichte*, Band 6 (Köln, 1972); Gerhard, "Ursachen und Folgen der Wandlungen im Währungssystems."
29. Franz Miltner – Heinrich Miltner – Josef Neumann, *Beschreibung der bisher bekannten böhmischen Privatmünzen und Medaillen* (Praha, 1852); Emanuela Nohejlová-Prátová, *Das Münzwesen Albrechts von Walenstein* (Graz, 1969).
30. Ferdinand Friedensburg – Hans Seger, *Schlesiens Münzen und Medaillen der neueren Zeit* (Breslau, 1901).
31. Revaz V. Kebuladze, "Europäische Münzen im Geldumlauf Georgiens vom 15. bis 18. Jahrhundert," *Hamburger Beiträge zur Numismatik*, Neue Folge, Heft 24/26, 1970/72 (Hamburg, 1977), pp. 151-162.
32. Günther Probst, *Österreichische Münz- und Geldgeschichte: Von den Anfängen bis 1918* (Wien, 1973), pp. 461-470; Bernd Sprenger, *Das Geld der Deutschen: Münzgeschichte Deutschlands* (Paderborn, 2002), p. 119.
33. Walter Schwinkowski, "Die Reichsünzreformstrebungen in den Jahren 1665-1670 und der Vertrag zu Zinna 1665," *Vierteljahrschrift für Sozial- und Wirtschaftsgeschichte* 14 (1918), pp. 1-87; Thomas Christmann, "Das Bemühungen von Kaiser und Reich um die Vereinheitlichung des Münzwesens (Zugleich ein Beitrag zum Rechtsetzungswerfahren im Heiligen Römischen Reich nach dem Westfälischen Frieden)," *Schriften zur Rechtsgeschichte*, Heft 41 (Berlin, 1988), pp. 89-124.
34. Peter Spufford, "Münzverschlechterung und Inflation im spätmittealterlichen und frühmodernen Europa," in: Michael North (Hg.), *Geldumlauf, Währungssysteme und Zahlungsverkehr in Nordwesteuropa 1300-1800* (Köln, 1989), pp. 109-126; Sprenger, *Das Geld der Deutschen*, pp. 126-127.
35. Lars O. Lagerquist, "The First European Banknotes (The Swedish Beginning in the 1660's)," *Rivista Italiana di Numismatica e Scienze Affini* 95 (1993) (Atti del Convegno Internazionale di Studi Numismatici in Occasione del Centenario della Società Numismatica Italiana 1892-1992), pp. 669-677.
36. Torgny Lindgren, *Riksbankens sedelhistoria 1668-1968* (Stockholm, 1968); Chown, *A History of Money*, p. 131; Gaettens, *Geschichte der Infla-*

tionen, pp. 127-146; Bertel Angström, *Plate Money – The World's Largest Currency* (Stockholm, 1986), pp. 12-29.

37. Иван Георгиевич Спасский, *Русская монетная система* [The Russian Monetary System] (Ленинград, 1962), pp. 126-133.
38. Федоров, *Монеты Прибалтики*, pp. 163, 209, 213, 231; Ivar Leimus, "Das Münzwesen Livlands im 16. Jahrhundert (1515-1581/94)," *Stockholm Studies in Numismatics* 1 (1995).
39. Ian Blanchard, *Russia's "Age of Silver": Precious-Metal Production and Economic Growth in the Eighteenth Century* (London, 1989).
40. Иван Георгиевич Спасский, *Талеры в русском денежном обращении 1654-1659 годов (Сводный каталог ефимков)* [The thalers in the Russian monetary system, 1654–1659 (General Catalogue of the Yefimoks)], Ленинград 1960; Ivan G. Spasskii, "The Yefimoks," in: Gregory G. Brunk (ed.), *World Countermarks on Medieval and Modern Coins (*Lawrence, MA, 1976), pp. 158-160; Willy Fuchs, "Die russischen Jefimiki [The Russian Yefimoks]," *Geldgeschichtliche Nachrichten* 14/70 (1979), pp. 49-54; Руслан Марковецкий, „Російскі эфимки (XV-XVII ст.) як історико-економічне джерело," in: Шуст Роман - Крижанівський Андрий - ШвецьВолодимир - Белопольский Сергій [red.], *Грошовий обіг і банківска справа в Україні - минуле та сучасність* (Матеріали міжнародної конференції: "Грошовий обіг і банківска справа в Україні - минуле та сучасність", яка відбулася у Львові 14-15 травня 2004 року) (Львів, 2005), pp. 160-165.
41. Федоров, *Монеты Прибалтики*, pp. 30-351.
42. Petr Vorel, *Stříbro v evropském peněžním oběhu 16. - 17. století (1472-1717)* [Silver in the European monetary circulation of the 16th and 17th centuries: 1472-1717] (Praha, 2009), p. 318, Map Nr. 4: „Evropa v systému mezikontinentálního obchodu se stříbrem v druhé polovině 17. století [The Europe as a part of the intercontinental trade with the silver in the second half of the 17th century]".
43. Kindleberger, *World Economic Primacy,* pp. 109-112.
44. K. N. Chaudhuri, "World Silver Flows and Monetary Factors as a Force of International Economic Integration, 1658-1758," in: W. Fisher – R. McInnis – J. Schneider (eds.), *The Emergence of a World Economy 1500-1914 – Papers of the IX International Congress of Economic History* (Stuttgart, 1986), pp. 61-82.

5

The Conventional Thaler and the World Market in the 18th and 19th Centuries

The development of the European monetary systems in the second half of the 17th century and the first half of the 18th century showed that the European economy still could not manage without precious metals as a value equivalent. The economic theories of mercantilism were also based on this assumption, by which a sufficient quantity of precious metal in a country was considered as a precondition of prosperity and of economic expansion – only, however, if it circulated in the form of minted coins and constituted an "engine" of production and trade.

From this perspective, in the first half of the 18th century, Central Europe, as part of the former Holy Roman Empire, presented a miserable picture. Theoretically, it was still a state unit that had its sovereign (the Roman Emperor) and a joint legislative body, the Imperial Assembly. The Imperial Assembly from the mid-17th century until the extinction of the Empire in 1806 even became a permanent institution, with the responsibility to also take measures in regard to the pan-Imperial currency. In actual fact, there did not exist such a force as could consolidate this internally, politically and religiously diverse grouping of several powerful states, free towns and dozens of insignificant secular and ecclesiastical principalities.

This state-of-affairs was manifested most notably in the monetary system. The Germany Princes of the Baroque period spent huge sums of money on the courtly splendor of their palaces, for imposing baroque residences, which frequently mimicked the style of the French kings. The Baroque courtly culture of the German Lands brought with it until then unimaginable developments in music, theater and philosophy, but with it also the de facto disintegration of the currency into many barely-convertible systems. Any prince could coined his own currency in any variety of metrological parameters and could enforce its circulation in the territory of his own "state," but two villages away it would not be possible to part with it.[1] No change to this development was to take place until the year 1740, following the death of Charles VI, the last Habsburg Emperor.[2]

Both the Habsburg empires built by Charles V and his brother Ferdinand I in the first half of the 16th century, entered the "age of reason" (as scholars described it later, in the 18th century) as backward areas of Europe that could not compete economically with their rivals in the struggle for a new redistribution of influence in the world. The seemingly inexhaustible sources of colonial silver brought mainland Spain into deep poverty because its rulers were unable to handle this wealth wisely. Neither did the Danubian monarchy do any better. Although from the late 17th century it experienced unprecedented success on the Balkan battlefields and rapidly increased its territory far to the southeast, the power boom of the Baroque Viennese court also had its downside. A counterbalance to success on the battlefield came in the form of a long-term tax requirement, with which the core entities of the Habsburg dominions were burdened. Production of handicrafts and trade in towns stagnated; the dependent status of the slavish population on their liege lords in the rural areas deepened; the demands of the state for conscription increased (because there was always a war being fought somewhere) and people of differing beliefs were harassed by religious repression in the course of the introduction of a single (Catholic) State Religion. These changes in the status of most of the population, however, were not a "privilege" of only the countries of the Catholic Habsburgs; similar developments were taking place in most of Central Europe.

In the first half of the 18th century the ruling power in most European countries was still built on dynastic principles and, for the further historical development of the Old Continent, the extinction of both of the branches of the Habsburg family in fairly quick succession (the Spanish in 1700, the Austrian in 1740) had crucial significance. The death of the last Habsburg and its consequences became another milestone on our journey through the history of the dollar, although major changes in this respect did not appear immediately in the year 1740.

Emperor Charles VI died without leaving an heir to the throne, therefore after his death a struggle was unleashed not only for the Imperial Throne, but also for the countries that the last Habsburg had ruled directly in Central Europe as the King of Bohemia, the King of Hungary and the Archduke of Austria, and also for the possessions in the Netherlands and Italy that had remained to him as to the former King of Spain from the heritage of the Spanish Habsburgs. The neighboring states (Bavaria, Saxony and Prussia) refused to respect the hereditary rights of Charles's eldest daughter Maria Theresa and with the support of France (which claimed entitlement to the Habsburg areas in the west of the Empire and in Italy) they divided up the northern part of the Habsburg monarchy.

Maria Theresa of Habsburg was not the first woman whose portrait appeared on the early modern European coins. Prior to her this honor was given to several Queens of England, Sweden's Queen Kristina and Russian Tsarinas in the early part of the 18th century. But she was a woman, whose portrait merchants viewed, created in relief on the silver thaler, when dealing in markets even many decades after her death, even at a distance of thousands of miles from her grave. Maria Theresa did nothing herself personally to particularly earn this privilege; at that time she was rather a symbol of the continuity of the government of the Habsburg family than a real driving force of history. The fact is, however, that but for this woman, there would not exist the peculiar phenomenon in the global market for precious metals known as the "Levant-taler."

This coin, originally called a "conventional thaler" in Europe, was established as part of the reform of the monetary system of the Habsburg monarchy at the beginning of the reign of Maria Theresa. Due to a variety of circumstances, however, it survived for a long time; not only throughout the reign of that monarch, but also the actual existence of the conventional currency (which became defunct in 1857) and, finally, even all the thaler currencies in Europe, that became obsolete in the early 1870's.

The Habsburg Empress Maria Theresa, married to the former Habsburg Governor of Hungary, the Duke of Lorraine Francis Stephen, was in 1740 face-to-face with a fateful decision. To yield to political coercion and military aggression and to settle for at least the remainder of the inheritance from her father, or to embark on an unequal struggle. As is well-known the Viennese Court chose the second alternative. Through skillful political activity and the mobilization of the Military Forces in

Hungary, in 1743 Maria Theresa gradually managed to recover her rule over most of the territory that had been ruled by her father until 1740. Remaining permanently lost were not only former possessions in Italy, but also in Silesia, the vast area northeast of the Bohemian Kingdom that, from the 14th century, had previously constituted part of the Lands of the Bohemian Crown.

The first phase of the military conflicts of this period was concluded by the Peace Treaty of 1748, by which the Viennese Court formally recognized the Prussian rule over Silesia and the County of Kladsko (Glatz). Both countries understood this agreement as only a temporary measure and began intensive preparations for a new war. The Habsburg Monarchy and Prussia, however, were amongst the most economically underdeveloped countries of Central Europe, and without significant reforms to their economic and social structures they could not expect any lasting success, even on the battlefield. Among the first measures that had to be undertaken was a currency reform, since, due to the lack of any strict control over the financial system of the state it was not possible subsequently to reform property taxes, income taxes or trade and export duties. A stable currency was also a prerequisite for targeted support for the production of goods and the development of manufacturing, the purpose of which would be to secure a sufficiency of goods in the market for domestic consumption and also, of course, supplies for the always insatiable army.

The Habsburg Monarchy after the end of war (in 1748) immediately instituted a modest reduction of the silver content of its coins. The weight of 28.82 g of the "Imperial" thalers produced in the territory of the Monarchy in 1659 was maintained, but their purity decreased by 2.5% (from 87.7% of Ag to 85.2% of Ag). A similar, though less significant, reduction of the silver content also took place was in respect of the lesser-value kreutzer coinage. However, this adjustment had not changed yet the basic principle of the old monetary system, in which the "Imperial" thaler was a coin with a varying payment strength, the value of which was adjudicated by government decree.[3]

The fundamental changes in the monetary system of the Habsburg monarchy and in Prussia therefore did not take place until 1750. This year was very significant in respect of the historical development of Western Europe and it has been accurately described as a milestone in the economic history of this region.[4]

Reforms to the monetary systems of the Holy Empire, although they did not take the same form in all parts of it, over the long-term introduced a system, whereby the unit weight of the silver became the common denominator. There was a problem, however, in that, dating from the Middle Ages, throughout Europe there had existed a large number of different weight standards. Although a conversion might be generally applicable, i.e. 1 mark = 2/3 of a pound, this depended on which pound or mark was being referred to. There were dozens of weight standards (specific "marks") in early modern Europe and this made it difficult to convert them.[5] The specific weight of a pound ranged usually between 230 and 255 grams, but some of them significantly deviated from these parameters, e.g. the Munich mark (224.49 g) and the Viennese mark (280.67 g).

In the case of the coins of the Habsburg Monarchy the weight basis until the mid-18th century was the Viennese mark (from this quantity of metal a specific number of coins were produced),[6] therefore it was very difficult (and at that time practically impossible) to maintain an exactly identical silver content with that of the coins of other countries, whose weight was based on a different mark (in the German lands usually the Cologne mark = 233.856 g).

Not until 1750 did the Viennese Court take significant steps towards the unification of its currency with its neighbor countries by adopting the Cologne mark as the primary unit of weight for its new currency, although the new thaler was also, in this sense, a compromise of sorts between the two prior standards. Between the Vienna and Cologne marks a weight ratio of approximately 10:12 was applied. Therefore, after 1750 the content of pure silver in a new Habsburg thaler, i.e. 23.38 g of pure silver was defined as 1/12 of that of the Viennese mark and as 1/10 of that of the Cologne mark. The weight ratio between the two marks (Cologne and Vienna) was also taken into account in determining the purity of sterling metal, for which the ratio between silver and copper was set as 5:1 (83.3% of Ag). From one of Viennese mark of sterling alloy, containing 83.3% of silver and 16.7% of copper, precisely 10 new thalers were produced. Soon afterwards, after Austria and Bavaria agreed upon their production at the Monetary Convention in 1753, the term "conventional thaler" was introduced to define these coins (see **Tab. XL/1**).[7]

Another new development in the monetary system of the Habsburg monarchy was the fixed definition of the nominal value of the thaler, which became no longer just a part of the monetary system, conducted in Rhine-gulden (1 Rhine-gulden = 60 kreutzers). The thaler, with a constant value of 120 kreutzers, was actually a double-guldiner; unlike in the North German and Scandinavian regions, in the Habsburg monarchy it did not represent a numerical monetary unit, but simply the designation of a particular type of coin. Nobody counted their money in thalers; all accounting operations and business transactions were conducted in the domestic currency, i.e. in Rhine-guldens and kreutzers. One Rhine-gulden in the new currency was identical in value to the minted silver half-taler, or to three silver 20-kreutzers or twelve 5-kreutzers.

The Currency reform in the Habsburg Monarchy in 1750 was entirely based on the same principles as those of the Third Imperial Minting Ordinance of Emperor Ferdinand I, dating from the year 1559. After a small-scale adjustment the new currency functioned for more than a century in the form in which it was introduced and conventional thalers from the years 1750-1857 remained legal tender in the territory of the Austro-Hungarian Empire until 1900.

That is to say that the Reform of 1750 differed from that of Ferdinand in 1559 in one fundamental aspect: Emperor Francis I of Lorraine (1745-1765) introduced the new currency only in the area that he actually dominated and which created a single economic area; i.e. in the Central European countries, whose ruler, de jure, was his wife Maria Theresa of Habsburg as the Queen of Bohemia (1743-1780) and Queen of Hungary and Archduchess of Austria (1740-1780). The new currency of the Habsburg monarchy was not conceived of as a pan-Imperial currency and it was not introduced even in the Habsburg possessions in the Netherlands and Italy. The previous monetary systems were retained in those countries; therefore the small coins that Francis I and Maria Theresa ordered to be produced for the Austrian Netherlands (i.e. present-day Belgium) could not be utilized in Prague, Budapest or Vienna.

In regard to the currency reform in the Austrian Netherlands carried out in 1755, the Viennese Court also gave greater consideration to the requirements of Western European money circulation. It introduced the minting of trade coins of the thaler type (also known as crown thalers or cross thalers), which differed considerably from the conventional Central European thalers in their higher content of silver, as they were intended to compete in the West European possessions of the Habsburgs with the French ecu.

Although the Austrian Habsburgs could not count in their Dutch possessions on the supply of precious metals from their overseas colonies as did their Spanish relatives during the 16th and 17th centuries (the target country for this exchange became France), in the mid-18th century the Habsburg monarchy belonged amongst the most important European producers of silver. The basis for this was primarily the newly opened silver mines in the South-Hungarian and Transylvanian mountains, mostly in the territory acquired during the wars against the Ottoman Empire at the cusp of the 17th and 18th centuries. Through the export of silver the Habsburg monarchy was able to make good its negative balance of payments.

Talers, made from 1750 on behalf of the Emperor Francis I of Lorraine and his wife, Maria Theresa of Habsburg, rapidly took over the position of the main Central European silver trading coin. The neighboring states also gradually adapted to this model. In 1753 Maria Theresa signed an agreement with the Bavarian Monarch concerning a common monetary convention, through which Bavaria then also issued their coins in accordance with the Austrian model. Based on this agreement the new currency was given the name "conventional currency," even though in actuality the Austro-Bavarian agreement on monetary union remained in effect for only one year.

A more significant expansion of the conventional currencies in the states of southern and southwestern Germany occurred in the 1760's, following the new Great War that destabilized most of the Central European economies. The majority of the states in the southern part of the former Holy Roman Empire that were motivated by power or were politically connected with the Habsburg Monarchy joined the "conventional currency" system. In no circumstances could it be anticipated that the Austrian model of a new currency would also be adopted by its former arch-enemy that was strengthening its position in the northeast of Germany – that is Prussia.

Monetary reform was also carried out in Prussia in 1750. The Prussian King Frederick II (1740-1786) invited the Dutch financier Johan Philip Graumann whom he had appointed in January 1750 as the General Director of the Mints in the Brandenburg-Prussian Monarchy, to undertake its implementation.[8]

In the second quarter of the 18th century silver coins of higher values were not produced for monetary circulation to any great extent in Prussia. The nation did not have its own silver resources and purchasing silver for coinage purposes was not advantageous. King Frederick William (1712-1740) had already ceased, in regard to the Prussian coinage, to respect the Leipzig Agreement of 1690 (that ratified the production of twelve thalers from one Cologne mark of pure silver) and ordered the minting of primarily small credit coins. Brandenburg double-groschens (on which was embossed a face value of "1/12 thaler")[9] were circulating as the coins with the highest face-value of the domestic legal tender, while the coins for the eastern part of the Prussian Monarchy were produced in accordance with the Polish monetary system. The absence of domestic tender was replaced by an influx of French silver ecus.

The reform of 1750 was therefore intended to unify the currency in all the constituent territories of Prussia, to remove foreign (mainly French) coins from circulation and to stabilize the Prussian coinage, on the basis of the renewal of production of full-bodied silver coins. The "Imperial" thaler ("Reichstaler" in German) remained the monetary unit of Prussia, and 14 of these thalers continued to be produced from one mark of pure silver. The Prussian thaler contained only 16.7 grams of silver and paid in the ratio of 14:10 to the thaler introduced in the Habsburg Monarchy during the same year (the conventional thaler = double-Rhine-gulden). Prussian coins in the denominations of 1, ½ and ¼ of thaler were produced as full-bodied tender; lower denominations (down to 1/48 thaler = 1/2 Prussian groschen) existed from the introduction of the new currency system as credit coins. In this respect, the Prussian reform differed substantially from that in Austria.[10]

What also differed was the vigor with which the Prussian King (who ruled his country in a military manner, whereby everything else was subordinate to the interests of the army) managed to meet his reform goals. By 1752 the Prussian monetary circulation had already been effectively "cleansed" of foreign coins. The raw material base did not change however and militant Prussia was obliged to purchase silver for the production of its coins on the precious metals markets of Saxony in Frankfurt and Leipzig. The optimistically initiated reform therefore began to crumble due to an insufficiency of silver. By the mid-1750's Prussia had already ceased minting full-bodied coins of the higher denominations. The Prussian "Imperial" thalers and their fractions were to be replaced in circulation by the newly introduced 8-groschen (with a nominal value of 1/3 of an Imperial thaler). The principal objective was achieved, however, and King Frederick II was given the opportunity to intervene much more effectively in the internal economy of his country, using the instruments of monetary policy, than during the previous decades. He was soon to take advantage of this situation during the Seven Years War (1756-1763), which he initiated in the manner of a "preventive attack" on the neighboring Habsburg Monarchy. That is to say that the reforms in the countries under the rule of Emperor Francis I of Lorraine and his wife Maria Theresa had been carried out quickly and successfully and the Prussian King did not want to wait for the opposition to gain additional strength.

All the European powers on both sides gradually became involved in the war, either militarily or by providing financial support. In the Habsburg lands, for a certain period of time, the war interrupted the promising reforms that had been initiated, while at the same time bringing about certain innovations that were to prove very practical during the postwar years; namely, the systematic substitution of copper credit tender for the small silver coinage from the year 1760 (which completely resolved the problem in regard to the foreign small coinage that was previously imported abundantly to the Monarchy) and the introduction of paper credit notes in 1762.

The Prussian Monarchy, in which the economic system had been completely subordinated to the needs of war, found itself in economic isolation and at war with most of its neighbor countries. It was able to continue to wage war primarily based on the financial support of Great Britain which provided the Prussian king (as the enemy of its French rival) annual support amounting to several million thalers, paid mostly in gold. Therefore, in the mints in the Prussian territory and in occupied Saxony mainly gold coins were produced; silver full-bodied coinage virtually disappeared from circulation. The production of currency was leased to private companies (partly also to Jewish businessmen) that flooded the monetary circulation of Prussia and the other states of northern Germany with small credit coins.

The Seven Years War in Europe that was concluded by the Peace Treaties of 1763 did not, in the end, change the disputed border between the two most powerful states of Central Europe. The importance of Prussia's power was significantly increased and, for several decades, it represented the most significant latent enemy of the Habsburg Monarchy, though the main direction of Prussian expansion in the last third of the 18th century was focused to the east, especially towards Poland.

After the end of the war, the Prussian King, through the Coin Edict of the 29th March 1764, restored the monetary system on basically the same principles as those of the reform of 1750. The "Imperial" thaler, which contained 1/14 of Cologne mark of pure silver, again formed the basis of the Prussian currency. Also considered as full-bodied coins were fractions of the thaler (down to 1/12 thaler); also retained was the groschen system (1 thaler = 24 groschens). To distinguish them from the inflationary war coins, the small currency units were called "good groschens" ("Guter groschen" in German).

During this postwar era, during which the monetary systems in Germany were reinstated, Prussia clearly diverged from the other countries of the Holy Roman Empire, most of which gradually acceded to the system of conventional currency, in accordance with the Austro-Bavarian model of the year 1753. For business purposes, however, conventional thalers and thalers based on the Burgundy model ("Albertustalers") were also produced in the Prussian mints, though in smaller quantities. In collectors' catalogs of this coinage is not usually differentiated in any way (a thaler is simply a thaler), although in actuality it fulfilled a variety of different functions in monetary circulation.[11]

As a result of the political developments in Central and Northern Europe during the second half of the 18th century the "taler" was utilized in several different forms, e.g. as a unit of account and for the actual minted coins, though they might have a differing content of silver. In accordance with their sequential developmental there were the following thalers:

The Conventional Thaler

This coin was created as a direct successor to the "Imperial" thaler through the reform of the monetary system of the Habsburg Monarchy in 1750. The adjective "conventional" was applied to it in 1753, when it was accepted into the Monetary Convention in the southern area of the Holy Roman Empire and in Bavaria. The basis of the currency was the conventional thaler, containing 23.38 g of Ag, divided into 120 kreutzers; all coins with kreutzer values were considered as full-bodied tender. The conventional currency itself, however, developed in a more complex manner than had been anticipated during the initial currency convention of 1753. In 1754 Bavaria already ceased to conform to this monetary convention and its kreutzer coinage contained less silver than corresponded to the conditions of the convention and therefore the payment strength of Bavarian kreutzers was reduced by 20% in comparison to that of the Austrian kreutzers.

While the other states in the northern and central parts of the Empire also minted conventional thalers (see **Tab. XL/2,3; Tab. XLI-XLIII**), at the same time they maintained their own monetary systems and did not adopt kreutzer units. The conventional thaler was a communal coin in these areas, with fixed payment strength. Most of the States in which conventional thalers were issued bore on them a direct indication of their silver content in German, usually in the form "10 EINE FEINE MARK," i.e. 1/10 of a mark of pure silver (meaning a Cologne mark). By the mid-1760's the conventional currency had been adopted by most of the States within the territory of the Holy Roman Empire, though in fact this large area was divided into three currency areas:

A) The Habsburg Monarchy:
The unit of account was the Rhine-gulden, worth 60 kreutzers; the conventional thaler was worth 2 Rhine-gulden = 120 kreutzers. A Cologne mark of pure silver (10 conventional thalers) was equivalent to 20 Rhine-gulden = 1200 kreutzers in small imperial coins.

B) Bavaria and the smaller states in southern and western Germany:
The unit of account was the gulden, worth 60 kreutzers; the conventional thaler was worth 2 2/5 guldens = 144 kreutzers. A Cologne mark of pure silver (10 conventional thalers) was equivalent to 24 guldens = 1440 kreutzers of small Bavarian coins.

C) The States of Central and Northern Germany:
The unit of account was the "Imperial" thaler, worth 24 groschens; the conventional thaler was worth 1 1/3 of an Imperial thaler = 32 groschens. A Cologne mark of pure silver (10 conventional thalers) was equivalent to 13½ "Imperial" thalers = 324 groschens.

The Crown Thaler, also called the Cross Thaler

This was a coin introduced in the South (Habsburg) Netherlands in 1755 as a full-bodied tender worth 9 escalins (shillings). It differed at first sight from other thaler coins through its powerful eye-catching symbol of the St. Andrew's or Burgundy Cross (whence the name "cross thaler"), between the arms of which the Royal Crown was depicted (whence the name "crown thaler"). Externally it was similar to the older Dutch patacon (the Albertustaler), but it contained a slightly higher content of silver (with a total weight of 29.44 g, with 87.3% of Ag, it contained 25.7 grams of pure silver). The Cross thaler was therefore recognized in the Habsburg Monarchy as legal tender of a higher value; it was worth 2 Rhine-gulden and 11 kreutzers of conventional currency. During the French Revolution and the subsequent Napoleonic Wars, production of the Cross thaler was also introduced at other Mints belonging to the Habsburg Monarchy, where it was produced for commercial purposes and used in tandem with the conventional thalers for the payment of mercenaries (see **Tab. XLIV/1-2**). Its production was discontinued in the early 19th century; it remained as legal tender in the Habsburg Monarchy however for nearly the next hundred years.

The Prussian Thaler

In addition to being unit of account, coins minted with this value were also introduced in 1750 by the Prussian King Frederick II and renewed again in 1764. During the last third of the 18th century it was circulating mainly in Brandenburg and in the Prussian Monarchy, and in that area of Poland that was occupied in the late 18th century by Prussia. A Cologne mark of pure silver was equivalent to 14 Prussian Imperial thalers (see **Tab. XLV/1**). This metrological standard, due to the increasing dominance of the power of Prussia in the German Lands, was applied over an increasingly wider area and in the middle of the 19th century it formed the basis for the principal German-Austrian common currency (called "unified currency," see below).

The Hanoverian Thaler

Hannover (and Brunswick–Lünneburg) continued to mint coins in accordance with the Coin Order of Leipzig from 1690, therefore a Cologne mark of pure silver was equivalent to 12 Hanoverian thalers. This thaler was at the same time a unit of account, divided into 36 "Mariangroschens"; on larger denomination coins the data were reported in both values (e.g. 2/3 of a thaler and also 24 Mariangroschens). In the late 18th century it was still explicitly stated on the larger coins that they were minted in accordance with the Imperial Coin Ordinance (i.e. the Coin

Order of Leipzig from 1690). Hannover and Brunswick were significant producers of silver, therefore their coinages were wide-spread in the western area of the Empire. In accordance with the personnel union the Ruler of these countries was the English Monarch. Hanoverian thalers, in accordance with the Coin Order of Leipzig from 1690, were minted until the early 19th century.

From the mid-1760's, the conventional thaler took over the role of the principal full-bodied coin in Germany. In the complex currency conditions of this region of Europe the indication of the amount of precious metal contained in full-bodied silver coins directly on the coins appeared to be a necessity. In addition to the older Imperial thalers from before 1750 in circulation (called "talers in species" or "speciestalers"), as in the 16th and 17th centuries, also circulating were various coinages of the thaler type. To determine their payment strength, however, it was no longer necessary to utilize valuation catalogs since the full-bodied thalers and the smaller coins had directly embossed on them the indication of their precious metal content, defined as fractions of a Cologne mark (233.8555 g).

Based on this system, the conventional currency survived, without any adjustments, such fundamental collapse of the power structures and the economies of most European countries as was brought about by the wars with Revolutionary and Napoleonic France at the cusp of the 18th and 19th centuries. The threatened war inflation devalued only credit tender (paper and metal). In most European countries (as previously in the 17th century in Sweden) two parallel monetary systems were established during the war (full-bodied tender and credit tender) and the mutual exchange ratio between them was evolved dynamically and generally also remained in effect during the post-war reconstruction.

The Napoleonic Wars fundamentally altered the political map of Europe. While the Peace Negotiations of the Vienna Congress sought to restore the prewar status quo, in many cases a return to the old system was no longer possible. Also significantly affected by the new situation was the development of the Central European currencies.

First, the Holy Roman Empire officially ceased to exist (1806). The ruler of the Habsburg Empire, the Holy Roman Emperor Francis II, had already been declared Emperor of Austria in 1804 (as Francis I). The number of State Units in the German territory diminished sharply and thereby many currency sub-systems that were still surviving from the 18th century disappeared. The process of the unification of Germany in the 19th century was primarily a matter of power and politics and it was most clearly reflected in the development of the currency.

The conventional currency had remained unchanged during the Habsburg Monarchy; both conventional and cross full-bodied silver thalers continued to be minted during the war, as well as in the times of deepest crisis, because the State Treasury needed them for business purposes, to pay for reparations and debts. Both paper and credit copper money were issued during the war in inflationary amounts and their purchasing power declined proportionately. The State bankruptcy of 1811 reduced the nominal value of the inflationary money to one-fifth of its previous value, and, though it was anticipated that through this course of action, during the subsequent war years, the currency would increase in value against the conventional silver currency, it was, however, devalued.

After the war, in 1816, the Imperial Court was obliged to officially confirm the existence of a dual parallel currency. All the financial data were still recorded in the old units, in Rhine-gulden = 60 kreutzers, but it become compulsory to indicate whether it was the conventional currency ("Convention Münze," abbreviated as "C.M.") or the Viennese currency ("Wiener Währung," abbreviated as "W.W."). In 1816 the exchange ratio between the two currencies was fixed at 1:2½; this relationship was maintained until 1857, when both these currencies ceased to exist. At that time the conventional thaler (see **Tab. XLVII/2-3**) was still a "double-Rhine-gulden C.M." in the conventional currency while in Viennese currency it was accepted as the equivalent of "five Rhine-guldens W.W."

It is easier to understand this development based on the example of the Habsburg Monarchy, because the units of account (i.e. Rhine-guldens) were named differently than were the units of the full-bodied silver coins (conventional thalers). A similar development also took place, however, in three other areas where the thaler was, at the same time, both a numerical monetary unit and a silver or, in the case of Hannover, gold full-bodied coin. At the time of the Napoleonic wars there were three large areas of contemporary Europe, in which a "dual" thaler of this nature existed: Prussia, the states of southwestern Germany and the Nordic region (Denmark, Sweden and Norway).

East-German Prussia was to play a decisive role in the further development of the thaler in Central Europe. Another currency reform took place in Prussia in the year 1821. The "Imperial" thaler remained the primary unit, carrying the same silver content (1/14 of a Cologne mark), that had been defined as early as in 1750. The thaler there was both a full-bodied coin and a unit of account, now divided into 30 groschens equivalent to 12 pfennigs (prior to 1821 it had been divided into 24 groschens). The Prussian monetary system was adopted by the other German states, with the exception of Saxony. The establishment of the German Customs Union ("Zollverein" in German) in 1834 became an important milestone on the path of the monetary integration of Germany. Over time, most of the States in the northern part of the former Holy Roman Empire were to become members of it (see **Tab. XLIX/1-2**).

Prussia had played a major integrative role in the creation of this new common economic area, therefore the common currency of the German Customs Union was derived from the Prussian thaler. The individual states retained their own monetary systems and units of account. These, however, had to be convertible to the "Unified" thaler (i.e. with a silver content of 1/14 Cologne mark, identical to the older Prussian "Imperial" thaler) or to the "Unified" double-taler (containing 1/7 of a Cologne mark of pure silver).

The conventional currency in the southern parts of the former Holy Roman Empire remained in its original form until the second half of the 1830's. It ceased to exist in 1837 through the concluding of the Mint Agreement at a conference in Munich by which the four southern German states (Bavaria, Baden, Württemberg and Nassau) agreed on the creation of their own single currency area, independent of both the Habsburg Monarchy currency and that of the German Customs Union. Thereby the South German Currency Union initiated its own common currency, the unit of which was the "guldiner."

By 1838, however, an agreement (known as the Dresden Coin Convention) had already been concluded between the two German monetary unions concerning the production of full-bodied means of payment with identical metrological parameters. The coins of the South German currency with a value of 3½ guldiners had the same silver content as a "Unified" double-taler. The "Unified" double-taler (equivalent to 3½ South German guldiners) became the principal full-bodied silver coin in the larger part of the German territory (see **Tab. XLIX/3**). It was coined by the Member States of both the Minting Unions and was accepted as the official currency throughout the entire territory. Through the monetary reform of the years 1840-1841 Saxony also accepted this model of a new unified currency; this confirmed the growth of the economic and political importance of Prussia in northern Germany.

The "Unified" silver thaler became both a symbol of the economic integration of Germany under Prussian leadership and the most important tender in the area of commerce. Gold coins were produced in the German region only as trading coins, while the paper currency had only limited territorial validity.

The concept of the political unification of all the Central European countries, in which German was the language spoken, was a manifestation of the strength of the German national movements in the 19th century. The rapidity of the process of monetary integration, however, also confirmed in practice the tremendous advantage that a large economic area without monetary and customs barriers provided for the development of production and trade. Although the individual ruling families of the German Principalities and kingdoms surrendered their sovereignty only reluctantly, in the name of integration, the rapid development of industry and trade and also the German ambitions to be a great-power dulled the former luster of the ruling aristocracy. The future destiny of the state was decided in the second half of the 19th century not only by the "Rulers by the Grace of God," but also, increasingly, by financiers, politicians and mining and industrial magnates.

The Habsburg Monarchy, headed during the revolutionary events of 1848 by the then very young Emperor Franz Joseph I (*1830, †1916), was still viewed halfway through the 19th century as a possible power center for the future unification of the German lands. The situation was complicated, however, in terms of the German national movements by the fact that the German-speaking population of the Habsburg Monarchy constituted only a significant minority. Apart from the area in which German was predominantly spoken, large parts of the monarchy were inhabited by Hungarians, Italians and Romanians. The largest proportion of the population of the state numerically, however, utilized as their native language one of the Slavic languages that closely resembled each other and, for members of these groups, were easy to understand in everyday communication (in the north of Monarchy: Czech, Slovak, Polish and Ukrainian; in the south of Monarchy: Slovenian, Croatian and Serbian). In terms of establishing a new "Europe of Nations" (as the then national-liberation and irredentist-type movements defined this concept) there was no reason why the Austrian Empire in its entirety should be constituted as a new, ethnically German nation.

An economic connection was in the interest of both parties, however. Therefore, in 1857, an extensive and somewhat complicated agreement was concluded on the establishment of a "Unified Currency."[12] This actually consisted of two mutually unconnected systems. The crown became the gold unit of the unified currency (only crowns and half-crowns were minted as purely commercial coins; no lower denominations were minted); the silver "Unified" thaler became the unit of the silver currency with a fixed payment strength in the monetary systems of the individual countries that adopted the unified currency.

The basis of the unified currency was silver as a precious metal, the price of which, in the years 1848-1870, was strengthening on the world market and appeared to be more stable than that of gold, which had also been greatly influenced by the export of gold from the abundant newly discovered American deposits.[13]

In the case of the Austrian Empire the adjustment of the internal currency relationships represented a very determined intervention as it introduced an entirely new currency with different values. First, de facto, the conventional currency, which in 1857 was actually in use only within the Austrian Empire, was withdrawn. In place of the unit of account the "Rhine-gulden = 60 kreutzers" a new decimal system was introduced: "Austrian gulden = 100 kreutzers." Conversion of the old monetary units to new was quite complicated (especially for kreutzers, which now had a lower value), because the amount of 1 Rhine-gulden from the old currency was converted into the new currency as 1 gulden and 5 kreutzers of Austrian currency, or (as it was then said), of the "Austrian number" (in German abbreviated as "ö.W.," i.e. "österreichische Währung").

The main reason for this adjustment, however, was the introduction of new silver full-bodied coins, "Unified" thalers, through the issuance of which (in addition to coins of the Austrian currency intended for internal circulation), the Austrian Empire united its monetary system with that of the German Customs Union. New thalers of unified currency (minted in "thaler" and "double-thaler" values) were virtually identical in their silver content with the older thalers of the German

Customs Union. The metric pound (in German "Pfund"), weighing 500 grams was chosen as their weight basis, for the simplification of the arithmetical calculations associated with the transition to the decimal system. The content of pure silver in the "Unified" thaler was no longer defined as 1/14 of a Cologne mark, but as a 1/30 of a metric pound. The inscription on the German federal thalers, which was "XXX EIN PFUND FEIN" (see **Tab. L**) also corresponded with this; analogically, on double-talers, it was "XV EIN PFUND FEIN."[14]

The newly introduced Austrian currency of "Unified" thalers (both domestic and foreign) was used within the Austrian Empire as circulation coins in the ratio of 1 "Unified" thaler = 1½ gulden ö.W. = 150 kreutzers ö.W. From 1858 silver "Unified" thalers already started to be produced in large quantities by the Habsburg Monarchy Mints (see **Tab. LII/1**). Also contributed to this were the newly discovered large reserves of silver ore, mined from deep mines around the Czech town of Příbram.

The quantity of Příbram silver mined during the 19th century greatly exceeded the volume of the mining in the Jáchymov region in the 16th century. The actual purchasing power of silver at the beginning of the 19th century was, however, substantially lower than it had been some 350 years previously, although the exchange ratio in the 16th century between gold and silver had oscillated at around the value of 1:15. By the 1870's this situation changed dramatically, however.

But the "life-span" of the thaler was terminated even prior to the global decline in the price of silver. The "Unified" thaler, which represented one of the potential means for the economic integration of Central Europe, died symbolically on the European battlefields at the cusp of the 1860's and the 1870's.

The first battleground was in the vicinity of the East Bohemian town of Hradec Králové, where, in 1867, the Prussian and Austrian armies clashed in a bloody battle. The Prussian victory in this brief war finally confirmed the crucial role played by Prussia in the establishment of a unified Germany, of which the Austrian Empire was no longer considered to be a part. Following this conflict the Habsburg Monarchy withdrew from a federal agreement on a Currency Union and ceased minting coins of the unified currency. Thereby, after nearly four centuries, the era ended of the production of silver thaler coins in the countries that had been previously ruled by the Habsburgs. The last Austrian

"Unified" thalers bear the date 1866 (see **Tab. LII/2**). The currency unit of the Monarchy remained the "gulden ö.W.". Older silver thalers, however, continued to circulate for some time as the official currency in the territory of the Habsburg Monarchy in three forms: cross thalers from the years 1755-1800 were worth 230 kreutzers ö.W., conventional thalers from years 1750-1856 were worth 210 kreutzers ö.W., and finally "Unified" thalers from the years 1857-1867 were worth 150 kreutzers ö.W.

The battlefields of the Franco-Prussian war of 1870-1871 became the next symbolic battleground. Victorious Prussia took advantage of its military superiority and achieved the reunification of Germany (excluding the Austrian Empire). A common currency, based on the decimal system, was created for the new German Empire: 1 Reichsmark = 100 pfennigs. Thereby the thaler of the South German Currency Union ceased to exist, both as a coin and a unit of account, and as the unified currency, which had functioned virtually unchanged in Germany, even after the secession of the Austrian Empire from the currency union.

In the unified German Empire the "Unified" thaler circulated for some time longer, as a coin with a payment strength of three Reichsmarks. The amount of silver contained in it was no longer of importance for its payment strength since the new Deutsche Mark was part of the monetary system, assured by gold. Abandonment of the silver monetary standard was caused by the increasing instability of the price of silver and its gradual fall.

The last area in Europe in which thalers were used as minted coins and as numerical monetary units remained in the Nordic countries. In Denmark, Norway and Sweden, there were similar monetary systems, the unit of account of which was "Imperial" thaler, i.e. "rigsdaler" (abbreviated to "Rgd."). In each of these countries the rigsdalers had a different payment strength; they circulated in all of them, however, in the following ratios: 1 Swedish Rgd. = ½ Norwegian Rgd. = ¼ Danish Rgd (see **Tab. XLVI/2**). In addition to these monetary units, also minted were full-bodied silver dalers called "rigsdaler species" (corresponding in their silver content with the Imperial thaler from prior to 1750; see **Tab. XLVI/3**). This Scandinavian thaler currency disappeared, however, at the same time as did the thalers in Germany. In 1872, the Scandinavian countries established their own monetary alliance, called the Scandinavian Monetary Union. Its principal monetary unit was the krone, divided into 100 öre and its conversion relationship, as of the founding of the Union, was 1 krone = 1¼ Reichsmark.

"Thaler" (and its variant forms – taler, daler, daalder, tolar, etc.) was, in Europe, the term, almost exclusively used to indicate a currency established on a silver basis or specifically a full-bodied silver coin bearing a mandatory content of precious metal.[15] The significant decline in silver prices on the world market in the 1870's destabilized all the currencies that were designated in this manner and also created problems for those currencies that used a bimetallic gold-silver system. Together with the fall of silver from its position as the precious metal of full-bodied coins that occurred because of the dramatic decline in the price of this metal in the early 1870's, the silver thaler remained only in the historical annals of the European Monetary Systems.

Notes

1. Konrad Schneider, "Frankfurt a. M. und die Geldkrise des 18. Jahrhunderts," *Scripta Mercaturae* 39 (2005), Nr. 1, pp. 1-44.
2. Volker Press, *Kriege und Krisen (Deutschland 1600-1715)* (München, 1991); Geoffrey Parker, "The Emergence of Modern Finance in Europe 1500-1730," in: Carlo M. Cipolla (ed.), *The Fontana Economic History of Europe II: The 16th and 17th Centuries* (London, 1974), pp. 527-594; Thomas DaCosta Kaufmann, *Höfe, Klöster und Städte: Kunst und Kultur in Mitteleuropa 1450-1800* (Köln, 1998), pp. 341-370, 407-430.
3. Günther Probst, *Österreichische Münz- und Geldgeschichte: Von den Anfängen bis 1918* (Wien, 1973), pp. 393-492.
4. Oskar Schwarzer, "Die Stellung 'Westeuropas' in der Weltwirtschaft 1750-1950," in: Michael North (red.), *Nordwesteuropa in der Weltwirtschaft 1750-1950* [Northwestern Europe in the World Economy 1750-1950] (Stuttgart, 1993), pp. 257-290.
5. Petr Vorel, *Stříbro v peněžním oběhu*, p. 66, Tab. Nr. 3 "Hlavní hmotnostní jednotky evropského mincovnictví raného novověku [The main units of weight in the European mint of the early modern era]."
6. Bernd Sprenger, *Das Geld der Deutschen: Geldgeschichte Deutschlands* (Paderborn, 1995), pp. 130-132.
7. Helmut Kahnt – Bernd Knorr, *Alte Maße, Münzen und Gewichte: ein Lexicon* (Leipzig, 1986), pp. 178-180; Eckart Schremmer, "Über 'stabiles Geld' (Eine wirtschaftshistorische Schicht)," *Vortragsreihe der Gesellschaft für Westfälische Wirtschaftsgeschichte e. V.*, Heft 29 (Dortmund, 1991), pp. 10-19.

8. Michael North, "Geldumlauf und Wirtschaftsregion (Untersuchungen am Beispiel Königreich Preußen und des Herzogtums Preußen in der Frühen Neuzeit)," *Hamburger Beiträge zur Numismatik*, Neue Folge, Heft 30/32, 1976/78 (Hamburg, 1985), pp. 71-88.
9. Chester L. Krause – Clifford Mishler_(ed. Colin R. Bruce), *Standard catalog of World Coins. World Coins Listings by date and mint 1701-1800* (Iola, 1996), pp. 398-403.
10. Sprenger, *Das Geld der Deutschen*, p. 136.
11. John S. Davenport, *German Talers 1700-1800* (London, 1979), pp. 259-266, Nr. 2581-2603.
12. Karl Helfferich, *Die Folgen des deutsch-österreichischen Münzvereins von 1857: Ein Beitrag zur Geld- und Währungstheorie* (Straßburg, 1894).
13. John F. Chown, *A History of Money from AD 800* (London, 1995), pp. 81-82.
14. Helfferich, *Die Folgen des deutsch-österreichischen Münzvereins von 1857: Ein Beitrag zur Geld- und Währungstheorie* (Straßburg, 1894); Sprenger, *Das Geld der Deutschen*, pp. 156-183.
15. Sprenger, *Das Geld der Deutschen*, tab. "Währungsgebiete und Münzsysteme in Deutschland am 1. 1. 1834," pp. 160.

6

Thalers and Dollars in America

The importation of precious metals from the American Continents, starting in the early 16th century, became one of the main economic factors affecting the overall economy of Europe and, through its long-term consequences, also its political development. It created instability in its monetary systems because both the precious metals lost their purchasing power. This resulted in sharp rises in the prices of food and of other commodities. This "price revolution," as this phenomenon is defined in literature, passed successively through the European economies, traveling steadily from west to east (in Central Europe it was significantly in evidence from the mid-16th century). One consequence of this also was the increased interest of trading companies in the Eastern European markets, where goods, the price of which had risen sharply in the west, could still be purchased very inexpensively for gold or silver.[1]

Together with the general rise in prices that also occurred in Central and Eastern Europe the ratio between the values of gold and silver changed. Therefore the efforts of the Austrian Habsburgs to maintain parity between the gold gulden and its silver equivalent (the guldiner) could not be sustained permanently. The influence of Spain also played an important role in this process: silver was markedly cheaper in the Spanish monetary system; the ratio of the price of gold to silver, at the cusp of the 15th and 16th centuries stabilized at 1:16. In Central Europe this ratio was different and oscillated at between cca. 1:10 and 1:11. Therefore it was advantageous to exchange Hungarian, Salzburg and Silesian gold ducats or gold coins from the Rhineland for Spanish silver coinage, to buy silver for the gold obtained, repeated over and over again. Such trades were worthwhile primarily when carried out in large volume, because, due to high transport costs, these transactions were not effective if they were conducted on a "retail" level.

An ideal area for conducting such trades proved to be a coastal area in the Netherlands that was a Spanish province. In these lands no significant amount of gold or silver has ever been mined. Yet here in the 16th century a dense network of mints appeared that were putting into circulation for the whole of Europe immense quantities of Dutch gold ducats and silver thalers. The financial center of the "old world" moved from the Italian City States to the coastline of the North Sea, as ships loaded with gold and silver from the Spanish colonies arrived there. The volume of gold imported in the first decades of the 16th century had reached the level of its entire European production and after the mid-16th century the imports of both precious metals began to greatly exceed it.

In the first decades following the conquest of the American Continents it was primarily gold, in the form of jewelry and vessels, that was imported into Europe, obtained from treasures stolen from the wealth of the advanced indigenous cultures of Central and South America. The vast majority of this was utilized immediately as pagament for minting Spanish coins. While searching for the mineral sources of the Aztec gold, however, Cortés' prospectors also discovered, in what is now Mexico, rich resources of silver. This ore with a high metal content, sometimes even appearing as veins of silver metal, could initially be extracted easily, sometimes even from surface deposits.

The Conquistadors themselves, of course, were not able to extract silver ore or to process it in metallurgical workshops. For this purpose it was necessary to procure experienced specialists from Europe. Already in 1523, however, shortly after the Fall of Aztec Tenochtitlan, Europeans initiated the ongoing mining of silver in the mountains close to the present location of the town of Taxco. Its intense exploitation was initially prevented by the shortage of a workforce. More and more reserves of silver ore were being discovered in the Mexican mountains, but there was no one to mine it and process it. The Colonial Mining Companies first utilized the labor of Indian prisoners captured in battle, whom they were purchasing from local indigenous rulers. Due to the high mortality-rate of the Indians who were struggling to get used to laboring in the ore mines, this strategy proved too costly. Therefore in 1534, the Spanish King Charles I (who was also the Emperor Charles V of Habsburg) issued a decree by which any indigenous people who manifested hostility to European colonizers and Catholic Church should be put into slavery. Complete supervision over the Ore Mines was taken over by Antonio de Mendoza, a member of an important family of the Spanish Nobility who had been appointed the Viceroy of the Spanish King in New Spain, as the area including today's Mexico, Guatemala and parts of the United States (Wyoming and California) was called. During Mendoza's tenure as Viceroy of Mexico (1535-1549) the volume of mining of American silver began to accelerate rapidly and from the mid-16th century the processing of American silver ore also accelerated due to the introduction in 1557 of a process called amalgamation.

Most of the American silver was imported into Europe, already in the form of minted coins, the production of which was introduced at the Central Mint (in present-day Mexico City), newly established in 1536 by the Viceroy Antonio de Mendoza. The extraction of precious metals, which was a priority of the Spanish Colonial Administration on the American Continent, also increased gradually in the Spanish Colonies in South America that covered a large area of Central and South America from present-day Panama to Argentina.[2] In Lima, in the Vice-Kingdom of Peru the minting of coins commenced in 1568. The best known and most profitable source of South American silver became the "Silver Mountain" in Potosi, Bolivia, where immense resources of silver were discovered in the year 1545. A special mint was established in the year 1574 for processing the local silver in the rapidly expanding town of Cerro de Potosi, at the foot of the mountain.[3]

It was the exploitation of the wealth of this Bolivian mountain that rattled the European silver market in the second half of the 16th century.[4] This is very clearly defined by the statistics concerning the average annual production from the mining of silver, which the most important production areas in Europe and in the Spanish Colonies supplied to the market in precious metals during the 16th century: from the 1520's to the mid-1540's the percentage ratio between the imported silver and that mined in Europe was approximately 18:82. From the late 1540's, however, the share of imported colonial silver began to rise sharply and by the late 16th century this ratio had reversed to approximately 12:88.[5]

In the second half of the 16th century, from the Colonial Mints in what are now Mexico,[6] Peru and Bolivia, hundreds of tons of silver coins were shipped to Europe.[7] However, in the European monetary circulation of that time there were virtually no "American" coins. How is that possible?

Like the Indian treasures from the early 16th century the tender produced in the American Mints served primarily as a base material for European coinage. In the case of the earliest mintage of the 16th and 17th centuries there were in fact no coins produced in a form that Europeans were accustomed to. What was sent to Europe were bulky embossed pieces of precious metal of only an approximately circular shape. Their production had to be rapid and it was not necessary to take the quality of the processing into account, since they were destined for subsequent melting. This provisional processing of the precious metal into a coin form was principally a technical measure, facilitating control over the market in precious metals produced in the American colonies. Trade in uncoined silver (and also in gold) from the American mines was strictly forbidden and subject to the supervision of the Officials of the Spanish Viceroy's Administration. By virtue of his regal status, one fifth of all the precious metal from the mining of silver belonged to the Spanish King.[8] Under the threat of severe penalties for non-adherence, all the silver mined had to be delivered to the Government Mints and processed there prior to being transported across the ocean. This was how "ship coins" came into being, as American coinage produced for export to Europe. They were in fact a semi-finished product of the mandatory quality and weight, that was not designed primarily for direct circulation, but was intended to simplify the subsequent processing of the precious metals into a standard coinage by the European Mints. That is why the coin blanks, intended for transport to Europe were produced within the metrological parameters of the Spanish currency.

During the first half of the 16th century the Spanish currency functioned on a three-tiered system consisting of golden coinage (the escudo), silver coinage (the real) and copper coinage (the maravedi) with a conversion ratio of 1 escudo = 16 reales and 1 real = 34 maravedi. Therefore even in the Spanish Overseas mints all the denominations were produced, including even the copper maravedi in small quantities, for the internal purposes of the Colonial Administration. Primarily minted for export to Europe, however, whither the vast majority of the production of the colonial mines was directed, were the highest common denominations of Spanish currency, i.e. octuples of the basic units: the gold 8-escudo coin and the silver 8-real coin. The large silver coin of the

Spanish monetary system with a value of 8 reales was called a "peso," which was an abbreviation from its original designation as a "peso de á ocho" i.e. "a piece of eight," understood as eight reales.

This system for processing precious metals in the Spanish Colonies was essentially retained until the 18th century. The systematic minting of technically high-quality coins made of precious metals was introduced in Mexico only from 1732. However, production of semi-finished products for export, "ship coins," also known as "cobs" continued in South and Central America; in the Peruvian mints until 1751, in Guatemala until 1753, in Potosi in Bolivia until as late as 1773 (see **Tab. LIII/1-3**).[9]

Spanish 8-real coins and their colonial version were similar in their size and weight to Central European thalers. In older times, prior to the mid-18th century, the designation "taler" was not used for 8-real coins; there was no reason why it should have been. In Spain and its colonies the thaler was referred to in Spanish as a "peso." The Spanish colonial 8-real coins did not appear in the 16th and 17th centuries in the monetary circulation of the Holy Roman Empire, Scandinavia, Poland or Hungary, in which all the large silver coins were called "talers." More specifically: they did not appear there in their original form as "ship coins," but indirectly as European, mainly Dutch coins that were produced from American colonial silver.

A significant change in the function of Spanish 8-real colonial silver coins brought about a change in the technology of their production in the second third of the 18th century. In their new form, as standard machine-minted coins of a regular shape (see **Tab. LIV/1**), Mexican and South American 8-real coins began to be used as the principal currency in the British Colonies in North America.

Until the discovery of rich reserves of gold and silver in the 19th century, extensive regions of North American did not have available any significant resources of precious metals of their own.[10] The British colonies on the East Coast of North America, that had been gradually founded and colonized since the early 17th century, initially did not have any inherent monetary system, nor their own currency. In formal terms the British currency was applicable there (1 pound = 20 shillings, 1 shilling = 12 pence), in which all accounts and receivables were denominated. In actuality, however, this money did not circulate there more widely. Exports from England to the Colonies had been strictly prohibited since

1695, independent resources of precious metals were not available to them and wholesale transactions were carried out through transfers between accounts.[11]

North American colonies were expected to produce requisite raw materials for their European metropolis, in exchange for which other European and Asian goods were supplied. The gradual development of the North American colonies, in which, mainly in the coastal areas, urban centers arose of a European type, required, however, the creation of some means of exchange. Without these the development of trade and of marketing was unimaginable. Europeans who were seeking to make their fortune in the North American Colonies were obviously familiar with the money from their original homelands and tried to replace them in some way. The internal economy of the North American colonies had to cope with a severe lack of precious metals.[12]

One method was to use alternative means of exchange, such as Indian wampum recognized in the 17th century as formal tender for the payment of small sums.[13] The general shortage of minted coins persisted in the North American colonies until the first half of the 18th century –even in 1730 in Virginia bundles of dried tobacco leaves were recognized as an official currency. Payments were not made directly with tobacco, but with vouchers, which were issued by the public tobacco warehouses established by the Colonial Administration, after the depositing of this commodity in a certain value.[14]

The oldest North American coins were produced from the year 1652 by the Mint in Boston in the territory of the Massachusetts Colony (later to become the State of the same name). This colony, whose inhabitants were mostly members of the Puritan Church, was the most active on the path towards creating an independent North American currency, but these efforts failed to meet with understanding, particularly in England itself. The production of Boston coins commenced, against the will of the Imperial Court as a manner of protest by the Massachusetts settlers against the British colonial monetary policy. In the first phase, imported English coins (the threepence, sixpence and shilling) were marked with the letters "NE" (i.e. "New England") and their value in pence ("III," "VI" or "XII").[15]

However, the volume of European coins that reached the American Continent, mostly in the luggage of the colonists themselves, was too small. Therefore the Boston Mint, run by John Hull, proceeded to manufacture its own coinage in values of from two to twelve pence. Primarily used for their production was Spanish colonial silver, which arrived on the North American mainland in various ways (mostly as pirate booty). Boston coins while respecting the English monetary system, otherwise differed significantly from European coinage. The obverse side bore the image of a pine tree while the reverse side showed the value of the coin in pence, in Roman numerals, and the year "1652."[16] It was inscribed with the words "MASATHVSETS IN NEW ENGLAND," starting on the face and finishing on the back (see **Tab. LIII/4**). These coins, produced until the mid-1680's without any change to the date shown, were declared the official currency by the Parliament of the Colony of Massachusetts. During three decades of activity at the Boston Mint coins worth about a million pounds were produced there.

Boston "pine" coins, however, despite their undoubted business and symbolic importance were not to become the basis for the creation an independent currency for the English colonies in America and in 1684, under pressure from the Royal Court, the production of this coinage was terminated. The Puritan community tried to replace the metal coins with credit paper currency. In 1686 John Blackwell had already founded a private Mortgage Bank in Boston. The banknotes produced by Blackwell did not inspire confidence, however, and in the monetary circulation they did not assert. More successful were the activities of the Massachusetts Colonial Parliament, which decided in 1690 to issue its own paper credit bills with a total nominal value of 7,000 pounds. Initially these were not intended for use as legal tender, but in times of scarcity of any other money they were used on a daily basis and they proved their excellence in the first years of their existence because their payment strength was backed by the payment authority of the State. This principle emerged as the best manner for the future in which the American Colonies and their internal monetary circulation could gradually became independent of England (or, from the beginning of the 18th century, of Great Britain).[17]

In this manner, under pressure to a certain extent, American "paper" currency was developed as an emergency solution, by means of which the local fast-growing multi-ethnic community had to cope with the shortage of precious metals, which were, according to the economic theory of the time known as mercantilism, the main measure of value and a guarantee of the stability of the currency. Other colonies that were issuing their credit bills also followed the example of Massachusetts. Efforts by British officials to restrict the issuance of these means of payment and for their replacement with minted coins proved impossible, since the monetary system still had a shortage of metal coins in. In the Colony of Massachusetts, where the officials of the British Administration tried to cancel the circulation of paper bills, because of a shortage of coins in 1735 settlers had to be permitted reimbursement of compulsory levies and of taxes in kind.

In peacetime, when standard business contracts were valid, the bank credit system functioned and the currency was assured by the authority of the state, a credit tender could fulfill the function of a means of exchange without any problem. In a time of war or of economic instability, however, a credit tender lost its reliability because a large amount of it could be produced relatively quickly and its payment strength was devalued by inflation. In the rapidly growing North American Colonies, a situation of this nature occurred in the mid-18th century, when a war conflict between the European powers (the Seven Years' War from 1756-1763) was transmitted to the American Continent.

Trading companies with intercontinental operations, of which the Dutch still retained a decisive share, in times of instability secured their available funds to a greater extent with precious metal and purchased the most important export commodity, produced at that time by the Spanish Colonies in Central and South America – i.e. precious metals in the form of trading coins. At the time of stabilization, following the end of hostilities, silver stocks were placed in circulation in large quantities in the North American Colonies, whose rapidly expanding production experienced a postwar boom. In this manner silver Mexican 8-real coins, which at that time were in large quantities exported mainly as trading silver to Asia and Africa, but later also to Great Britain, entered the monetary circulation of the North American Colonies.

The Spanish colonial coins gained confidence amongst American settlers because of their stable content of precious metal. That is to say that they were not a standard common tender, circulating at a specific nominal value, but trading coins, monetized precious metal, in the case of which, for commercial reasons, it was desirable for their producer to maintain their consistent production parameters over many decades.

Unlike the older semi-finished coined products, destined for export to Europe as bullion (especially for minting Dutch trading thalers), the Mexican 8-real coins of the new type were already being minted regularly in the mid-18th century as standard European coins of a high quality. Also machine finishing of their edges was carried out, in accordance with which it was obvious at first glance, and without weighing, whether or not the coin had been fraudulently "lightened" by cutting its peripheral area, as was common in the case of the older irregularly shaped "ship coins."

Mexican 8-real coins, i.e. the silver peso, at the beginning of the last third of the 18th century thereby became the most important type of coin used for cash payments in the North American colonies. These coins were also reaching the British Colonies, especially by sea in connection with exchange for the goods that the rapidly expanding Early American industrial centers (especially the towns and harbors on the coast) were able to offer. Maritime trade at that time was mainly conducted by Dutch companies, which had traditionally, already since the 16th century, dominated the market in the precious metals supplied to Europe (and later to Asia and Africa) from the Spanish Colonies. As a result of the economic and political changes in Europe, however, it was no longer worthwhile to ship South American silver to Dutch ports, nor to coin Dutch thalers from it (in Flemish "daalder") and nor to export these to the east, to Russia, to the southeast, to the Ottoman Empire and beyond to East Asia, where the Netherlands was building its Colonial Empire in the territory of today's Indonesia. It was less expensive to let the actual production costs be borne by the Spanish Colonial Mints and for commercial purposes to use the final product directly, i.e. the high quality minted silver coins. Therefore, the Spanish colonial coins began to replace the older and formerly very popular Dutch thalers in the intercontinental trade in silver.

These coinages, however, were of a similar type; the Dutch thalers and the Spanish 8-real coins were of a similar size and weight, though they differed in their content of silver. So in that part of the Colonial World, where communication was conducted mainly in the Germanic languages (in this case Dutch and English), the Mexican 8-real coin started to be called a "daalder" and as a phonetic transcription of this Dutch word, in English a "dollar." Therefore, in the North American Colonies, large silver coins were called by this name, under which the Dutch brought them to pay for goods – i.e. dollars.

At this stage in the circulation of the Spanish 8-real coins in the American colonies it was no longer an independent monetary unit. The word “dollar” was used only to refer to this particular type of silver coin. For the soldiers, colonialists and adventurers who were arriving in North America from Central Europe and Scandinavia[18] during the second half of the 18th century such a designation seemed obvious and natural, since in their countries of origin they were also used to calling all the big silver coins “talers.”

Indeed, in Central Europe (and also specifically in the Czech lands) the 8-real coins had already, for a long time, been known as “talers.” For example, in official decrees dating from the years 1753-1755 regulating the circulation and purchasing value in the Czech lands of foreign coins made from precious metals, the silver 8-real coin had been described as “Spanish thalers minted in Europe and Colonial or Mexican pesos coming from the Americas.” At that time the domestic thaler, which was a coin of a conventional currency had a payment strength of 2 Rhine-gulden (= 120 kreutzers), while the 8-real coin paid a little more, 124 kreutzers.[19]

From the literature there can be no doubt that the term “dollar” was derived from the word “tolar” or “taler” that originated in the 1520’s in the Czech and German language environment as the name given to a large silver coin minted in the West Bohemian Town of Jáchymov. However, there are various explanations, about the manner in which this term became a synonym for the silver Mexican peso (the 8-real coin) and subsequently for the main currency unit of the United States of America.

The direct transfer of the name of the coin from the Mexican or South American region in connection with monetary exchange between the American Continents in the 18th century is very unlikely. In the Spanish designation “taler” was never used at all to define the silver 8-real coins and, with rare exceptions, the other Romance languages also did not adopt it.[20]

According to another hypothesis the main credit for the expansion of the use of the word “dollar” in America originated with settlers from Scotland who used this term for the large silver British five-shilling coin (otherwise known as a “crown”) as a certain manner of protest against the British Government in Scotland.[21] This hypothesis, however, I consider as improbable. It is true that when a large Scottish coinage or the

English silver crowns, minted after 1551, appeared on rare occasions in circulation in Central Europe, they were called thalers there (as also were other similar coinages). In collecting catalogs one type of Scottish coin from the 17th century, is directly designated as a "dollar."[22] In Great Britain, however, including in Scotland, this term was not used until the second half of the 18th century when five-shilling coins were called "crowns." Indeed characteristic of the British monetary system of the 18th century was the minting of gold coins made from precious metal imported from the Portuguese Colonies. Thanks to these links and its plenitude of gold Great Britain was the first country which in the early 19th century switched entirely to a monometallic currency assured by gold.[23] The nation had no major source of silver as did France, its greatest political rival, and as soon as in 1751 the coinage of English silver crowns (five-shillings, 30.0002 grams of 92.5% Ag) was interrupted for many decades, as was the case in regard to most other silver coins. As a result of the complete absence of silver in the British monetary circulation during the reign of George III (1760-1820), Spanish colonial coinage (i.e. the 8-real coins, then generally described on the world market as "Pillar Dollars") appeared in large quantities in lieu of domestic silver coins, the importation of which was undertaken by Dutch companies as part of the credit provided to Great Britain by the Netherlands. The circulation of the "Pillar Dollars" was officially sanctioned in 1797. From that year the 8-real coins were stamped with a small contramark depicting George III and were valued at 4 shillings and 9 pence (while containing less silver than the older five-shilling coins).[24]

These coinages were also called dollars in Great Britain, because they were imported there as dollars. The usage of the term was imported in association with the Spanish 8-real coins; it is difficult to directly associate the appearance of the term "dollar" with the British five-shillings since, in the late 18th century, the "Mexican dollar" was worth only 4¾ shillings in Great Britain. In 1804 the payment strength of the "Pillar Dollar" was officially increased to 5 shillings. At the same time the Bank of England issued its own British dollars for circulation. Silver from the "Spanish dollars" was utilized for the production of this denomination; the coin bore a nominal designation in British currency ("FIVE SHILLINGS") and also the term "DOLLAR." British dollars were produced in this form (bearing the date 1804)[25] until 1811, when they were replaced in wartime replaced by bank tokens (jetons) with a nominal value of 5 shillings and 6 pence. The regular production of British coins was not reestablished until after the Napoleonic Wars, when the British pound (from 1816) became the first world currency to be based solely on the gold standard. Henceforth, for restricted circulation in Great Britain and its Colonies, the silver content of the shilling coins did not have essential significance; regular minting of silver five-shilling coins was restarted in 1818, maintaining a purity of 92.5%, while the weight was decreased to 28.2759 g).[26]

The term "dollar" was therefore, in fact, imported to the Great Britain in the late 18th century from the American context, not vice-versa. I consider the arguments supporting the decisive role of the Dutch in the expansion of the use of the term dollar in the North American context as more credible.[27] Even in the first half of the 16th century, the term "taler = daaler = dollar" was used as a synonym for the large silver trading tender employed in the market for precious metals. In the mid-18th century it was the Dutch who played the most important role in this industry and were also major creditors of the British Royal Crown.[28]

The disputes concerning the monetary system of the North American Colonies and stubborn efforts to prevent the circulation of colonial paper credit as a means of payment were major impulses for efforts to achieve political and economic independence from the British metropolis. Benjamin Franklin himself, already in his youth, was an ardent supporter of U.S. paper currency as state-guaranteed legal tender. One of the first measures that the new government acceded to, during the struggle for Independence from Great Britain, was issuing its own banknotes and coins and creating a new currency.[29]

The British pound was the official tender of the North American colonies until the year 1775. Pounds, shillings and pence, issued by the individual provinces or towns or by banks were also the official credit tender. At the time of the struggle for independence by the American Colonies the issue of currency as well as the name that it should carry was a primary political issue; therefore for political reasons the new currency could not be issued in the former British monetary units.

The first tender of the new independent state was placed in circulation on the basis of a Resolution of the II. Continental Congress in Philadelphia of the 10th of May 1775. It took the form of paper bills ("Continental Currency Bills"), dated 1776 and their nominal value was expressed in dollars and their fractions and multiples, from 1/6 to 80 dollars..[30]

The new American currency actually constituted vouchers for goods, similar to the previously issued "tobacco" paper money. The goods referred to in the Resolution of the Congress at this time were precious metals, i.e. gold and silver. The government bills had a declared value, determined according to one of these three options:

1) an exact number of mechanically minted Mexican silver dollars;

2) uncoined silver, the quantity of which was equivalent to the precious metal contained in the appropriate number of these Mexican coins;

3) an amount of gold, that was currently equivalent in value to such an amount of silver (a mandatory exchange ratio between gold and silver was not determined, however).

The currency vouchers with compulsory circulation in the newly established states were supposed to be subsequently reimbursed to their holders in one of these three possible ways. It was at that time that the term "dollar" first appeared on U.S. paper tender. The relevant statutory provision from 1775, however, did not define a new monetary unit, but an equivalent to a specific amount of precious metal, i.e. the silver contained in a Spanish 8-real coin, which, in accordance with analogous European coins was called a dollar.

Paper vouchers for precious metals dated 1776 carried a symbolic representation of the new American unity, consisting of a chain with thirteen links bearing the names of the individual states of the newly formed Union together with a three-line inscription "We Are One." In addition to the printing of paper money a proposal also arose for the minting of new coins with a motif of the unity of the thirteen U.S. states on its obverse side as had been used for the paper bills. The term "dollar," however, is still absent on these coins; in the inscription on the reverse side appeared only the text "CONTINENTAL CURRENCY" (i.e. the currency of the Continental Congress, which functioned during the years 1776-1781 as the first U.S. Government). This coin was to become a full-bodied domestic equivalent to the paper bills in exchange for silver, as had been anticipated as a future development by the Resolution of Congress of May 1775.[31]

This "continental dollar" (as it is now described in collectors' catalogs) was not to reach circulation, however. It was preserved only in the form of tin specimens made for testing in several slightly differing types and variations. Apparently also made experimentally were silver specimens (today three original specimens are known), though actual production of silver dollars of the Continental Currency of 1776, in reality, was never commenced. The war situation forced the government to increase the quantity of paper money in circulation and the first common U.S. paper currency was gradually devalued by wartime inflation.

Following the collapse of the Continental Currency each of the thirteen states within the American Confederacy was permitted to issue its own currency in 1781. Thereby in the years 1781-1788 many local small coinages were created (all without showing any indication of their nominal value). Some were imitations of small British coins; others bore a significant inscription and a visual symbol of independence from the former homeland.[32] From 1785 circulation of the Spanish 8-real coin (see **Tab. LIV/2**) as legal tender was officially permitted in certain individual states, as had in fact been anticipated by the Resolution of Congress of 1775. However, this coin did not constitute an equivalent to the paper dollar of the Continental Currency and its payment strength against credit bills grew significantly, to the level of 1:100 by the cusp of the 1780's and 1790's.

Only after the stabilization of the political and economic situation did the U.S. government proceed to re-establish the domestic currency. This was carried out through the "Mint Act" of the 2nd April 1792. This law actually declared the dollar as the new currency unit of the USA, divisible into hundredths, i.e. cents. The introduction of the decimal currency system (1 dollar = 10 kreutzers = 100 cents) represented significant progress and the simplification of financial activities.[33] The colonial home-country itself (i.e. Great Britain) was at that time still using the complex monetary system that was derived from the medieval weight units of precious metal (one pound = 20 shillings = 240 pence). Equally complex lower-level monetary units were also used to define the payment strength of European thalers.[34]

The value of the new monetary unit, the U.S. dollar, however, unlike in 1775, was no longer primarily expressed in silver as the equivalent of 24.82319 grams of pure silver (the amount then contained in the Mexican 8-real coin), but as its equivalent in gold. One dollar was equivalent to 1.6038 grams of pure gold. At the same time a fixed ratio of both metals (1:15) was established, thereby the dollar was also equivalent to 24.057 g of pure silver. The new U.S. currency was established as a bimetallic system.

Under this provision the minting of full-bodied gold coins as multiples of dollars began during the last decade of the 18th century (from 1795 in values of between 2.5 and 10 dollars) and also (from 1794) of silver dollars weighing 26.96 grams with a purity of 89.24% of Ag. At the cusp of the 18th and 19th centuries silver dollars were minted in a relatively high volume (see **Tab. LV/1**), amounting to hundreds of thousands of items. The cost of producing silver one-dollar coins was relatively high and their minting in this form ceased as early as in 1804. The function of the dollar coins in circulation was easily substituted by paper notes of equivalent value, and Mexican silver coins were also circulating in large quantities. U.S. dollars had a slightly lower content of precious metal (by 3.08%) than the Mexican 8-real coins (dollars) minted at that time (see **Tab. LIV/3**). As a result of the gradual decline in the price of silver at the cusp of the 18th and 19th centuries, the value of the metal in the Mexican silver dollar more closely approached its equivalent in gold. Therefore both of these types of silver coins (the U.S. dollar and the Mexican peso) circulated in the United States simultaneously.

The use of foreign silver coins, however, did not solve the problems that were entailed by the use of the bimetallic system of currency, based on the free convertibility of gold and silver coins at a fixed ratio. At the beginning of the 19th century, golden dollars were in circulation evaluated more highly than the paper and silver tender by a factor of cca. 5%.

After the change in the fixed exchange ratio between gold and silver in the USA (which was adjusted in 1834 from its original level from 1792 of 1:15 to 1:16) it became worthwhile to export silver coins, since in other countries silver was more expensive than it was in the USA. Within a few months following the establishment of the new parity between the two precious metals in 1834, silver coins completely disappeared from monetary circulation. The minting of silver dollars was not renewed until the value of silver also began to rise again in the USA.[35]

Also associated with the restoration of the mass production of silver U.S. dollars at the end of the 1830's was the termination in the United States of the legal circulation of foreign coins made of precious metals. New types of U.S. dollars were then minted in an unchanged form during the years 1839-1873, although the number of units issued, in comparison with the rapidly growing U.S. population and the expansion of the territory in which they were valid, was not very large. The main volume of the means of payment was then not constituted of silver dollar coins but of gold coinage and even more of paper money convertible for gold, issued by a dense network of banks in the individual states of the U.S. Federation.

Although the fledgling American Federation in 1792 officially chose as the name of the main unit of its new currency that of the older silver European trading coin (the thaler) that was secondarily applied to the Mexican colonial 8-real coins, the U.S. dollars had another, more modern, function in the monetary circulation. They "inherited," however, a certain small but significant detail from the Mexican 8-real coin, still in use today: namely, the "$" symbol, indicating the "dollar" monetary unit (whether American or otherwise; e.g. an analogous symbol is also used for the Mexican peso).[36]

The inspiration for this symbol was the reverse side of the Mexican 8-real coin depicting the Pillars of Hercules that were located on the coin on both sides of the land hemispheres. Each of the pillars is wrapped with an inscription tape in the shape of the letter "S," which together constitute a model for the "$" symbol.[37] American settlers used the image that they saw minted on the coin as shorthand for the "Mexican dollar," usually without knowing anything of its original symbolic meaning.[38]

The Pillars of Hercules, standing in ancient times on both sides of the Straits of Gibraltar, also enjoyed great popularity with the Emperor Charles V of Habsburg (who ruled Spain from 1516 to 1556).[39] The pillars were intended to symbolize the ambition of Spain as a world-power and especially its colonial expansion overseas to the west, beyond the Pillars of Hercules. This concept is expressed in the Latin motto "PLUS ULTRA" (in modern German "NOCH WEITER," i.e. "further beyond"), which since the days of Charles V has been associated with that pair of pillars (decorated by two crowns, Spanish and Roman, i.e. the Imperial) and widely depicted in celebratory graphics of the period. The same motif occasionally also appears on coins that were minted in Europe in the reign of Emperor Charles V; this motif, however, became typical of the colonial Spanish coins of its overseas possessions, more precisely of the above-mentioned "ship coins." From the inception of their coinage in 1536, the two Pillars of Hercules and the simple inscription "PLUS ULTRA" (but without the inscription tape) appeared on their reverse side.

However it was not until the introduction of the machine coining of 8-real coins in Mexico in 1732 that the reverse side of coins was changed into the form in which these coins were imported in large quantities into the British colonies in America, i.e. with a Pillar of Hercules on each sides of the Earth's hemispheres and the inscription tape wrapped around them with the words "PLUS" (on the left column) and "ULTRA" (on the right). In some other Spanish Colonies in South America the reverse side remained unchanged till even later, the longest period was in Guatemala, where coins struck in accordance with the original design were minted from 1536 until the end of the Colonial Administration in 1821.[40]

Most of the Central and South American Republics that emerged following the collapse of the Spanish Colonial Empire during the first quarter of the 19th century, retained the old currency unit, i.e. the "peso" or 8-real coin, at least at the beginning of their existence. The appearance of the new coins was obviously altered, as they could no longer bear the image of the Spanish King or symbols of the unity of the Spanish Empire on both sides of the Atlantic. This dilemma was best epitomized (in a slightly different form in each case) by the new Peruvian and Chilean pesos – in the center of the large silver coin was placed just one of the Pillars of Hercules (see **Tab. LV/2**).

Notes

1. Georg Wiebe, *Zur Geschichte der Preisrevolution des XVI. und XVII. Jahrhunderts* (Leipzig, 1895); F. Braudel – F. Spooner, "Prices in Europe from 1450 to 1750," in: E. E. Rich – C. Wilson (cpl.), *The Cambridge Economic History of Europe,* Vol. VI: *The Economy of Expanding Europe in the 16th and 17th Centuries* (Cambridge, 1967), pp. 378-486; D. Fisher, "The Price Revolution: A Monetary Interpretation," *Journal of Economic History* 49 (1989), pp. 883-902; Carlo M. Cipolla, *Die Odyssee des spanischen Silbers: Conquistadoeres, Piraten, Kaufleute* (Berlin, 1996), p. 54.
2. Carlos Marichal, "The Spanish-American Silver Peso: Export Commodity and Global Money of the Ancien Regime, 1550-1800," in: Steven Topik – Carlos Marichal – Frank Zephyr (eds.), *From Silver to Cocaine: Latin American Commodity Chains and the Building of the World Economy, 1500-2000* (Durham, 2006), pp. 25-52, Map "Royal mints in colonial Spanish America, 1535-1810," p. 31.

3. Dennis O. Flynn, "Spanish-American silver and world markets in the sixteenth century," *Economic Forum* 10, no. 2 (Salt Lake City, Utah, 1979-1980), pp. 46-72; Jeffrey A. Cole, *The Potosí Mita 1573-1700: Compulsory Indian Labor in the Andes* (Stanford, 1985); Jane E. Mangan, *Trading Roles: Gender, Ethnicity, and the Urban Economy in Colonial Potosí* (Durham, 2005), p. 195, Table 10 "Potosí Silver Production, by Decade, 1561-1710 (in Pesos of 272 Maravedís)."
4. Michael North (Hg.), *Von Aktie bis Zoll: Ein historisches Lexikon des Geldes* (München, 1995), pp. 364-365 "Amerikanische Silberproduktion 1530-1800."
5. Günter Ludwig – Günter Wermusch, *Silber: Aus der Geschichte einer Edelmetalls* (Berlin, 1986), pp. 14; Cipolla, *Die Odyssee des spanischen Silbers*, pp. 49, tab. "Geschätzer Wert der aus den Kolonien in Lateinamerika nach Spanien importierten Waren und Edelmetalle" and p. 54, tab. "Import Spaniens von Gold und Silber aus den amerikanischen Kolonien (in Tonnen)"; Viktor Miller zu Aichholz – August von Loehr – Eduard Holzmair, *Österreichische Münzprägungen 1519-1932* (Wien, 1948), p. XXIII, "Edelmetallproduktion 1493-1600."
6. Peter J. Bakewell, *Silver Mining and Society in Colonial Mexico, Zacatecas 1546-1700* (Cambridge: Cambridge Latin American Studies, 1971); Fréderique Langue, *Los señores de Zacatecas – Una aristocrática minera del siglo XVIII novohispano* (México, 1999), pp. 21-27, Map 2 "Localización de los principales centros mineros de la Nueva España" (p. 19); John TePaske, "Early Spanish Colonial Mints: Mexico, Santo Domingo, Lima, Potosí," in: Jan Lucassen (ed.), *Wages and Currency: Global Comparison from Antiquity to the Twentieth Century* (Bern, 2007), pp. 265-292, Map 11.1 "Spanish America 1500-1800" (p. 266).
7. Cipolla, *Die Odyssee des spanischen Silbers*, pp. 19-23, 79-88; Joe Cribb – Barrie Cook – Ian Carradice, *The Coin Atlas: A comprehensive View of the Coins of the World throughout History* (London, 1999), pp. 289-290; Seawall Menzel, *Cobs, Pieces of Eight and Treasure Coins: The Early Spanish-American Mints and their Coinages 1536-1773* (New York, 2004), p. 5, "From Ore to Coins to the King," and p. 14, Map "The Ten Early Spanish-American Mints (1536-1773)."
8. Ludwig – Wermusch, *Silber*, pp. 164-202.
9. Seawall Menzel, *Cobs, Pieces of Eight and Treasure Coins*; Daniel Sedwick – Frank Sedwick, *The Practical Book of Cobs* (2007, 4th edition).
10. Douglas C. North, *The Economic Growth of the United States 1790-1860* (New York, 1966), p. 255, tab. H-IX, "California gold production and gold Exports 1848-1860."
11. Stanley L. Engerman, "Mercantilism and overseas trade 1700-1800," in: Roderick Floud – Donald McCloskey (eds.), *The Economic History of*

Britain since 1700 (Cambridge, 1994), p. 182-202; John F. Chown, *A History of Money from AD 800* (London, 1995), p. 60-63; John J. Cusker, "British Mercantilist Policy and the American Colonies," in: Stanley L. Engerman – Robert E. Gallman (eds.), *The Cambridge Economic History of the United States,* Vol. I.: *The Colonial Era* (Cambridge, 1996), pp. 337-362.

12. William Letwin, "Monetary Practice and Theory of the North American Colonies during the 17th and 18th Centuries," in: Vera Bagnoli Barbagli (ed.), *La Moneta nell'economia Europea secoli XIII-XVIII (Atti della "Settima Settimana di studio" 11-17 aprile 1975)*, Istituto Internazionale di storia economica "F. datini" Prato, Serie II – Atti delle "Settimane di Studi" e altri Convegni 7, Firenze 1981, pp. 439-469.
13. Scott Kenneth, *Counterfeiting in Colonial America* (Philadelphia, 2000), pp. 13-45, Chapter 2: "Wampum, Boston Money, and Foreign Coin."
14. William G. Summer, *A History of American Currency* (New York, 1874; reprint 1968), pp. 3-5.
15. Summer, *A History of American Currency*, p. 11-14; Arthur Nussbaum, *A History of the Dollar* (New York, 1957), p. 7-8; Chown, *A History of Money*, p. 216-219; Frances Williams Browin, *Coins Have Tales to Tell: The Story of American Coins* (Philadelphia, 1966), p. 24 (picture Nr. 16).
16. J. Earl Massey, *America's Money: The Story of Our Coins and Currency* (New York, 1968), pp. 43-45.
17. Summer, *A History of American Currency*, p. 18-25.
18. John G. Gagliardo, "Germans and Agriculture in Colonial Pennsylvania," in: Harry N. Schreiber (ed.), *United States Economic History – Selected Readings* (New York, 1964), p. 4-28; Michael North, *Kommunikation, Handel, Geld und Banken in der Frühen Neuzeit*, Enzyklopädie deutscher Geschichte, Bd. 59 (München, 2000), p. 14-36; Carlos Marichal, *Bankruptcy of Empire: Mexican Silver and the Wars Between Spain, Britain and France 1760-1810* (Cambridge, 2007).
19. Kliment Čermák – Bedřich Skrbek, *Mince Království českého za panování rodu habsburského od roku 1526* [The Coins of the Kingdom of Bohemia during the Rule of the Habsburg House from 1526] (Pardubice, 1891-1923), II, pp. 790-809.
20. Frank Nuessel, "Currency Designations in Spanish-Speaking Nations," *The Numismatist*, November 1986, p. 2260-2265.
21. Tyll Kroha, *Grosses Lexikon der Numismatik* (Gütersloh, 1997), p. 123; Jack Weatherfort, *Eine kurze Geschichte des Geldes und der Währungen – Von der Anfängen bis in die Gegenwart* (Zürich, 1999), p. 149; Mary Ellen Snodgrass, *Coins and Currency – An Historical Encyclopedia* (London, 2003), pp. 130-131.

22. R. Scott Carlton, *The International Encyclopaedic Dictionary of Numismatics* (Iola, 1996), p. 60; Chester L. Krause – Clifford Mishler (ed. Colin R. Bruce), *Standard Catalog of World Coins. World Coin Listings by date and mint 1601-1700* (Iola, 1996), p. 1001.
23. Nicholas Mayhew, *Sterling: The Rise and Fall of a Currency* (London, 1999), p. 103-104, 123-124.
24. Krause –Mishler, *Standard Catalog of World Crowns and Talers from 1601*, p. 777-781.
25. Wood Howland, "The Bank of England Counterstamp on United States Money," in: Gregory G. Brunk (ed.), *World Countermarks on Medieval and Modern Coins* (Lawrence, MA, 1976), pp. 158-160; Willy Fuchs, "Die russischen Jefimiki" [The Russian Yefimoks], *Geldgeschichtliche Nachrichten* 14/70 (1979), pp. 161-163.
26. Peter Seaby, *Standard Catalogue of British Coins,* Vol. I: *England and United Kingdom, excluding Scottish, Irish and the Island Coinages* (London, 1969), p. 202-208; Richard Lobel – Mark Davidson – Allan Hailstone – Eleni Calligas, *Coincraft's Standard Catalogue of English & UK Coins 1066 to Date* (London, 1995), p. 441-442; Nussbaum, A *History of the Dollar*, pp. 10-11.
27. R. Scott Carlton, *The International Encyclopaedic Dictionary of Numismatics* (Iola, 1996), p. 73; Cipolla, *Die Odyssee des spanischen Silbers*, p. 67.
28. Stephen Zarlenga, *Der Mythos von Geld: die Geschichte der Macht: Vom Tauschhandel zum Euro: eine Geschichte des Geldes und der Währungen* (Zürich, 1999), p. 181-184.
29. Carl von Hock, *Die Finanzen und die Finanzgeschichte der Vereinigten Staaten von Amerika* (Stuttgart, 1867); William G. Summer, *A History of American Currency*; Nussbaum, *A History of the Dollar*; Chown, *A History of Money from AD 800.*
30. Chown, *A History of Money*, p. 220; Summer, *A History of American Currency*, p. 15-16; Nussbaum, *A History of the Dollar*, p. 33-34.
31. Richard Doty, *America's Money, America's Story: A Chronicle of American Numismatic History* (Atlanta, 2008, 2nd edition), pp. 37-42.
32. Walter Breen, *Complete Encyclopedia of U. S. and Colonial Coins* (New York, 1988); Summer, *A History of American Currency*, p. 43-59.
33. Massey, *America's Money*, pp. 87-90; Thomas W. Becker, *The Coin Makers: The Development of Coinage from Earliest Times – With New Section on Private Mints* (New York, 1970), pp. 144-147.
34. Hock, *Die Finanzen und die Finanzgeschichte der Vereinigten Staaten von Amerika*, p. 355-357; Summer, *A History of American Currency*, p. 60-61; Nussbaum, *A History of the Dollar*, p. 52; Weatherfort, *Eine kurze Geschichte des Geldes,* p. 149.

35. Summer, *A History of American Currency*, p. 108-110; Chown, *A History of Money*, pp. 81-82, 159-190, tab. "Growth of US Banks and circulation of US $ 1792-1830" (p. 183).
36. Alvaro J. Moreno, *$ – El Signo de Pesos: Cuál es su origen y qué representa?* (Mexico, 1965).
37. Doty, *America's Money*, p. 35.
38. Clyde Hubbart, "Colonial Coinage of Mexico 1536-1732/Monedas Coloniales de 1536 a 1732", in: *Monedas Mexicanas* (Mexico, 1960), p. 13-18; Clara Semple, *A Silver Legend: The Story of the Maria Theresa Thaler* (Manchester, 2006), p. 10.
39. Wilfried Seipel (red.), *Kaiser Karl V. (1500-1558): Macht und Ohnmacht Europas*, Kunsthistorisches Museum Wien, 15. Juni bis 10. September 2000 (Wien, 2000).
40. José Tamborell Jr., "Colonial Coins from 1700 to 1821/Las Monedas Coloniales de 1700 a 1821," in: *Monedas Mexicanas* (Mexico, 1960), p. 19-21.

7

The Dollar and its Expansion in the 19th and 20th Centuries

In the early 1870's the price of silver in the European market started to fall sharply. In order to protect their currencies, all the developed countries quickly began to restrict the free convertibility of silver for gold and to gradually introduce currency systems based on the gold standard.[1] Cheap silver was abundant everywhere, since the old silver coins, including all the former Central European thalers, were withdrawn from circulation on a massive scale. As a result of these reforms, all the European thaler currencies, in rapid succession, ceased to exist.

Although after 1872 nowhere in Europe was money counted in thalers, silver thalers (or dollars) continued to be produced in large and ever-increasing quantities. At the cusp of the 19th and 20th centuries coins of this type were even produced in states in which, in the early modern period, the thaler currency had never been officially accepted (Great Britain) or in countries that had long ago given up using the original thaler coins (Italy). A substantial proportion of the silver that was found in the European monetary circulation at the time of the cancellation of the thaler currency was remelted and re-minted into the form of silver thalers or dollars. How did this come about?

The reason is not so difficult to find, even if, to explain this apparently illogical monetary development, we need to delve a little deeper, back into the past, specifically to the 18th century. Precious metals were at that time (as in previous and subsequent centuries) common trading goods on the world market.[2] Officially designated bullion of a considerable weight (e.g. "gold bars") was not yet in use to any great extent for trading, as it is today, but instead trading coins were minted, the quality of which was guaranteed by their issuer. Thereby the content of precious metal in trading coins remained stable, unlike in coins that were intended for regular payments. The Treasury could improve its situation by "lightening" the silver content of coins, but only in respect of those that were circulating at an officially determined nominal value.[3] Such activities in regard to trading coins did not make much sense, because the customer was buying them only as precious metal and the concealed reduction of the purity of the silver (while maintaining the other parameters) would constitute fraud that would soon be discovered.[4]

Even in the market for precious metals there was competition and any deviation from the guaranteed quality aroused mistrust and a subsequent loss of market share. Therefore the quantity of precious metal in trading coins remained constant for a long period, even if the issuer (sovereign, state) experienced economic crisis or war was ravaging the country. For similar reasons the design of such coinage also remained unchanged. The long tradition and duration of tender of a certain type (containing a constant amount of precious metal) was the guarantee of a certain stability and increased the popularity of specific types of silver trading coins. This was, by-and-large not only an economic consideration but also a psychological issue.

The Central-European Habsburg Monarchy, since its actual inception in 1526, had engaged in perpetual war with the Ottoman Empire. The Balkan border remained for decades the scene of bloody fighting, but neither political propaganda nor prohibition against commercial contact with the "mortal enemy of European Christendom" (as the Ottoman Empire was described), were to remain a persistent obstacle to the traditional exchange of goods between Europe and the Middle East. Silver Imperial thalers were already exported to the Turkish Empire during the 16th century[5] because it was possible to purchase with them exotic oriental goods and also gold, which was traditionally cheaper in the Orient (and to immediately monetize these favorably in Europe). In the second half of the 17th century trade with the Turkish Possessions in the Near East and in North Africa took on a new aspect and became an important source of income for the Viennese Court Treasury.[6]

The Habsburg Monarchy was not the only European country that was successfully exporting its silver coins to the Ottoman Empire and also further south in Africa. From reports that have been preserved it is evident that even at the cusp of the 17th and 18th centuries, Habsburg coins constituted a relatively small share from amongst the silver tender circulating in the Near East and in North Africa.[7]

This situation changed, however, during the last third of the 18th century.

In 1763 a long period of wars came to an end and the power position of the Habsburg-Lorraine dynasty stabilized. Although Emperor Francis I of Lorraine, known for his interest in business and in economic reform, died shortly thereafter (†1765), his son, Emperor Joseph II (1765-1790), successfully continued with his efforts for the economic advancement of the Habsburg Monarchy.

At the end of the life of Emperor Francis I, his monetary reform from the years 1750-1753 began to be successfully implemented in the Holy Roman Empire. By the mid-1760's, most of the German States had adopted the conventional currency. The conventional thaler became a new unifying currency element in Central Europe that not only swiftly displaced the previously widespread French thaler coinage from the German lands, but also from the realm of long-distance trading in precious metals.

The decisive French share in the export of silver coins began to decline, together with a reduction in the importation of Spanish colonial silver. In the second half of the 18th century, a substantial portion of the Mexican silver that, during previous periods, had mostly been imported into Europe as a raw material for minting, either remained on the American Continent or was exported to Asia. The French share in the export of silver to the Levant area was quickly absorbed by other European states, whether or not they were themselves significant producers of metallurgical silver (the Habsburg Monarchy) or were simply traders in precious metals (e.g. Venice, Holland). The temporary drop in the French export of silver reached bottom during the period of government crisis in the 1780's, during which the export of precious metals from the country was specifically forbidden and subject to severe penalties.[8] During the French Revolution and the subsequent revolutionary wars in France the production of silver coins of the thaler type (the ecu) ceased entirely and was replaced by the franc denominational system.[9]

Silver French thalers (ecus) that were produced from Spanish colonial silver in large quantities and of a unified design, during the first two thirds of the 18th century started gradually disappearing from the supplies of European silver to South-West Asia and North-Eastern Africa. At first glance the French trading coins from that period still appeared the same; they differed only in the numeral attached to the name of the reigning Louis, their year of issuance and their mint mark (see **Tab. XXXVIII/1,2**). Conventional thalers started to be imported from Europe in their place, each containing one tenth of a Cologne mark of pure silver.

Although all the conventional thalers had an identical content of silver, their external appearance varied considerably. These coins were issued by several dozens of secular and ecclesiastical rulers and Imperial Cities and, in aggregate, they constituted a variegated collection of coins with depictions of various rulers and their coats-of-arms and those of towns and also depicting other scenes (see **Tab. XL-XLIII**). Only a few understood their inscriptions in Latin and in the German language in this linguistically and culturally diverse (mostly Islamic) environment. In this manner, the new silver coins were gaining acceptance only gradually and details that might have seemed irrelevant to Europeans also played a significant role in their degree of popularity.

The conventional thalers of the Habsburg Monarchy were finally victorious in the struggle over the export of European silver to the Levant market; more precisely it was just one particular type that was popular: namely the conventional thaler, on the face side of which was depicted a smiling Queen with somewhat revealed exuberant Baroque breasts and on the reverse side the double-headed Imperial Eagle (see **Tab. LII/3**). There was a lesser degree of interest in coinages bearing depictions of Emperor Francis I or of the other German Princes and Kings; the rulers on the South-Western and Northern African Coasts preferred payment from their European trading partners in silver thalers depicting Maria Theresa. The reason was purely psychological; there is no doubt that they liked this conventional thaler more than the others because a woman was depicted on it, something that was not exactly commonplace within the Islamic environment.[10]

These coins were therefore imitated by trading competitors, even during the lifetime of Maria Theresa († 1780). Thalers with similar significantly profiled depictions of women were produced by competing suppliers, e.g. Venice in northern Italy (1756), subsequently the Dalmatian port city of Dubrovnik (see **Tab. XLVIII/1**) and ultimately, also very similar iconographically, were the first silver dollar coins that were minted in the USA, in the late 18th century (see **Tab. LV/1**). For commercial reasons, the subsequent sovereigns of the Habsburg Monarchy also permitted the minting of conventional thalers bearing the name and image of the deceased Maria Theresa with an ante-dated year of minting, 1780, and the contramark "S.F" that had been used only by the Mint in Günzburg in Burgau (together with their own conventional thalers of the interim years, bearing the real mint mark from where they were produced).

These coins, which became known as "Levant thalers," in the early 19th century were also officially valid throughout the area of the Austrian Empire, in addition to all the coins of the conventional currency produced on behalf of the reigning Emperor and carrying the current date, i.e. the conventional thaler = 120 kreutzers of the conventional currency. Although the technology of coin production had already made significant progress during the first half of the 19th century, the "Levant thalers" imitated the older, simpler minting style, including a relief inscription around the edge of the coin.

The vast majority of these coins, however, were destined for export to Africa and Asia. This particular type of conventional thaler, therefore, also "survived" the abolition of conventional currency in 1857, since Austria had obtained a notable exception to the Minting Convention by which all the participating states made a commitment to produce silver coins only in accordance with the metrological parameters of their federal currency: i.e. that it could also continue to produce "Levant thalers" for trading purposes. These were coins intended for export to the Turkish Empire, so their production (in addition to their minting at the actual Viennese Mint) was concentrated in the southern area of the monarchy, in Milan and Venice. From 1780 this new coinage, the Levant thaler, was produced in large quantities at many Royal Mints in what was then the Habsburg-Lorraine Monarchy; in addition to Vienna, where they were minted continuously from 1780 until 1937, also in Günzburg in Burgau in today' Germany (1780-1802), Upper Hungarian Kremnica in today's Slovakia (1781-1786), Transylvanian Karlsburg, i.e. today's Gyula Fehérvár in Romania (1785-1803), Northern Italian Milan (1789-1802 and 1820-1859) and Venice (1820-1866) in present-day Italy, and lastly at the mint in Prague, the Capital of today's Czech Republic (1836-1842).

As a result of the political and economic changes during the second half of the 19th century, the structure, the economy and the monetary system of the Danubian Monarchy were evolving rapidly, while the "Levant thaler" was being produced continuously, in ever larger amounts. Following the loss of the Northern Italian possessions it was coined only in Vienna. In 1900, it ceased to be accepted as the official currency of the Austro-Hungarian Crown and continued in production solely as a trading coin, with which it was not possible to make direct payments y in Austria-Hungary. A rather curious situation then emerged. Although these coins ceased to be valid in their country of origin, from the late 18th century onwards they gradually became the absolutely dominant and universally accepted means of payment in the vast territories of southwestern Asia and in the North African and West African world, including some French and British colonial areas of interest. However, in addition to these relatively nearby territories, the conventional Maria Theresa thaler was also exported far overseas, especially by Dutch merchants. Thereby (labeled with a contramark) it remains legal tender in present-day Indonesia (Java, Madura) which at that time were Dutch colonies.[11]

Neither in the newly emerging independent states, nor in the dependent colonial territories were the Levant thalers removed from circulation and replaced by new currencies or by the tender (francs, pounds) of the Colonial Powers until the gradual disintegration of the Ottoman Empire took place, commencing in the 19th century. However large areas of south-eastern Africa (Ethiopia, Somalia) and of Anatolia (Yemen, Saudi Arabia, Oman, the United Arab Emirates) remained, where "Levant thalers" continued in use as the main means of monetary exchange even during the first half of the 20th century, i.e. even after the Second World War.

Other European countries took advantage of this situation and for trading with this region, rich in raw materials, they also started to produce, for this purpose (exactly in accordance with the Austrian model) "Levant thalers" bearing the image of Maria Theresa, and the date 1780. Italy was the first country to adopt this practice since it needed these coins to assert its colonial interests in what is now Ethiopia. The older Ethiopian or Italian coinages that were produced at the cusp of the 19th and 20th centuries to replace the Levant thaler in the monetary circulation (5 liras = 1 thalero) had not brought about the desired effect. Therefore in Rome, during the years 1935-1939, copies of the Maria Theresa silver thalers were minted, which were then exported in large quantities to occupied Abyssinia.[12]

The Italian example was already time-tested and the objections of Austria were not accepted because the "Levant thaler" did not constitute official tender in Austria. Their production was temporarily halted by the Vienna Mint in 1937. However, the failure of the Austrians to provide these items, was immediately taken advantage of by the competition. Maria Theresa thalers with the date 1780 embossed on them were therefore produced in Brussels in Belgium (1937-1938) and in Utrecht in Holland (1939). However, Great Britain, where the coins were minted in London (1936-1961), became by far the largest producer of them, while during the war the British Mint in Mumbai, India also produced these coins on a temporary basis from 1940-1941 for the eastern area of the circulation of the "Levant thaler" in Anatolia.

The "Levant thaler" became the unrivaled most popular coin of all the monetary systems worldwide and was produced in exactly the same form (i.e. in terms of its appearance and metrological parameters and still dated with the original year), over the largest area and in the greatest volume. To this day, it is not known even how many of these coins were produced during the years 1780-1961 (when their coinage in London was terminated); estimates range widely between 330 and 800 million units.[13] The specific places and periods of production of these coins are very difficult to determine, however, and possible only with the help of specialized catalogs.[14]

At the Vienna Mint the production of these coins was restarted in 1946[15] and you can now purchase newly minted "Levant thalers" while taking a stroll through the historic center of Vienna. Although they have still the same design and content of silver, you cannot use them for buying anything in Austria; they serve only as tourist souvenirs.

The "Levant thaler" thereby symbolically prolongs the "life" of its original ancestor, i.e. the Czech thaler from Jáchymov. It bears the same name of thaler. And when you look closely at the reverse side of the Levant thaler, specifically the emblem located on the chest of the imperial eagle, you will also find the symbol of the Kingdom of Bohemia; the same symbol with the appearance of a double-tailed silver lion with a golden crown that also decorated the original Jáchymov thalers from 1520 that carried the name King Louis Jagiello.

The "Levant thaler" dominated the monetary systems of the Near East and of Northern and Eastern Africa as their main currency until the end of the 19th century.[16] This coin, however, did not penetrate further east on a significant scale; although the principles of trading in precious metals were the same as they are here the Asian market was dominated by different powers. In India, China, Japan and throughout this entire area the price of silver in comparison with that of gold was much cheaper than it was in Europe and the U.S. From the 1870's, when the price of silver collapsed in both Europe and the U.S., it was advantageous to export silver to places where it was still relatively highly valued – i.e. to India and East Asia. The tremendous river of silver that began to flow into this region was, however, not only exchanged in bulk for gold or oriental goods and spices, but also became the value equivalent in the ever-expanding trade in narcotics.[17]

In East Asia payment was traditionally made using bronze and paper credit money. Large trading transactions were carried out using precious metals by weight.[18] Therefore in the 17th and 18th centuries Mexican and Latin American colonial coins gained great popularity in these regions a, either in the form of roughly minted "ship coins" or later the higher quality Mexican 8-real coins.[19] Also in Asia, since the 17th century, coinage of this type was known as "daaler," because the import of these coins (as well as the importation of Dutch silver thalers) was carried out by Dutch traders. Although the significance of the Dutch business activities was overshadowed in the 19th century by the British colonial expansion, the denotation of large silver coins using the term "daaler" (i.e. transcribed in English as "dollar") remained and was traditionally used in the Asian region.[20]

The United States of America was relatively late in bringing its silver reserves to the advantageous Asian markets. The reason for this was that in previous times, until the 1870's, U.S. silver dollars were not minted in large quantities. Prior to the discovery of silver in the mountains of Nevada during the second half of the 19th century, the U.S. had no major source of this precious metal. In its bimetallic gold-silver monetary system the mass minting of silver dollars was not economically advantageous, since, due to the increase in the price of silver in the 19th century, the intrinsic value of one silver dollar coin (i.e. the value of the metal that it contained) was greater than $1. The silver dollar however was still coined, even during the Civil War, North versus South, but only in relatively small quantities.[21]

The economic problems brought about during the years of Civil War between 1861 and 1865, however, required certain changes to the American monetary system. The main new feature (for the first time since 1775) was the introduction of paper money, guaranteed by the

State (called state notes), that were put into circulation by both of the warring factions. After the end of war the state notes from the North (the "greenbacks") became the legal tender throughout the U.S.; the validity of the Southern paper legal tender was nullified, without any compensation. Unlike banknotes the state notes were not freely convertible for precious metals. Temporarily, therefore, a dual currency emerged, by which the exchange rate of full-bodied gold dollars to paper state notes was in the ratio of 1:2.85 (in 1864). Before parity could again be achieved between the payment strength of the state notes and metal coins made from precious metals (which happened in around the year 1879), the U.S. currency had to undergo fundamental reforms.[22]

In the early 1870's the price of silver in the European market began to fall sharply. In countries with a bimetallic system this development caused considerable problems, since silver coins were rapidly losing their intrinsic value and becoming solely a credit tender. This was the major weakness of the bimetallic monetary system with a fixed exchange ratio between gold and silver (in the U.S. at that time 1:16). Although in previous decades this system had managed to absorb minor fluctuations in the market prices of the two metals, it was not able to cope with the precipitous fall in the price of silver during the 1870's due to which the Federal thaler currency in Central Europe, guaranteed by silver, also collapsed.

The problems with silver dollars in the U.S. were solved temporarily by the new Coinage Act of February 12, 1873. In accordance with this law, the currency of the United States continued to be based solely on gold and the minting of silver dollar coins for circulation was terminated. However, the price of silver on the Euro-American market for precious metals fell so swiftly[23] that all the developed countries tried as rapidly as possible to take advantage of the significant price differences and to utilize their surplus of cheap silver in the Asian market. For this purpose, in 1873, a new type of silver dollar was introduced in the U.S., called the "Trade Dollar." While maintaining the same level of purity (90%) it had a higher weight (27.22 g), i.e. half a gram more than the dollar coins minted during the years 1836-1873. This coin, however, did not have the function of legal tender in the U.S.; it was simply trading silver for export and trade in the Asian regions. For these reasons, data concerning its weight and purity were stamped on the coin: "420 GRAINS 900 FINE" (i.e. 420 grains = 27.22 grams of silver with a purity of 90%).

The U.S. trade dollar was produced in this form until 1885 (see **Tab. LVII/1**).[24]

For similar reasons Great Britain also introduced its own minting of "Trade Dollars" during the second half of the 19th century.[25] The first coinages of this type were silver British dollars produced during the years 1863-1866 for Hong Kong, the main British colonial port in China. British Hong Kong dollars were metrologically based on the Spanish colonial 8-real coins with which they were intended to compete in the Asian market. They did so well in circulation that in 1895 Great Britain launched the mass production of "Trade Dollars" for the Chinese and Malaysian markets.

American and British trade dollars were exported to East Asia in large quantities. Well minted coins with a stable silver content gradually superseded both the older coinage (especially that of Mexican and South American origin) and also the precious metal bullion. The metrological model of the "Trade Dollar" was then imitated in the domestic Chinese and Japanese coins, also called "dollars." In the vast area of East Asia silver Asian dollars were manufactured until the 1930's in many types and variants. On some types directly stamped in English was "ONE DOLLAR" (or information concerning the weight and fineness or the payment strength in terms of the older domestic currency). In everyday language, however, the terms "yuan" or "yen" (i.e. round thing) began to be used to describe the large silver dollars and they later became a numerical monetary unit in China, Taiwan and Japan. The terms "yuan" or "yen" and "dollar" were for quite a long time synonyms for the same coin in these areas.[26]

The Chinese island of Taiwan played a very important role for the European trade with East Asia, where the Dutch, as early as in 1620, began to build their trading bases. Through Dutch trading, European, Mexican and South American silver was already in the 17th and 18th centuries flowing via Taiwan to China and Japan. Also produced in Taiwan were the oldest Asian dollars, already, from the cusp of 1830's and 1840's, minted in the form of standard silver coins with stable parameters. Imported to China were mostly silver 8-real coins from the Spanish colonies and also Dutch coinage.

The dual naming of means of payment used in the 19th century remained in effect in Taiwan. Taiwan money bears the designation "Yuan," but in the business world it is normally referred to as the "Taiwan Dollar" (see **Tab. LXVIII/4**). A similar situation also exists in regard to the currency of the East Asian Sultanate of Brunei. The local tender has its own name (the "ringgit"), but it is officially known as the "Brunei Dollar" (see **Tab. LXXVII/2**) Unlike in Taiwan, however, the Brunei coins and banknotes bear denominations defined according to both the monetary systems.

While the Taiwan dollar from the first half of the 19th century bore only Asian motifs and inscriptions in Chinese alphabet, minted dollars of the European type, produced by modern technology from the 1860's, began to infiltrate the monetary systems in Asia (see **Tab. LVI/3,4**). At first it was a "Trade Dollar," which was minted from 1866 by the British Colonial Administration in Hong Kong. During the years 1875-1877 Japan imitated this coinage for trading purposes (with the English inscription "Trade Dollar," but with Japanese motifs). Silver coins of this type were also minted in Japan later (until the First World War), but were consistently referred to using the name of the domestic currency unit, i.e. the "yen."[27]

In the largest country of that region, Imperial China, the production of its own Chinese dollars did not commence until the early 20th century. Chinese dollars also in many cases bore the English text "ONE DOLLAR," even after the inception of the Republic and also later following the introduction of communist rule. The last silver Chinese dollars were minted in 1934 (**see Tab. LVIII**). The monetary system remained in its original form of colonial silver dollars for the longest period in Hong Kong, where until the present time the dollar is still the monetary unit, although it is no longer produced from silver (see **Tab. LXVII**).

The cessation of the usage of the traditional silver dollar coinage in the U.S. and its replacement in 1873 by the mass-produced dollar trading coin, the "Trade Dollar," seemingly signaled the end of the U.S. silver dollar. But in fact this situation did not last for a long time. Even after the discontinuation of the bimetallic system and the transition to guaranteeing the American currency with gold, the law by which it was possible to have silver dollar coins produced from privately owned silver remained in force. Due to a rapid drop in silver prices in 1878 the intrinsic value of the regular silver dollars produced before 1873 fell below the level of $1. Thereby it began to be worthwhile to import silver, obtained on the world market for precious metals, in large volumes into the U.S. since, after the payment of a relatively low seigniorage, it was possible to purchase silver dollars with it with the identical content of precious metal, but of a much higher nominal value than that for which the silver was purchased.

Such transactions were not of course relevant to just a pouch of Austro-Hungarian silver guldiners that someone had brought with him to America on his way to a new life. This speculative "silver dollar game" was played by the large trading and mining companies that supplied silver on the global market. In America itself this represented a relatively large quantity of silver, which in the 1870's the mining companies making use of the mineral resources from the "Big Silver Bonanza" of Nevada wanted to play with in the market.[28] In 1878 these interest groups managed to politically influence the restoration of the minting of silver dollars in huge volumes. The new coins differed from the older silver coinage in their new concept of an obverse and a reverse side; the content of precious metal remained unchanged. However, the price of silver declined so rapidly that by 1879 the U.S. Government was already obliged to repeal the Act on the free monetization of silver, in order that a flood of silver dollars should not affect the laboriously achieved parity between paper banknotes, the gold dollar coinage (during the years 1849-1889 the dollar was also produced as a small gold coin, see **Tab. LVI/1**) and other metal tender.[29]

From 1878 U.S. silver dollars were produced in large quantities, but the vast majority of them were not put into circulation at the time of their production. They represented only monetized silver and were stored in bank safes. Therefore it was not necessary to change their external appearance nor their content of silver: during the years 1878-1921 the same silver "Morgan Dollar" (named after the author of its graphic design, see **Tab. LVII/2**) was still produced, although the value of the dollar, expressed in gold, had changed. Only in 1921 was the design modernized and the silver dollar coin was produced in a new version, known as the "Peace Dollar" (1921-1935, see **Tab. LVII/3**). But this type was also never used in large quantities for actual payment, even though it was legal tender. Dollar coins were not very popular in monetary circulation because of their weight and a certain distrust of the coinage based on its lower value of silver. The main means of exchange in American monetary circulation was paper currency, starting with the dollar bill.

In the late 19th century one dollar represented quite a sum of money and therefore it was popular in the form of a paper bill, freely convertible into gold (see **Tab. LXV**). A certain dislike for the one dollar coin and the greater popularity of paper notes, had not changed, moreover, even more than a hundred years later when, currently in the U.S., you can neither buy much for a dollar nor obtain gold coins for paper money at the bank.

In the time of economic problems caused by the global economic crisis of 1929, the majority of world currencies abandoned the gold standard, i.e. directly guaranteeing the currency with gold.[30] In 1933 the U.S. decided to abandon the gold standard (established in 1873). In the following year (1934) the dollar was devalued by more than 40% in relation to the value of gold. This additionally caused the collapse of the long-maintained parity between notes and gold coins.[31] The cost of the precious metal used in gold dollar coins rose to well above their face value. Gold dollar coins were no longer produced or used in circulation. In 1935 the coinage of silver dollars was terminated. However, the U.S. dollar was the only world currency that maintained its exchange rate for gold in a ratio of 1 troy ounce (31.1 g) = $35 in paper bills. Also due to this unique status, during the second third of the 20th century, the U.S. dollar gained a dominant position in the global economy, though the main reason for this confidence in the U.S. currency during this period was the economic growth and the importance of the U.S. as a world power.[32]

The free convertibility of the U.S. dollar into gold increasingly appeared as an economic anachronism. The total world production of industrially mined gold rose rapidly during the second half of the 20th century and the U.S. itself was no longer its major producer. South Africa and the former Soviet Union became by far the most significant holders of the "golden purse." In 1971 the convertibility of the U.S. dollar into gold was abandoned. This ended the era of precious metals being a direct monetary equivalent; after 1971 gold (like silver) became just one of many commodities on the world market.[33]

Fluctuations in the market price of gold and silver, which for monetary exchange in the era of silver thalers in 16th to 19th centuries were one of the crucial factors, today have a similar effect as does a sudden rise or fall in the price of oil, cotton or coffee. They are influenced by supply and demand, and also by political developments in different parts of the world. In fact the extraordinary expansion of the dollar as the monetary unit of many countries that took place during the 20th century had virtually nothing to do with trading in silver or gold. It was the result of political changes and related policy decisions concerning new forms of national currencies in the independent and/or emerging countries, particularly those in the Americas and in Oceania.

The vast majority of countries in which payments are now conducted in a dollar currency were, in fact, formerly British colonies; in most of these newly introduced dollars replaced the former colonial currency based on the British pound. Choosing the dollar as a new decimal currency unit (unlike the British pound, which was divided into 20 shillings of twelve pence) was viewed as a symbol of independence, following the U.S. model. In 1775 the dollar replaced the British pound in the former British colonies of North America; in many countries that were still under British influence during the 20th century local dollar currencies replaced the British pound.

The exceptions to this constitute only a few of today's dollar currencies outside America.

The first of these are the currencies of states that came into existence on the northwest coast of Africa as refuges for black Americans freed from slavery. The oldest of these is Sierra Leone, already established in 1791 by the British trading company (the Sierra Leone Company). Silver coins bearing this date and the inscription "1 dollar" were minted for the needs of the inhabitants of this British Colony. Their production, however, was only symbolic and ended with this first minting.

The U.S. dollar took permanent root in neighboring Liberia, which was established in 1822 as a new homeland for former American slaves - this concept was also expressed by the name given to the new state and the fact that it was not a colony. As a result of the nation's direct contact with the American culture the U.S. dollar actually became the currency of Liberia. Liberian dollars started to be minted in 1833. In addition to these coins, however, large quantities of British coins and of British coinage produced for colonies in West Africa were also circulating in the country. The inception of a real independent Liberian dollar currency took place in 1960 (see **Tab. LXIII/1**).

In 1895 Great Britain introduced a common dollar currency for its colonies in East Asia and for export to China and Japan pursuant to the older model of the Hong Kong dollar. Silver Trade Dollars minted in

Bombay also became the official currency of Hong Kong. Their production continued till 1935. After the disintegration of the British Colonial Empire the Hong Kong dollar remained the currency unit of the last British colony and has continued to be used there as an independent currency even after the termination of the British Administration of Hong Kong (1997).

In Asia in addition to the Hong Kong dollar, the Taiwanese yen (dollar) and the Brunei ringgit (dollar), dollar currency also exists in Singapore. Singapore had also been a British colony; the introduction of a dollar currency was decided following the establishment of the independent Republic of Singapore in 1967 (see **Tab. LXV/1,2**).

All other current dollar currencies in other continents were introduced in a similar manner to the Singaporean currency, in countries that were formerly British colonies or still remain part of the British Commonwealth. The vast majority of these (with the exception of Canada, Belize and Fiji) had not been established prior to the 1960's and 1970's.

Canada is the other nation in North America, where dollars are used. Formally the British Queen remains the Monarch of this vast country. The British monetary system, however, was applicable only until the year 1870, when the dollar was introduced in Canada based on the U.S. influence. In the first stage of the existence of the Canadian dollar currency, metal dollars were not produced, only small coins up to the value of half a dollar. The first silver Canadian dollar bearing a picture of a typical Indian canoe saw the light of day in 1937. Canadian dollars were then minted in this form until 1966 (see **Tab. LXXIX**). Canada remained the last country in the world where silver dollars were minted as standard currency. Given its relatively low durability however (the coins are subject to significant wear and tear), this metal is not suitable for everyday coins and the production of silver legal tender is unnecessarily expensive. Therefore Canada, like most other countries, commenced the production of coins made of base metals with gold and silver reserved for minting commemorative and collectible coins.

Another independent dollar currency was established in 1963 in today's Zimbabwe (formerly Southern Rhodesia) in southern Africa. As in other British colonies in southern Africa the British pound was used there as currency and in addition to this, from the 1920's onwards, coins from neighboring South Africa were widely circulated there. The currency of Southern Rhodesia as a British colony was established in 1932 in accordance with the British model. The Pound currency system remained in the form of a Central African currency of the Federation established in the years 1953-1963 by today's nations of Zambia (formerly Northern Rhodesia), Malawi (formerly Nyasaland) and Zimbabwe (formerly Southern Rhodesia). After the collapse of this Federation in 1963 a new currency was established in independent Zimbabwe, which still remained as part of the British Commonwealth, replacing the older British shilling system with the dollar (1 dollar = 10 shillings = 100 cents). Following the Civil War in the 1970's the new independent republic was named Zimbabwe (instead of Southern Rhodesia), and since 1980 it has established the dollar, divided into 100 cents, as its currency (see **Tab. LXIII/2**). Recently, however, the Zimbabwean dollar currency has earned a notorious first place for its inflation rate, which exceeded all previously known world records, including the horrific inflation in Germany following the First World War.

Another former British colony on the African continent, which, after its declaration of independence introduced a dollar currency, is Gambia in West Africa. The local currency, the "dollar," adapted to the native language as "dalasi" (see **Tab. LXIII/3**), was introduced after the nation's establishment as an independent republic in 1970; the small coins are not called cents but, in Gambian, "bututs."

Also variegated is the "family" of dollar currencies in the nations south of the U.S. and in the Australian-Oceanic region. It appears like a jumble of various dollar currencies, produced by any or all of the island mini-states. The situation, in fact, is simpler because the vast majority of such "dollar currencies" are not independent currencies, but they are only the commercial product of business activities by which currency is not created for the purpose of making payments, but as a collectible item and a souvenir for tourists. Such activities, however, are typical not only for the Caribbean and Oceania - several similar examples can be found in Europe; e.g. the Vatican, San Marino and Liechtenstein also issue their own money, but it is not utilized in the actual monetary circulation.

In these regions in practice only a few dollar currencies are utilized; the vast majority of the others are simply "fictitious" currencies, only existing in the form of annual collectible editions, or sometimes only as commemorative coins of different denominations made of silver, gold, or from base metals. Some formally independent states do not even have their own currency and used the tender of their major neighbors on a long-term basis; an instance of this, for example, is the use of the U.S. dollar as the official currency of Puerto Rico (1898), of the U.S. Virgin Islands (since 1917), of Ecuador, of Micronesia, of the Marshall Islands and of a few other small island countries (including Palau, Guam, Johnston Atoll, Midway and the Turks and Caicos Islands).

In the vast Caribbean, there are also many small island states that issue their own dollars, but only a few of them actually have their own dollar currency.

One of these is the Bermuda dollar, established in 1970, shortly after the declaration of independence by this isolated island nation (1968). It took over from the former local currency (the Bermuda pound), which had existed in the form of paper legal tender since 1914. Together with the introduction of a dollar decimal system, small Bermuda cent coins started to be minted for circulation; the dollar denominations are in paper banknotes. Silver Bermuda one-dollar coins of many different types are issued as commemorative coinage, maintaining a uniform design and the appearance of "silver dollars" (see **Tab. LXII**).

The Bahamian dollar, which is even a few years older, also underwent a similar process. The Bahamas were a British Colony that had its own currency, denominated in pounds and shillings. The abolition of the Colonial Administration in 1964 encouraged a currency reform and the subsequent introduction of Bahamian dollars (1966). Bahamian dollars are minted as coins of base metal for normal circulation; also coined, apart from these, are gold and silver denominations as collectible items (see **Tab. LXXI**).

The Jamaican dollar is amongst the most wide-spread currencies in use in the Caribbean. Jamaica belonged amongst the most important British Colonies in Central America. Used as currency there in the 18th century were Spanish colonial 8-real coins that (as in Great Britain) were provided with contramarks. Although Jamaica had already gained its political independence in 1962, it did not accede to the reform of its own currency and make the transition from the British pound system to the decimal dollar system until 1969 (see **Tab. LXXII/2,3**). Jamaican dollar coins exist in many metrological types, because they are produced as coinage for monetary circulation. Reflected in their external form are inflation and the necessity to save on production costs; therefore, since

1976, Jamaican dollars have been getting smaller and are being made from cheaper materials. The higher dollar denominations are produced from precious metals as commemorative coinage; this includes the "big coins" made of high-quality silver (92.5%) and weighing 136.08 grams, issued in the years 1978-1985 with a nominal value of 25 Jamaican dollars and, since 1986, (with the same parameters) in a nominal value of 100 Jamaican dollars.

The nearby Cayman Islands, independent of Jamaica, also used the Jamaican dollar as the currency for their internal circulation. Since 1973 the Cayman Islands have minted their own small coins and dollars; in the early years however only as annual editions and as commemorative coinage for collectible purposes. Today, however, the "Cayman Islands dollar" (see **Tab. LXXIII/1**) is an independent currency with a much greater purchasing power than that of the Jamaican dollar.

Close to Jamaica, on the mainland of Central America, another former British colony can be found, previously called British Honduras, now Belize, in accordance with the name of its capital city. Initially the monetary development in this state was similar to that of Jamaica. There, too, contramarked (with the letters "G.R") Spanish colonial 8-real coins were used for internal circulation. At the beginning of the British Administration Jamaica and British Honduras even formed a single colony. This situation changed dramatically after 1884 when British Honduras was declared a separate Crown Colony of Great Britain. As a result of its very close economic relations with neighboring Guatemala, the Guatemalan silver peso (for which the English used the term "dollar," as they did also for the Mexican peso, see **Tab. LV/3**) was declared the official currency of British Honduras in 1894. At the same time the colonial administration issued its own paper money for British Honduras, denominated in dollars. Since 1894 this state has had its independent dollar currency; until 1924, however, in addition to the official Honduran dollars, U.S. dollars were also in circulation. At the time of the disintegration of the British Colonial Empire, the former British Honduras was renamed Belize, though it did not achieve political independence until 1981. These changes, however, had no impact on the outward form of the local dollars; only the name of the issuing state was altered (see Tab. **LXXIII/2**).

In terms of territorial range the most widely used currency in the Caribbean is the "Dollar of East-Caribbean States." This currency is valid in many of the island statelets, which were previously British colonies, stretching southeast from the British Virgin Islands to Grenada. This constitutes a total of ten island countries (sequentially from northwest to southeast): the British Virgin Islands, Anguilla, Barbuda, Antigua, Saint Kitts and Nevis, Montserrat, Dominica, Saint Lucia, Saint Vincent and Grenada. These countries individually gained their independence between 1967 - 1972 and remain part of the British Commonwealth. The common currency of East Caribbean was introduced there in 1955 in accordance with the British model and also "survived" the introduction of the decimal system in Great Britain itself (in 1971). As the last of the currencies, based on the system "one pound = 20 shillings = 240 pence," it was abolished through a reform in 1981, by which was introduced the East Caribbean dollar, divided into hundred cents (see **Tab. LXXIV/1,2**). Each of the Caribbean island countries listed mints its own commemorative coins in dollar denominations that are not intended for monetary circulation (see **Tab. LXXIV/3**).

The East Caribbean currency based on the pound system has also been used since 1955 by the island states at the southeastern edge of the Caribbean, i.e. Barbados and the Trinidad and Tobago archipelago. These two countries, however, left the island monetary union even prior to the introduction of East Caribbean dollar; Trinidad and Tobago in 1966 (see **Tab. LXXV/1, 2**) and Barbados in 1973 (see **Tab. LXXV/3**). Both these countries have their own valid dollar currencies; the dollars are made as regular circulating coins, and of course also, from precious metals, in the form of memorial and commemorative coinage.

In the northeastern part of South America lies Guyana, the former British Guiana. Its complex monetary development corresponds to its location at the intersection of the colonial interests of the Netherlands, Spain and Great Britain. Even in the 19th century, commonly used there simultaneously were coins from the Spanish colonies, and of Dutch and British coinages. The main currency, however, until the First World War, remained the British pound. Although Great Britain minted a small silver four-pence (1838-1945) for British Guiana in large quantities, these did not constitute an actual independent monetary system. After the First World War, the colonial administration issued its own paper currency in British Guiana worth 1 and 2 dollars (first issued in 1916, later several more times, also with higher denominations and in more modern versions). This tender also, however, did not become the basis of an independent currency and, after the Second World War, the British currency was again restored there. With the reform of the colonial system, in 1952 British Guiana established its own government and the East Caribbean pound currency referred to above was introduced as the official currency. Only after gaining full independence in 1965, when the name of the state was also changed to today's Guyana, was a fundamental monetary reform undertaken. In 1966 the decimal currency system was introduced, the main unit of which was the Guyana dollar. Since the introduction of the new currency the "Bank of Guyana" has issued dollar coins; in the first years of its existence as an independent state in the form of large copper-nickel coinage. At present, the Guyana dollar is a small copper coin (see **Tab. LXXVI**).

Australia and the major part of Oceania remain part of the British Commonwealth until present day. The development of the local currencies was obviously influenced by the former colonial status of these countries. The primary dollar currencies of this region are the Australian and the New Zealand dollars; the others all have only a limited scope or are not used at all as tender.

Amongst the former British possessions in the Pacific only the monetary development of the island state of Fiji represents a significant exception. This country used its own pound currency system even prior to its direct affiliation within the British sphere of influence, which was established in 1874 on the basis of the agreement of the tribal King Thakombau. Though this island nation during almost the entire following century remained a part of the British Empire (British pounds were used there and, from 1910, also Australian pounds), it still retained its own currency, which, however, was also derived from the British pound system (banknotes since 1873 and from 1934 also small coins). The dollar currency system was introduced in Fiji in a full range of denominations in 1969; in addition to common dollar coins and banknotes also issued of course are commemorative coins and occasional coins made from precious metals (see **Tab. LXXII/1**).

Unlike in Fiji, specific local currencies were not introduced into the monetary circulation in the southern areas of British influence in Australasia and Oceania until the early 20th century; the local tender of these British colonies remained the British pound.

In 1910 the Australian pound currency was placed in full circulation (both coins and banknotes) in accordance with the British model.

For a quarter of a century Australian currency was used in the majority of the British colonial dominions in Australasia and Oceania; from it were gradually derived the currencies of the other colonies in this region. This situation remained basically unchanged until 1966, when the Australian pound was replaced by a new decimal system based on the Australian dollar (see **Tab. LXIX/1,2**). The Australian dollar is the official monetary unit of Australia and also of several other island states, which later declared their own independence and then issued their own coins in dollar values (but not paper notes, which continue to be Australian dollar notes). These are the island states of Tuvalu (independent since 1978), Kiribati (1979) and Nauru (1993). In addition, the Australian dollar is valid as the official currency of several other small island countries (Cocos Islands, Heard and McDonald, Norfolk and Christmas Islands).

The Australian dollar was also previously the official currency of the Solomon Islands. After its declaration of independence (1976) its own currency was introduced in 1977, the Solomon Islands dollar (see **Tab. LX/3**).

In New Zealand the Australia pound was used as legal tender until 1933, when it was replaced by the new New Zealand pound, in a full range of denominations range. New Zealand also followed Australia in the introduction of the decimal system - therefore in 1967 the New Zealand dollar was born (see **Tab. LIX** and **LXX**). This monetary unit is also the official tender of several neighboring island states that issue their own coins (or banknotes) of the dollar system only as annual editions and as commemorative coinage: the Cook Islands (since 1972), Niue (since 1974), the Tokelau Islands (since 1978, see **Tab. LX/1**) and Pitcairn Island (since 1988, see **Tab. LX/2**).

The New Zealand dollar became the main currency unit of the island state of Western Samoa in 1972, i.e. several years after its declaration of independence (1962). Only in 1967 did Western Samoa introduce its own dollar currency. The name of the main denomination, however, was adapted to the local pronunciation, therefore the local dollar is called a "tala" (see **Tab. LXI/1,2**).

New dollar currencies, however, are being initiated even now, not only through a declaration of formal independence by a small island, which then starts to coin its own dollars for collectors and tourists (see **Tab. LXIX/3**; Tab. **LXI/3**).

The youngest real dollar currency in the world is the Namibian dollar, the new currency of Namibia in southern Africa, placed in circulation at the close of the 20th century. Namibia was a country that belonged from the 19th century within the British sphere of influence. No specific currency was issued for this colony were and normally British tender circulated there; after 1880 (when this country became a German protectorate) German marks were used there and, increasingly, also money of neighboring South Africa. Namibia was occupied by the Republic of South Africa until 1994. It was only the political changes that took place in the Republic of South Africa at the end of the 20th century that in fact enabled the creation of an independent Namibia. This vast African country that, throughout its history, did not have its own currency, chose as its new monetary unit the "Namibian Dollar" (abbreviated as "N$"; its payment strength was linked to that of the South African rand that continued to circulate in Namibia even after the establishment of its independent currency). In this case also the choice of a new monetary unit was not influenced by economic factors and the dollar represented a symbolic expression of independence, as is the case for most other dollar currencies (see **Tab. LXIII/4**).

The emergence of a new currency is usually related either to the establishment of a new state entity or to significant political changes. Therefore the majority most of today's dollar currencies were created in the 1960's and 1970's when most of the countries that until then had constituted part of the British colonial system became independent. New states and new currencies were created in a similar manner in the former areas of French and Dutch colonial influence. None of these, however, chose the "dollar" as their new currency unit; this choice seemingly is always influenced by cultural and linguistic traditions.

Newly independent countries also appeared in Europe during the last decade of the 20th century. This came about as a result of the disintegration of the former Soviet Union, the previous Federal Republics of which became independent, and additionally as a result of the rather friendly division of Czechoslovakia into the Czech Republic and Slovakia and due to the protracted military conflict in the former Socialist Federal Republic of Yugoslavia. Most of the newly created states felt the need to express their new sovereignty by also changing the name of their currency. Some of them returned to historical roots and often used unusual names for their new currencies, the meanings of which, however, can be deduced fairly easily (Ukrainian "karbovanets" or today's "grzywnas," Croatian "kuna," etc.).

The emergence of new currencies, however, was affected not only by the division of some European countries, but also by their broader integration. When reflecting at the end of the 20th century on a new form of a common European currency, in connection with the economic integration of the European Union, the suggested "European thaler" appeared to be the big favorite. Some European countries have even started minting their new "eurotalers," but in fact they never became a legal tender.

Only one of the new countries of Central and Eastern Europe did remember the "good old" thaler ("tolar"). The Republic of Slovenia introduced a new thaler currency immediately after declaration and military defense of its independence in 1991. The implementation of the Slovenian thaler, however, was not inspired by the current dollar, as has been the case of new overseas currencies in the late 20th century. By the choice of this monetary unit Slovenia demonstrated its ancient cultural affinity with Central Europe, in the economies of which the silver thaler had provided a significant unifying element since the 16th century. Historically speaking, Slovenia had every right to the symbolic "appropriation" of the thaler since neither the Czech Republic nor Austria and eventually not even the European Union chose to do so. The territory of present-day Slovenia had belonged since the Middle Ages to the Habsburg Monarchy and so historical indicia related to the Slovenian territory can also be found on the "father of European thalers," the Tyrolean guldiner of 1486. A substantial area of today's Slovenia was historically Carniola (named after the Castle in Kranj, located close to the capital, Ljubljana); it was also the southern area of historic Styria, part of the Windic March (in the west part of Slovenia) and also the southern part of the historical Carinthia. Therefore, for a short period, a hundred and twenty years after the demise of the federal thaler currency in united Germany (1871), Central Europe enjoyed the new thaler in the country that in the medieval and early modern period constituted the extreme southeastern boundary of the former Holy Roman Empire. The new Slovenian tolar (see **Tab. LXXVIII/1,2**), however, did not survive long enough to even reach its "age of majority," since it ceased to exist in 2007, when Slovenia adopted the common currency system of the European Union, the Euro.

With the exception of that brief life-span of the Slovenian tolar, nowhere in Europe was the thaler currency officially used for nearly a half century. Despite this evident "time gap" it is possible to trace an unbroken thread of direct kinship that links all of today's dollars and thalers with their early modern age silver predecessors. That circle had, in a symbolic manner, even been completed.

In 1986 the U.S. began to mint a new trading silver coin. On its obverse side it bears the inscription "1 OZ FINE SILVER – ONE DOLLAR" (see tab. **LXXX/2**). In the market for precious metals this coinage naturally has a higher value than one dollar and this monetary unit is only symbolically engraved in this manner. However, it has the same content of precious metal (one troy ounce, i.e. 31.1 g) and basically the same function (monetized trading silver) as that of the Tyrolean guldiner - uncialis from 1486.

At the end of this book, let me offer a small idea.

The dollar is now the world's most wide-spread monetary unit, although in each of the more than twenty dollar currencies existing at the beginning of the 21st century it represents a different value. The world economy, despite its fluctuations, is increasingly closely linked and, in the long term, it is heading towards the creation of a common currency that could be utilized without regard to political boundaries (if there even will be any of these in several centuries from now) or linguistic and cultural differences.

Could the dollar become such a global currency? I think not, even without taking into account the current problems of the financial market, the first symptoms of which appeared in late 2008 in the banking world, in regard to the U.S. dollar.

It has to be acknowledged that the thaler/dollar has a long tradition as a monetary unit since it has already existed for almost half a millennium. During its history it has been utilized in some form in most of the inhabited lands. At present, a substantial part of the economic potential of humanity is held in dollar currencies (either as physically circulating tender or in bank accounts or other financial assets). In my opinion, however, it will not become a global currency. I see no obstacle to the process of the integration of the world economy. This will undoubtedly intensify, since despite all the crisis fluctuations this will be better for all concerned. The problem will probably not even be in regard to the physical form of the global currency, because some economically based equivalent has always been found as a means of assessing the market value of goods. Humankind can probably succeed in adopting a common currency, but will it ever be able to agree on a name for it?

The experiences of the late 20th century have shown how difficult this is and how hard it is to seek for compromises in these circumstances. The path of many national currencies via the "ecu" to today's "Euro" has not been easy. It has turned out that even not such a large group of European countries that have very similar cultural norms and common historical roots, has not been able to even choose a traditional name for its common currency. For diplomatic and political reasons the new currency cannot be franc, crown, mark, lira, zloty or peseta and, who knows why, not even thaler. An artificially created name for the common European currency, the Euro, functions in the Germanic and Slavic languages as if it were an incompletely pronounced word that is missing a section of it and that is virtually impossible to decline. What then could be the name for a currency that should be embraced not only in Paris and Kiev, but also in Mumbai, in Osaka, in Pretoria or in Yerevan?

Tough to answer. Inspiration, however, could perhaps be found in the silver dollar. This coin has already once, in its past, played a role as a global monetary medium.

Go back, for example, to more than two centuries ago, when thirteen former North American Colonies fought for their independence. If you were then to embark on a journey around the world, I would recommend taking with you Mexican dollars to cover your travel expenses. Gold coins could also be good, but you would have to exchange them, perhaps with difficulty, for the domestic currencies of certain countries. But not Mexican dollars; with these it would be possible to pay directly almost everywhere in the world where they were familiar with the currency. However, you should not be surprised how many different names this "universal coin" has. Somewhere it is called "peso," somewhere else "piastre." In Central Europe it is the "Spanish thaler minted in America," in the British Isles and in the U.S. the "dollar," in Italy "tallero" or "scudo." In French-speaking countries it is called the "ecu," in China "Yuan," in Japan "Yen" and who knows how many local names we could discover. The silver thaler with the symbol of the Pillars of Hercules was trusted in every country. It was a tender of lasting value. With this thaler you did not have to worry about inflation, caused by the careless issuance of fiat money and the indebtedness of the state budget. With it you did not have to worry about the fluctuations in exchange rates because everywhere it retained its payment strength in regard to a variegated medley of the provincial currencies of the then known world.

So it did not matter that it had such a diverse designation in so many languages. Should someone in Jamaica or in the Peruvian Andes not understand you sufficiently, it was enough to write on a piece of paper or with a stick in the sand the universally known "$" symbol and everyone knew immediately that you meant the silver dollar. It was not necessary to give the universally valid world money a common name. Even without the name it performed its function equally well in Toruń as in Beijing and even in Texas. And what else could we desire of such a global currency?

Notes

1. Adolf Soetbeer, *Edelmetall-Produktion und Wertverhältnisse zwischen Gold und Silber seit der Entdeckung Amerika's bis zur Gegenwart* (Gotha, 1879).
2. Fernand Braudel, *Civilization and Capitalism 15th-18th Century, Volume II, The Wheels of Commerce* (London, 2002), pp. 194-203.
3. John F. Chown, *A History of Money from AD 800* (London, 1995), p. 76.
4. Carlo M. Cipolla, *Die Odyssee des spanischen Silbers – Conquistadoeres, Piraten, Kaufleute* (Berlin, 1996), pp. 116-118.
5. Holm Sundhaussen, "'Die Preisrevolution' im Osmanischen Reich während der zweiten Hälfte des 16. Jahrhunderts – 'Importierte' oder intern verursachte Inflation? (Zu einer These Ö. Barkans)," *Südost-Forschungen* 42 (1983), pp. 169-181; Şevket Pamuk, *A Monetary History of the Ottoman Empire* (Cambridge, 2004), p. 144, Tab. "The exchange rate of European coins expressed in akçes 1584-1731."
6. Ronald C. Jennings, "Loans and Credit in Early 17th-Century Ottoman Judicial Records (The Sharia Court of Anatolian Kayseri)," *Journal of the Economic and Social History of the Orient* 16 (1973), pp.. 168-216; Şevket Pamuk, "The Disintegration of the Ottoman monetary System During the Seventeenth Century," in: Dennis O. Flynn – Arturo Giráldez (eds.), *Metals and Monies in an Emerging Global Economy, An Expanding World – The European Impact on World History 1450-1800*, Volume 14 (Aldershot, 1997), pp. 317-332.
7. Charles Fawcett, "Seventeenth Century Dollar Symbols in the Levant," *The Numismatic Chronicle* (1947), pp. 186-189; Lutz Ilisch, "Levantinische Gegenstempel auf französischen Münzen des 17. Jahrhunderts

– Der Timminhandel in zeitgenössischen Berichten," in: Thomas Fischer – Peter Ilisch (ed.), *Lagom (Festschrift für Peter Berghaus zum 60. Geburstag am 20. November 1979)* (Münster, 1981), pp. 315-326.

8. Chown, *A History of Money*, p. 68; Stanley L. Engerman, "Mercantilism and overseas trade 1700-1800," in: Roderick Floud – Donald McCloskey (eds.), *The Economic History of Britain since 1700* (Cambridge, 1994), pp. 182-202.
9. Chown, *A History of Money*, pp. 74-88, 232-234; Chester L. Krause – Clifford Mishler (ed. Colin R. Bruce), *Standard catalog of World Coins. World Coin Listings by Date and Mint 1701-1800* (Iola, 1996), pp. 179-184.
10. Carl Ernst, "Der Levantinerthaler," *Numismatische Zeitschrift* 4 (1872) (Wien, 1875), pp. 271-295; Carl Peez – Josef Raudnitz, *Geschichte der Maria-Theresien-Thalers* (Wien, 1898).
11. Franz Leypold, "Das Verbreitungsgebiet des Maria-Theresien-Talers," *Numismatische Zeitschrift* 94 (1980), p.p 63-64; Wolfgang Heß – Dietrich Klose, *Vom Taler zum Dollar 1486-1986* (München, 1986), pp. 195-196.
12. Richard Pankhurst, "The Perpetuation of the Maria Theresa Dollar and Currency Problems in Italian-Occupied Ethiopia 1936-1941," *Journal of Ethiopian Studies* 8/2 (1970), pp. 89-117.
13. Jeffrey E. Stokes, "Die Nachprägungen des Maria-Theresien-Talers in englischem Auftrag aus Wien, London, Brüssel, Bombay und Birmingham," *Numismatische Zeitschrift* 94 (1980), pp. 65-73; Werner Biermann, "International Commerce in East Africa c. 1500 to the 1870s," *Social Research on Africa* 5 (1998), pp. 1-68; Jack Weatherford, *Eine kurze Geschichte des Geldes und der Währungen – Von der Anfängen bis in die Gegenwart* (Zürich, 1999), p. 148; Giles Pope, "The Maria Theresa Dollar in the Late Nineteenth and Early Twentieth Centuries," in: Karl Bachinger – Dieter Stiefel (Hgg.), *Auf Heller und Cent – Beiträge zur Finanz- und Währungsgeschichte* (Frankfurt, 2001), pp. 253-278.
14. Walter Hafner, *Lexicon of the Maria Theresien Taler 1780* (Wien, 1984).
15. Clara Semple, *A Silver Legend: The Story of the Maria Theresa Thaler* (Manchester, 2006), p. 46, Table 1: "Reported Mintages of Maria Theresa Thalers for Habsburg or Austrian Mints."
16. Philippe Flandrin, *Les Thalers d'Argent: Histoire d'une monnaie commune* (Paris, 1997), pp. 167-187.
17. Joseph Edkins, *Chinese Currency* (London, 1890), pp. 21-23; Cipolla, *Die Odyssee des spanischen Silbers,* pp. 121-122.
18. Arjan van Aelst, "A South-Chinese Currency Zone between the Twelfth and Nineteenth Centuries," in: Jan Lucassen (ed.), *Wages and Currency: Global Comparison from Antiquity to the Twentieth Century* (Bern, 2007), pp. 97-112.

19. J. B. Caldecott, "The Spanish Dollar as Adapted for Money in our West Indian Colonies," *The British Numismatic Journal* 1 (1904), pp. 287-298.
20. Takeshi Hamashita, "Silver in regional economies and the world economy (East Asia in the sixteenth to nineteenth centuries)," in: Takeshi Hamashita (Linda Grove – Mark Selden, eds.), *China, East Asia and the Global Economy (Regional and historical perspectives)* (London, 2008), pp. 39-56.
21. William G. Summer, *A History of American Currency* (New York, 1874; reprint 1968), pp. 109-111; Günter Ludwig – Günter Wermusch, *Silber: Aus der Geschichte einer Edelmetall* (Berlin, 1986), pp. 212-246; Chown, *A History of Money*, pp. 81-82, 93-97, 246-255.
22. J. Earl Massey, *America's Money: The Story of Our Coins and Currency* (New York, 1968), pp. 151-170.
23. John Amos (ed.), *Coin World Almanac – First Edition* (Sidney, 1975), Tab. "Price of Silver per Troy Ounce in New York, 1874-1973," pp. 216-217.
24. Weatherford, *Eine kurze Geschichte des Geldes*, p. 153; Massey, *America's Money*, pp. 176-180.
25. Krause – Mishler, *Standard Catalog of World Crowns and Talers*, pp. 806-807; Michael North (Hg.), *Von Aktie bis Zoll: Ein historisches Lexikon des Geldes* (München, 1995), pp. 87-88.
26. Edkins, *Chinese Currency*, pp. 16-26; Richard. N. J. Wright, "The Silver Dragon Coinage of the Chinese Provinces 1888-1949," *The Numismatic Chronicle* (1979), pp. 167-200; Heß – Klose, *Vom Taler zum Dollar 1486-1986*, p. 192.
27. John Demarais, "The British Trade Dollars in Hong Kong and Malaya," *Numismatic International* 16 (1982), Nr. 10, pp. 303-307; Richard N. J. Wright, "The Introduction of Chinas Modern Silver Coinage," *Coin & Medal News* 24 (1987), Nr. 10, pp. 61-64.
28. Carl von Hock, *Die Finanzen und die Finanzgeschichte der Vereinigten Staaten von Amerika* (Stuttgart, 1867), pp. 712-713, Tab. "Ausweise über das Münzwesen und den Verkehr mit edlen Metallen"; Ludwig – Wermusch, pp. 212-246.
29. Arthur Nussbaum, *A History of the Dollar* (New York, 1957).
30. Gustav Cassel, T*he Downfall of the Gold Standard* (Oxford, 1936), pp. 181-190, 217-224.
31. Massey, *America's Money*, pp. 217-220.
32. Chown, *A History of Money*, p. 270; Frances Williams Browin, *Coins have Tales to Tell: The Story of American Coins* (Philadelphia, 1966), pp. 109-116.
33. Summer, *A History of American Currency*, pp. 88-89; Andrew Hacker, *Money: Who Has How Much and Why* (New York, 1997), Tab.: "The 20 Wealthiest Americans Who Are Self-Made or Largely So – Personal Worth in 1996," p. 96.

Recommended Reading

General

Bozorgnia, S. M. H. *The Role of Precious Metals in European Economic Development: From Roman Times to the Eve of the Industrial Revolution.* Volume 192 in "Contributions in Economics and Economic History." Connecticut: Greenwood Press, 1998.

Del Mar, Alexander. *History of Monetary Systems: Record of Actual Experiments in Money made by Various States of the Ancient and Modern World.* Chicago, 1896; reprint Orono, 1983.

_____. *A History of the Precious Metals*. New York, 1902; reprint 1969.

_____. *Money and Civilization (or, a History of the monetary laws and systems of various states since the Dark Ages, and their influence upon civilization)*. New York, 1867; reprint 1969.

Deraeve, Jacques and Jean-Marie Duvosquel, eds. *One Money for Europe – XIth International Numismatic Congress*. Brussels, 1991.

Eagleton, Catherine and Jonathan Williams. *Money, A History*. London, 2007.

Flynn, Dennis O., Arturo Giráldez and Richard von Glahn, eds. *Global Connections and Monetary History, 1470-1800*. Aldershot, 2003.

Heß, Wolfgang und Dietrich Klose. *Vom Taler zum Dollar 1486-1986.* München, 1986.

Chown, John F. *A History of Money from AD 800*. London, 1995.

Kindleberger, Charles P. *A Financial History of Western Europe*. London, 2006.

_____. *World Economic Primacy: 1500 to 1990*. New York: Oxford University Press, 1996.

Lucassen, Jan. ed. *Wages and Currency: Global Comparison from Antiquity to the Twentieth Century*. Bern, 2007.

Means, Howard. *Money and Power: The History of Business*. New York, 2001.

North, Michael. *Das Geld und seine Geschichte: Vom Mittelalter bis zur Gegenwart.* München, 1994.

Porteous, John. *Münzen: Geschichte und Bedeutung in Wirtschaft, Politik und Kultur*. Frankfurt am Main, 1969.

Redish, Angela. *Bimetallism – An Economic and Historical Analysis*. New York, 2006.

Seavoy, Ronald E. *Origins and Growth of the Global Economy: From the Fifteenth Century Onward*. London, 2003.

Thompson, James Westfal. *Economic and Social History of Europe in the Later Middle Ages, 1300-1530*. New York. 1958.

Weatherfort, Jack. *The History of Money*. New York, 1997.

Zarlenga, Stephen. *Der Mythos von Geld – die Geschichte der Macht: Vom Tauschhandel zum Euro: eine Geschichte des Geldes und der Währungen*. Zürich, 1999.

Encyclopaedian Views and Dictionaries of Numismatics

Carlton, R. Scott. *The International Encyclopaedic Dictionary of Numismatics*. Iola, 1996.

Cribb, Joe. *Money*. London, 1990.

_____., Barrie Cook and Ian Carradice. *The Coin Atlas: A Comprehensive View of the Coins of the World Throughout History*. London, 1999.

Hobson, Burton and Robert Obojski. *Illustrated Encyclopedia of World Coins*. New York, 1970.

Kroha, Tyll. *Grosses Lexikon der Numismatik*. Gütersloh, 1997.

Mackay, James. *2500 Coins of the World*. London, 2008.

North, Michael, Hg. *Von Aktie bis Zoll – Ein historisches Lexikon des Geldes*. München, 1995.

Snodgrass, Mary Ellen. *Coins and Currency: An Historical Encyclopedia*.London, 2003.

Catalogs of Thalers and Dollars

Davenport, John S. *European Crowns, 1484-1600*. Frankfurt am Main, 1985.

_____. *European Crowns, 1600-1700*. Galesburg, 1974.

_____. *European Crowns, 1700-1800*. Galesburg, 1971.

_____. *German Talers, 1500-1600*. Frankfurt am Main, 1979.

_____. *German Secular Talers, 1600-1700*. Frankfurt am Main, 1976.

Davenport, John S. *German Talers, 1700-1800*. London, 1979.

_____. *The Dollars of Africa, Asia and Oceania*. Galesburg, 1969.

Divo, Jean Paul. *Die Taler der Schweiz*. Zurich, 1966.

Egg, Erich. *Der Tiroler Taler (Die Prägungen der Münzstätte Hall in Tirol 1477-1809)*. Innsbruck, 1972.

Hafner, Walter. *Lexicon of the Maria Theresien Taler, 1780*. Wien, 1984.

Heinrich, Heinz und Wolfgang Steguweit. *Alte Taler des Münzkabinetts Gotha*. Gotha, 1983.

Osbon, James B. *Jim Osbon's Silver Dollar Encyclopedia*. Richmond, 1976.

Schnee, Gernot. *Sächsische Taler, 1500-1800*. Frankfurt, 1982.

Спасский, Иван Георгиевич. *Русские ефимки (Исследование и каталог)* [Russian Yefimoks (Essay and catalogue)]. Новосибирск, 1988.

Voglhuber, Rudolf. *Taler und Schautaler des Erzhauses Habsburg von Erzherzog Sigismund v. Tirol 1484 bis Kaiser Franz Josef I, 1896*. Frankfurt am Main, 1971.

Wayte, Raymond. *The Silver Dollars of North and South America*. New York, 1964.

Chapter 1
European Silver Coins at the Turn of the 15th and 16th Centuries

Ammann, Gert und Meinrad Pizzinini, Hgg. *Der Herzog und sein Taler. Erzherzog Sigmund der Münzreiche: Politik - Münzwesen - Kunst*. Innsbruck, 1986.

Erich, Egg, Hg. *Der Tiroler Thaler (Die Prägungen der Münzstätte Hall in Tirol 1477-1809)*. Innsbruck, 1972.

Ingenhaeff, Wolfgang und Johann Bair, Hgg. "Schwazer Silber – Vergeudeter Reichtum? (Verschwenderische Habsburger in Anhängigkeit vom oberdeutschen Kapital an der Zeitwende vom Mittelalter zur Neuzeit)." Schwazer Silber - 1. International Bargbausymposium Schwaz 2002 (Tagungsband). Schwaz, 2003.

Moeser, Karl und Fritz Dworschak. "Die große Münzreform unter Erzherzog Sigismund von Tirol (Die ersten großen Silber- und deutschen Bildnismünzen aus der Münzstätte Hall im Inntal)." *Oesterreichisches Münz- und Geldwesen im Mittelalter VII*. Wien, 1936.

Moser, Heinz, Hellmut Rizzoli und Heinz Tursky. *Tiroler Münzbuch. Die Geschichte des Geldes aus den Prägestätten des alttirolischen Raumes*. Innsbruck, 1984.

Spufford, Peter. *How Rarely did Medieval Merchants use Coin?* Utrecht, 2008.

_____. *Money and its Use in Medieval Europe*. Cambridge, 1989.

Chapter 2
The First Appearance of the Taler in Jáchymov

Hásková, Jarmila. "Die Währungs- und Münzentwicklung unter den Jagellonen in Böhmen 1471-1526." *Sborník Národního muzea v Praze,* řada A, č.1/2. Praha, 1969.

Nemeškal, Lubomír. *Jáchymovská mincovna v 1. polovině 16. století (1519/1520-1561) – Význam ražby tolaru* [The Mint of Jáchymov during the 1st Half of the 16th Century (1517/1520 – 1561) – The Importance of the Minting of Thaler]. Praha, 1964.

_____. *Počátek ražby českého tolaru a konec ražby pražského groše (1469-1561) – Peněžně – historická studie* [The Beginning of Minting of the Czech Thaler and the Termination of Minting of the Prague Groschen (1469-1561) – Essay on Monetary History]. Praha, 1997.

_____. and Petr Vorel. *Dějiny jáchymovské mincovny a katalog ražeb I. 1519/1520 – 1619* [History of the Jáchymov Mint and catalogue of coinage from the years 1519/1520-1619]. Pardubice, 2010.

Vorel, Petr. *Od pražského groše ke koruně české 1300-2000 (Průvodce dějinami peněz v českých zemích)* [From the Prague Groschen to the Czech Crown, 1300-2000 (Monetary History of the Czech Lands)]. Praha, 2004 (2nd edition).

Chapter 3
The Struggle over the Taler in Central Europe in the 16th Century

Blaich, Fritz. *Die Reichsmonopolgesetzgebung im Zeitalter Karls V: Ihre ordnungspolitische Problematik*. Stuttgart, 1967.

Edelmayer, Friedrich, Maximilian Lanzinner und Peter Rauscher, Hgg. *Finanzen und Herrschaft – Materielle Grundlagen fürstlicher Politik in den habsburgischen Ländern und im Heiligen Römischen Reich im 16. Jahrhundert.* Wien, 2003 .

Ehrenberger, Richard. *Das Zeitalter der Fugger – Geldkapital und Creditverkehr im 16. Jahrhundert I-II*. Jena, 1896.

Hamilton, Earl J. *American Treasure and the Price Revolution in Spain 1501-1650.* New York, 1970.

Nemeškal, Lubomír. *Snahy o mincovní unifikaci v 16. století* [Pursuit of Monetary Unification during the 16th Century]. Praha, 2001.

Schrötter, Friedrich. "Das Münzwesen des Deutschen Reichs von 1500 bis 1566," *Jahrbuch für Gesetzgebung, Verwaltung und Volkswirtschaft im Deutschen Reich* 35 (1911), pp. 129-172; 36, (1912) pp. 99-128.

Vorel, Petr. *Monetary Circulation in Central Europe at the Beginning of the Early Modern Age – Attempts to Establish a Shared Currency as an Aspect of the Political Culture of the 16th Century (1524-1573)*. Pardubice, 2006.

Wiebe, Georg. *Zur Geschichte der Preisrevolution des XVI. und XVII. Jahrhunderts*. Leipzig, 1895.

Chapter 4
Talers and the European Wars during the 16th to the 18th Centuries

Blanchard, Ian, *Russia's "Age of Silver": Precious-Metal Production and Economic Growth in the Eighteenth Century*. London, 1989.

Christmann, Thomas. *Das Bemühungen von Kaiser und Reich um die Vereinheitlichung des Münzwesens*. Berlin, 1988.

Israel, Jonathan I. *Dutch Primacy in World Trade, 1585-1740*. Oxford, 1990.

Schwinkowski, Walter. *Die Reichsmünzreformbestrebungen in den Jahren 1665-1670 und der Vertrag zu Zinna 1667*. Berlin, 1916.

Sprenger, Bernd. *Das Geld der Deutschen: Münzgeschichte Deutschlands*. Paderborn, 2002 (3rd edition).

Subrahmanyam, Sanjay, ed. *Merchant Networks in the Early Modern World*. Aldershot, 1996 (reprint 2005).

Vorel, Petr. *Stříbro v evropském peněžním oběhu 16. - 17. století (1472-1717)* [Silver in the European monetary circulation of the 16th and 17th centuries (1472-1717)]. Praha, 2009.

Zanden, Jan Luiten van. *The Long Road to the Industrial Revolution: The European Economy in a Global Perspective, 1000-1800*. Leiden, 2009.

Chapter 5
The Conventional Taler and the World Market in the 18th and 19th Century

Cunz, Reiner. *Vom Taler zur Mark: Einführung in die Münz- und Geldgeschichte Nordwestdeutschlands von 1500 bis 1900*. Hannover, 1996.

Flandrin, Philippe. *Les Thalers d'Argent: Histoire d'une monnaie commune.* Paris, 1997.

Helfferich, Karl. *Die Folgen des deutsch-österreichischen Münzvereins von 1857: Ein Beitrag zur Geld- und Währungstheorie.* Straßburg, 1894._

Marichal, Carlos. *Bankruptcy of Empire: Mexican Silver and the Wars Between Spain, Britain and France, 1760-1810.* Cambridge, 2007.

North, Michael, Hg. *Nordwesteuropa in der Weltwirtschaft 1750-1950.* Stuttgart, 1993.

Rittmann, Herbert. *Deutsche Münz- und Geldgeschichte der Neuzeit bis 1914.* Solingen, 2003.

Schremmer, Eckart, Hg. *Geld und Währung vom 16. Jh. bis zur Gegenwart.* Stuttgart, 1993.

Stein, Stanley J. and Barbara H. Stein. *Silver, Trade and War: Spain and America in the Making of Early Modern Europe.* Baltimore, 2000.

Chapter 6
Talers and Dollars in America

Browin, Frances Williams. *Coins have Tales to Tell: The Story of American Coins.* Philadelphia, 1966.

Scott, Kenneth. *Counterfeiting in Colonial America.* Philadelphia, 2000.

Summer, William G. *A History of American Currency.* New York, 1874 (reprint 1968).

Nussbaum, Arthur. *A History of the Dollar.* New York, 1957.

Menzel, Sewall. *Cobs, Pieces of Eight and Treasure Coins: The Early Spanish-American Mints and their Coinages, 1536-1773.* New York, 2004.

North, Douglas C. *The Economic Growth of the United States 1790-1860.* New York, 1966.

Perez, Gilbert S. *The "dos mundos" Pillar Dollars.* Manila, 1948.

Sedwick, Daniel and Frank Sedwick. *The Practical Book of Cobs.* Winter Park, 2007 (4th edition).

Chapter 7
The Dollar and its Expansion in the 19th and 20th Centuries

Semple, Clara. *A Silver Legend: The Story of the Maria Theresa Thaler.* Manchester, 2006.

Doty, Richard. *America's Money, America's Story: A Chronicle of American Numismatic History*. Atlanta, 2008 (2nd edition).

Hirt, Walter. *Leben mit dem Dollar?* Zürich, 1989 (2nd edition).

Hock, Carl von. *Die Finanzen und die Finanzgeschichte der Vereinigten Staaten von Amerika*. Stuttgart, 1867.

Massey, J. Earl. *America's Money (The Story of Our Coins and Currency.* New York, 1968.

Peez, Carl und Josef Raudnitz. *Geschichte der Maria-Theresien-Thalers*. Wien, 1898.

Zischka, Anton. *Der Dollar – Glanz und Elend einer Währung*. München, 1986.

List of Plates

VIII	Holy Roman Empire, Principality of Saxony: 1/4 of taler from 1545
	Holy Roman Empire, Principality of Saxony: taler from 1538
	Holy Roman Empire, County of Mansfeld: taler from 1547
IX	Holy Roman Empire, Principality of Brandenburg–Franken–Schwabach: taler from 1544
	Holy Roman Empire, County of Öttingen: taler from 1541, minted in the name of Emperor Charles V
	Holy Roman Empire, County of Henneberg: taler from 1555, minted in the name of Emperor Charles V
X	Holy Roman Empire, City of Kaufbeuren: taler from 1543, minted in the name of Emperor Charles V
	Holy Roman Empire, City of Donauwörth: taler from 1546, minted in the name of Emperor Charles V
	Holy Roman Empire, City of Hammeln: taler from 1558, minted in the name of Emperor Charles V
XI	Front page of the Second Imperial Minting Order of 1551
XII	Holy Roman Empire, Duchy of Tyrol: Ferdinand I of Habsburg, Imperial guldiner (taler), minted 1556
	Similar Imperial guldiner (taler), minted in Tyrol, 1558.
	Kingdom of Bohemia, Jáchymov: Ferdinand I of Habsburg, taler, 1556
XIII	Ferdinand I of Habsburg, guldiner (60-kreutzer), minted 1560 in Tyrol and 1564 in Bohemia
	Holy Roman Empire, City of Colmar: guldiner (60-kreutzer), minted 1571 in the name of Emperor Maximilian II
	Holy Roman Empire, City of Freiburg in Briesgau: guldiner (60-kreutzer), minted 1571 in the name of the long-defunct Emperor Ferdinand I

XIV	Holy Roman Empire, City of Lübeck: taler, 1568, minted in the name of Emperor Maximilian II. Kingdom of Bohemia: Maximilian II, taler 1575, minted after the monetary reform from 1573 Holy Roman Empire, County of Mansfeld: taler, 1577
XV	Holy Roman Empire, Principality of Braunschweig–Lünneburg: talers, 1586 and 1604 Holy Roman Empire, secularized archbishopric Magdeburg: Joachim Friedrich of Brandenburg, taler, 1595
XVI	Holy Roman Empire, Principality of Saxony: talers, 1575, 1593 and 1594
XVII	Holy Roman Empire, Principality of Saxony: talers, 1598, 1609 and 1618
XVIII	Kingdom of Bohemia: Rudolf II, talers, 1580 and 1606 Lands of the Bohemian Crown, Silesian territorial Principality of Legnica–Brzeg: taler, 1607
XIX	Italy, Principality of Toscana: taler, 1595 Spanish Netherlands: "spannish Philips talers," minted in Brabant (1557) and in Geldern (1575)
XX	United Provinces of the Netherlands, Holland: Imperial taler ("Rijksdaalder"), 1592 Spanish Netherlands: Philip II, Burgundy taler ("patacon"), 1584 Spanish Netherlands: Archduke Albrecht of Habsburg, undated Burgundy taler (also called "patacon" or "Albertustaler"), minted 1598–1621

XXI	Spanish Netherlands: Philip III, Burgundy talers ("patacons"), minted in Tornau 1622 and in Brabant 1626 and 1638
XXII	United Provinces of the Netherlands: Imperial talers ("Rijksdaalders"), minted in Overijssel (1620) and West Friesland (1621)
	United Provinces of the Netherlands, Province of Overijssel: Imperial taler ("Rijksdaalder"), 1662
XXIII	United Provinces of the Netherlands: "lion" talers ("Leeuwedaalders"), minted in the City of Kampen (1648) and in the Province of Holland (1653)
	Kingdom of Denmark: King Frederick III, taler, 1656
XXIV	Kingdom of Bohemia: inflationary coins minted in 1621: 120-kreutzer and 150-kreutzer
	Holy Roman Empire, Principality of Saxony: inflationary coin minted in 1622
XXV	Lands of the Bohemian Crown, Principality of Silesia: four-cornered, one-sided inflationary coins minted in the name of Silesian Evangelical Estates in 1621
	Kingdom of Bohemia: Ferdinand II, taler, 1621, full-value silver taler, minted concurrently with the inflationary coins
	Kingdom of Bohemia: Ferdinand II, taler, 1624, full-value silver taler, minted after the State Bankruptcy of 1623
XXVI	Kingdom of Bohemia: silver talers minted by the Schlick family in 1627 and 1645
	Kingdom of Bohemia, Duchy of Český Krumlov: Duke John Ulrich of Eggenberg, taler, 1629

XXXIV	Principality of Silesia: talers of Emperor Leopold I (1705) and Charles VI (1714) Holy Roman Empire, Principality of Saxony: Frederick August II, King of Poland, taler, 1718
XXXV	Kingdom of Bohemia: talers of Emperor Joseph I (1707) and Emperor Charles VI (1714 and 1720)
XXXVI	Austria: silver taler minted by the family of Schwarzenberg in 1696 and 1741 Holy Roman Empire, Archbishopric of Salzburg: taler, 1694
XXXVII	Kingdom of France: silver talers ("ecu"), minted 1691 and 1694 Russia: Tsar Peter I, silver ruble (taler), 1725
XXXVIII	Kingdom of France: silver talers ("ecu"), minted 1728 and 1776 Livonia: Livonian silver ruble (taler), 1757
XXXIX	Holy Roman Empire, Principality of Saxony: 1/3 of a taler, 1674 Kingdom of Sweden: "talers of silver currency," minted 1718 Holy Roman Empire, Principality of Saxony: August III, King of Poland, 2/3 of a taler, 1763
XL	Bavaria: conventional taler, 1755 Saxony: Frederick Christian, King of Poland, conventional taler, 1763 Saxony: Duke Xavier, administrator of Kingdom of Poland, conventional taler, 1764
XLI	Germany, City of Nürnberg: conventional talers, 1764, 1761 and 1763, minted in the name of Emperor Francis I of Lorraine

XLII	Germany, City of Regensburg: conventional taler, 1756, minted in the name of Emperor Francis I of Lorraine
	Germany: conventional talers of the Cities of Mühlhausen (1767) and Nürnberg (1768), minted in the name of Emperor Joseph II of Lorraine
XLIII	Germany, Bishopric of Würzburg: conventional taler, 1770
	Germany, Principality of Pfalz–Sulzbach: conventional taler, 1772
	Germany, Principality of Saxony: conventional taler, 1790
XLIV	South (Habsburg) Netherlands: Cross taler (called "Crown taler"), minted in Brussels, 1787
	Habsburg monarchy, Burgau: Cross taler (called "Crown taler"), minted in Günzburg, 17894
	Italy, Duchy of Toscana: conventional taler, 1799
XLV	Germany, Kingdom of Prussia: Prussian taler, 1785
	Germany, Kingdom of Prussia: conventional taler, 1795
	Kingdom of France: silver taler ("ecu"), 1792
XLVI	Germany, City of Hamburg: 32-schilling of Hamburg currency, 1809
	Kingdom of Denmark: King Frederic VI, Danish taler, 1813
	Kingdom of Denmark: King Frederic VI, full-bodied Imperial taler ("en rigsdaler species"), 1838
XLVII	Germany, Bavaria: conventional taler, 1803
	Habsburg monarchy: conventional talers, 1831 and 1853

XLVIII	Dalmatia, City of Dubrovnik: conventional taler, 1794 Germany, Kingdom of Saxony: conventional talers, 1823 and 1831
XLIX	"Unified" silver talers of the German Customs Union, minted 1840 in the Kingdom of Prussia and in the Kingdom of Hannover Germany, Kingdom of Prussia: "Unified" double-taler, 1841
L	Germany: "Unified" talers after 1857: Kingdom of Bavaria (1871) City of Frankfurt am Main (1865), Kingdom of Hannover (1859) Kingdom of Saxony (1861), Kingdom of Württemberg (1866)
LI	Germany, Kingdom of Prussia: banknote 1 taler, 1861
LII	Habsburg monarchy: Emperor Franz Joseph I, "Unified" talers, 1858 (Mint Vienna) and 1866 (Mint Kremnica) "Levant thaler"minted in Günzburg in the name of Empress Maria Theresa in 1780
LIII	Silver Spanish colonial 8-real "ship coins" (called "cobs"), minted in Potosi (today's Bolivia): 1678, undated and 1768 North America, New England – Massachusetts Colony: 12-pence, 1652, minted in Boston
LIV	Mexico: machine-minted 8-real colonial silver coins (called "peso" or "Pillar Dollar"), 1755, 1791 and 1806

LV	USA: silver dollar, 1795 Chile: peso (silver dollar), 1818 Guatemala: 8-real ("peso"), 1829
LVI	USA: gold coins: 1 dollar (1851) and 10 dollars (1893) Great Britain: "Trade Dollars," 1900 and 1903
LVII	USA: silver dollars: "Trade Dollar" (1877), "Morgan Dollar" (1885) and "Peace Dollar" (1922)
LVIII	China: silver dollars ("yuans") from the first third of the 20th century, 1908, 1914 and 1934
LIX	New Zealand: 1 dollar coins, 1967, 1969 and 1977
LX	Dollar coins in Oceania: Tokelau Islands (1981), Pitcairn Island (1988) and Solomon Islands (1977)
LXI	Samoa and Sisifo: dollar coins, 1969 and 1970 Cocos Islands: 1 dollar, 2004
LXII	Bermuda: dollar coins, 1972, 1989 and 1992
LXIII	Dollar coins of Liberia (1962), Zimbabwe (1980), Gambia (1987) and Namibia (1993)
LLXIV	USA: dollar coins 1976, 1979, 2000, 2007 (undated, President Adams) and 2009 (undated, President Harrison)
LXV	USA: 1 dollar treasury note, 1869

LXVI	China: 10 dollar banknote, 1923 China–Canton: 1 dollar banknote, 1949
LXVII	Hong Kong: 1 dollar banknote, 1957, and 1 dollar coin, 1994
LXVIII	Singapore: undated current 1 dollar banknote and 1 dollar coin, 1988 Taiwan: 1 dollar coin, 1960
LXIX	Australia: undated 1 dollar banknote (1983), and 1 dollar coin, 1984 Galapagos Islands: 1 dollar coin, 2008
LXX	New Zealand: undated 1 dollar banknote and 1 dollar coin, 1986
LXXI	Bahamas: 1 dollar banknote, 2001, current 1 dollar coin, 1976, and gold 1 dollar coin, 1995
LXXII	Fiji: 1 dollar coin, 1969 Jamaica: 1 dollar banknote, 1989, and 1 dollar coin, 1976
LXXIII	Cayman Islands: 1 dollar banknote Belize: 1 dollar banknote, 1990
LXXIV	East Caribbean Currency: undated 1 dollar banknote (1965) and 1 dollar coin, 1991 British Virgin Islands, 1 dollar coin 1973

LXXV Trinidad and Tobago: undated 1 dollar banknote (1985) and 1 dollar coin, 1979

Barbados: 1 dollar coin, 1974

LXXVI Guyana: undated 1 dollar banknote (1989) and 1 dollar coins, 1970 and 1996

LXXVII Tonga: undated current “1 $” banknote (“1 pa’anga”)

Brunei: “1 $” banknote (“1 ringgit”), 1996

LXXVIII Slovenia: 1 tolar coin, 2004, and undated 1 tolar banknote

Portugal: “5 $” coin (“5 escudos”), 1988

LXXIX Canada: 1 dollar banknote, 1973, and 1 dollar silver coin, 1965

LXXX USA: 1 dollar banknote, 2001

USA: 1 dollar trading silver coin (“1 troy ounce of fine silver”), 2002

Austria: Hall in Tirol, historical downtown
and the tower of the mint (at the back)

Holy Roman Empire, County of Tyrol: silver guldiners minted
by Duke Sigismund of Tirol in 1484 and 1486
(woodcuts from a valuation-book published in 1572 in Saxony)

Duchy of Savoie: teston of Duke Charles I, minted 1482–1490

Holy Roman Empire, Principality of Saxony: the first Saxon Guldengroschen, minted at the beginning of the 16th century

Kingdom of Hungary: King Vladislav Jagiello, silver guldiner, 1506

Czech Republic: Valley of Saint Joachim

Kingdom of Bohemia: the oldest design of the Czech Taler,
minted in the name of King Louis Jagiello in Jáchymov, 1520

Czech Republic, Jáchymov: the House of Mint
from the first half of the 16th century

Kingdom of Bohemia: silver taler, minted 1526

Kingdom of Bohemia, Jáchymov: silver medal ("death taler"),
minted in commemoration of Stephan Schlick after 1526

Kingdom of Bohemia, Jáchymov: silver taler minted by Schlick family
in 1527 in the name of King Ferdinand I of Habsburg

Holy Roman Empire, Archduchy of Upper Austria:
Ferdinand I of Habsburg, pfundner (12 kreutzers), 1530

Kingdom of Bohemia, Jáchymov: Ferdinand I of Habsburg, taler, 1529

Kingdom of Bohemia, County of Kladsko (Glatz):
John of Pernštejn, taler from 1542

Lands of the Bohemian Crown, Principality of Silesia,
City of Wrocław (Breslau): taler from 1545

Holy Roman Empire, Principality of Saxony: ¼ of taler from 1545

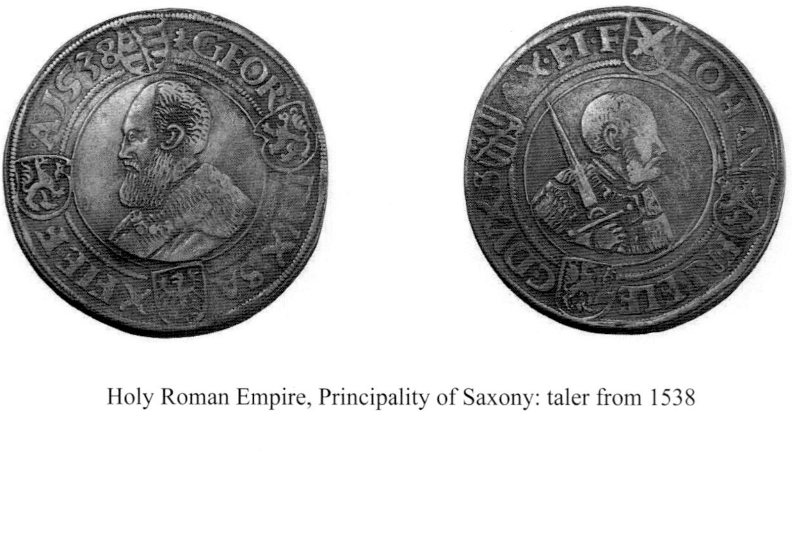

Holy Roman Empire, Principality of Saxony: taler from 1538

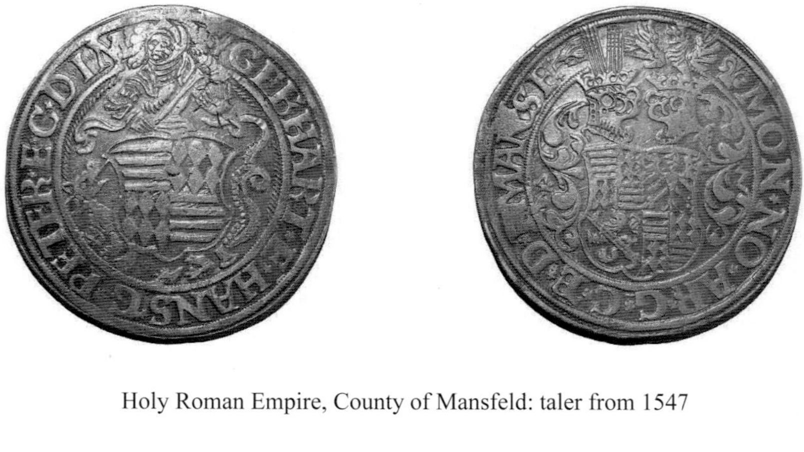

Holy Roman Empire, County of Mansfeld: taler from 1547

Holy Roman Empire, Principality of Brandenburg–Franken–Schwabach:
taler from 1544

Holy Roman Empire, County of Öttingen: taler from 1541,
minted in the name of Emperor Charles V

Holy Roman Empire, County of Henneberg: taler from 1555,
minted in the name of Emperor Charles V

Holy Roman Empire, City of Kaufbeuren: taler from 1543,
minted in the name of Emperor Charles V

Holy Roman Empire, City of Donauwörth: taler from 1546,
minted in the name of Emperor Charles V

Holy Roman Empire, City of Hammeln:
taler from 1558, minted in the name of Emperor Charles V
Nominal numerical value ("24 groschen") is directly imprinted on the coin

Kaiser Karl des fünfften
Newe Müntzordnung/

Sampt Valuierung der
Guldin vnd Silberin Müntzen/Vnd
darauff eruolgtem Kaiserlichen Edict/
zů Augspurg/ alles im Jar
M. D. LI. auf-
gericht vnd auß
gangen.

Cum Gratia & Priuilegio Imperiali.

Getruckt zů Augspurg / durch
Philipp Vlhart.

Front page of the Second Imperial Minting Order of 1551

Holy Roman Empire, Duchy of Tyrol: Ferdinand I of Habsburg,
Imperial guldiner (taler), minted 1556. Nominal numerical value ("72 kreutzers")
is directly imprinted on the coin; on the reverse side is depicted the single-headed
Imperial Eagle, heraldic symbol of the Roman King

Similar Imperial guldiner (taler), minted in Tyrol, 1558, but on the reverse side
is depicted the double-headed Imperial Eagle, heraldic symbol of the Emperor

Kingdom of Bohemia, Jáchymov: Ferdinand I of Habsburg, taler, 1556

Ferdinand I of Habsburg, guldiner (60-kreutzer), minted 1560 in Tyrol
and 1564 in Bohemia. Nominal numerical value ("60 kreutzers")
is directly imprinted on the coin

Holy Roman Empire, City of Colmar: guldiner (60-kreutzer),
minted 1571 in the name of Emperor Maximilian II

Holy Roman Empire, City of Freiburg in Briesgau: guldiner (60-kreutzer),
minted 1571 in the name of the long-defunct Emperor Ferdinand I

Holy Roman Empire, City of Lübeck: taler, 1568,
minted in the name of Emperor Maximilian II. Nominal numerical value
("27 schilling, 6 pfennig") is directly imprinted on the coin

Kingdom of Bohemia: Maximilian II, taler 1575,
minted after the monetary reform from 1573

Holy Roman Empire, County of Mansfeld: taler, 1577

Holy Roman Empire, Principality of Braunschweig–Lünneburg:
talers, 1586 and 1604

Holy Roman Empire, secularized archbishopric Magdeburg:
Joachim Friedrich of Brandenburg, taler, 1595

Holy Roman Empire, Principality of Saxony: talers, 1575, 1593 and 1594

Holy Roman Empire, Principality of Saxony:
talers, 1598, 1609 and 1618

Kingdom of Bohemia: Rudolf II, talers, 1580 and 1606

Lands of the Bohemian Crown, Silesian territorial
Principality of Legnica–Brzeg: taler, 1607

Italy, Principality of Toscana: taler, 1595

Spanish Netherlands: "spannish Philips talers,"
minted in Brabant (1557) and in Geldern (1575)

United Provinces of the Netherlands, Holland: Imperial taler („Rijksdaalder"), 1592

Spanish Netherlands: Philip II, Burgundy taler ("patacon"), 1584

Spanish Netherlands: Archduke Albrecht of Habsburg, undated
Burgundy taler (also called "patacon" or "Albertustaler"), minted 1598–1621

Spanish Netherlands: Philip III, Burgundy talers ("patacons"),
minted in Tornau 1622 and in Brabant 1626 and 1638

United Provinces of the Netherlands: Imperial talers ("Rijksdaalders"), minted in Overijssel (1620) and West Friesland (1621)

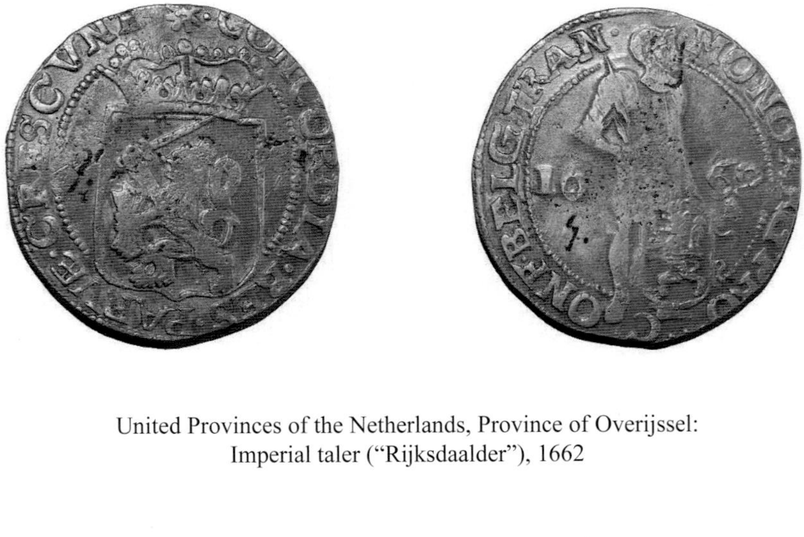

United Provinces of the Netherlands, Province of Overijssel: Imperial taler ("Rijksdaalder"), 1662

United Provinces of the Netherlands: “lion” talers (“Leeuwedaalders”), minted in the City of Kampen (1648) and in the Province of Holland (1653)

Kingdom of Denmark: King Frederick III, taler, 1656

Kingdom of Bohemia: inflationary coins minted in 1621:
120-kreutzer and 150-kreutzer
Nominal numerical value is directly imprinted on the coin

Holy Roman Empire, Principality of Saxony: inflationary coin minted in 1622:
Nominal numerical value ("40 groschen") is directly imprinted on the coin

Lands of the Bohemian Crown, Principality of Silesia: four-cornered, one-sided inflationary coins minted in the name of Silesian Evangelical Estates in 1621
Nominal numerical value is directly imprinted on the coin:
6 Silesian talers [= 432 kreutzers] and ¾ of Silesian taler [= 54 kreutzers]

Kingdom of Bohemia: Ferdinand II, taler, 1621, full-value silver taler, minted concurrently with the inflationary coins

Kingdom of Bohemia: Ferdinand II, taler, 1624, full-value silver taler, minted after the State Bankruptcy of 1623

Kingdom of Bohemia: silver talers
minted by the Schlick family in 1627 and 1645

Kingdom of Bohemia, Duchy of Český Krumlov:
Duke John Ulrich of Eggenberg, taler, 1629

Holy Roman Empire, Duchy of Mansfeld: taler, 1619

Holy Roman Empire, Convent of Quedlinburg: taler, 1624

Holy Roman Empire, Archbishopric of Salzburg: taler, 1624

Holy Roman Empire, Principality of Saxony:
talers from 1624, 1625 and 1629

Holy Roman Empire, City of Hamburg: taler, 1621
Nominal numerical value ("32 schillings") is directly imprinted on the coin

Holy Roman Empire, City of Frankfurt am Main: taler, 1623

Holy Roman Empire, City of Augsburg: taler, 1642

Switzerland, City of St. Gallen: taler, 1620

Lands of the Bohemian Crown, Principality of Silesia:
Ferdinand II, taler, 1630

Holy Roman Empire, Principality of Saxony: ½ taler, 1630

Holy Roman Empire, Duchy of Tyrol:
Archduke Ferdinand of Habsburg, undated taler, minted 1564–1595

Holy Roman Empire, Duchy of Tyrol: silver talers of Archduke Leopold of Habsburg (1632) and of Archduke Sigismund Francis (1665)

Kingdom of France: silver talers ("ecu"), minted 1642 and 1647

United Provinces of the Netherlands, Province of Zeeland: double-taler, 1690
Nominal numerical value ("10 schillings") is directly imprinted on the coin

Holy Roman Empire, Principality of Saxony:
talers, minted 1653, 1658 and 1665

Principality of Silesia: talers of Emperor Leopold I (1705)
and Charles VI (1714)

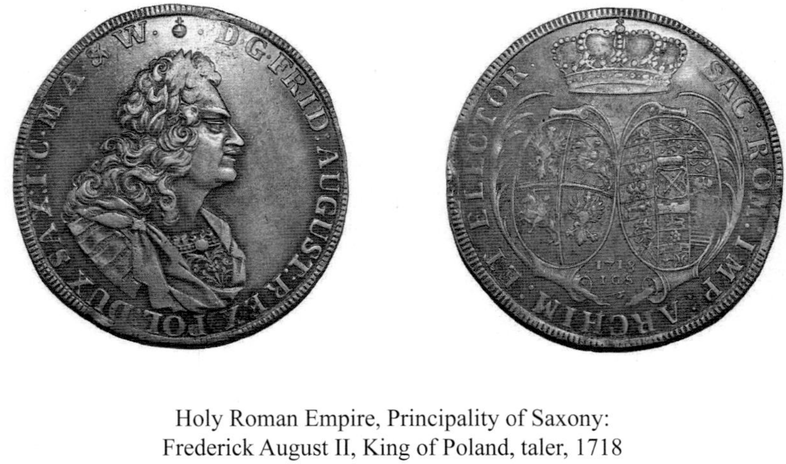

Holy Roman Empire, Principality of Saxony:
Frederick August II, King of Poland, taler, 1718

Kingdom of Bohemia: talers of Emperor Joseph I (1707)
and Emperor Charles VI (1714 and 1720)

Austria: silver taler minted by the family
of Schwarzenberg in 1696 and 1741

Holy Roman Empire, Archbishopric of Salzburg: taler, 1694

Kingdom of France: silver talers ("ecu"), minted 1691 and 1694

Russia: Tsar Peter I, silver ruble (taler), 1725

Kingdom of France: silver talers ("ecu"), minted 1728 and 1776

Livonia: Livonian silver ruble (taler), 1757
Nominal numerical value ("96 kopeks") is directly imprinted on the coin

Holy Roman Empire, Principality of Saxony: ⅓ of a taler, 1674
Nominal numerical value ("⅓ of the unit of account "Imperial taler"
[= 30 kreutzers]") is directly imprinted on the coin

Kingdom of Sweden: "talers of silver currency," minted 1718
Small copper credit coins, whose nominal numerical value
("1 daler silvermynt") in imprinted on the coins

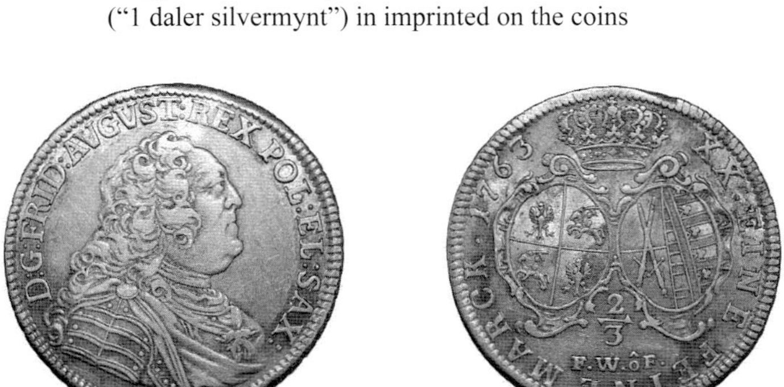

Holy Roman Empire, Principality of Saxony:
August III, King of Poland, ⅔ of a taler, 1763
Nominal numerical value ("⅔ of the unit of account "Imperial taler"
[= 60 kreutzers]") is directly imprinted on the coin

Bavaria: conventional taler, 1755

Saxony: Frederick Christian, King of Poland, conventional taler, 1763

Saxony: Duke Xavier, administrator of Kingdom of Poland,
conventional taler, 1764

Germany, City of Nürnberg: conventional talers, 1764, 1761 and 1763,
minted in the name of Emperor Francis I of Lorraine

Germany, City of Regensburg: conventional taler, 1756,
minted in the name of Emperor Francis I of Lorraine

Germany: conventional talers of the Cities of Mühlhausen (1767) and
Nürnberg (1768), minted in the name of Emperor Joseph II of Lorraine

Germany, Bishopric of Würzburg: conventional taler, 1770

Germany, Principality of Pfalz–Sulzbach: conventional taler, 1772

Germany, Principality of Saxony: conventional taler, 1790

South (Habsburg) Netherlands: Cross taler (called "Crown taler"),
minted in Brussels, 1787

Habsburg monarchy, Burgau: Cross taler (called "Crown taler"),
minted in Günzburg, 17894

Italy, Duchy of Toscana: conventional taler, 1799

Germany, Kingdom of Prussia: Prussian taler, 1785
Nominal numerical value ("one Imperial taler"
[the Prussian unit of account]) is imprinted on the coin

Germany, Kingdom of Prussia: conventional taler, 1795

Kingdom of France: silver taler („ecu"), 1792

Germany, City of Hamburg: 32-schilling of Hamburg currency, 1809
Silver content (“1/17 of a Cologne mark of pure silver”) is imprinted on the coin

Kingdom of Denmark: King Frederic VI, Danish taler, 1813
Nominal numerical value (“en rigsbankdaler”
[the Danish unit of account]) is imprinted on the coin

Kingdom of Denmark: King Frederic VI, full-bodied Imperial taler
(“en rigsdaler species”), 1838, corresponding in the silver content
with the Imperial taler from prior to 1750

Germany, Bavaria: conventional taler, 1803

Habsburg monarchy: conventional talers, 1831 and 1853

Dalmatia, City of Dubrovnik: conventional taler, 1794

Germany, Kingdom of Saxony: conventional talers, 1823 and 1831

"Unified" silver talers of the German Customs Union,
minted 1840 in the Kingdom of Prussia and in the Kingdom of Hannover
Silver content ("1/14 of a Cologne mark of pure silver") is imprinted on the coin

Germany, Kingdom of Prussia: "Unified" double-taler, 1841
Imprinted on the coins are: silver content ("1/7 of a Cologne mark of pure silver"),
nominal value in the German Custom Union currency ("2 talers")
and nominal value in South German currency ("3 ½ guldiners")

L

Germany: "Unified" talers after 1857: Kingdom of Bavaria (1871),
City of Frankfurt am Main (1865), Kingdom of Hannover (1859),
Kingdom of Saxony (1861), Kingdom of Württemberg (1866)
Imprinted on the coins are: silver content ("$\frac{1}{30}$ of a metric pound of pure silver")
and nominal value in the "Unified Currency" ("1 unified taler")

Germany, Kingdom of Prussia: banknote 1 taler, 1861

Habsburg monarchy: Emperor Franz Joseph I, “Unified” talers, 1858
(Mint Vienna, today’s Austria) and 1866 (Mint Kremnica, today’s Slovakia)

“Levant thaler” was initially the conventional taler of Habsburg monarchy,
minted in Günzburg in the name of Empress Maria Theresa in 1780

Silver Spanish colonial 8-real "ship coins" (called "cobs"),
minted in Potosi (today's Bolivia): 1678, undated and 1768

North America, New England – Massachusetts Colony:
12-pence, 1652, minted in Boston

Mexico: machine-minted 8-real colonial silver coins
(called “peso” or “Pillar Dollar”), 1755, 1791 and 1806

USA: silver dollar, 1795

Chile: peso (silver dollar), 1818

Guatemala: 8-real ("peso"), 1829

USA: gold coins: 1 dollar, 1851, and 10 dollars (called "eagle"), 1893

Great Britain: "Trade Dollars," 1900 and 1903,
minted for export of silver to China and Malaya

USA: silver dollars: “Trade Dollar” (1877),
“Morgan Dollar” (1885) and “Peace Dollar” (1922)

China: silver dollars ("yuans") from the first third
of the 20th century, 1908, 1914 and 1934

New Zealand: 1 dollar coins, 1967, 1969 and 1977

Dollar coins in Oceania: Tokelau Islands (1981),
Pitcairn Island (1988) and Solomon Islands (1977)

Samoa and Sisifo: dollar coins, 1969 and 1970

Cocos Islands: 1 dollar, 2004

Bermuda: dollar coins, 1972, 1989 and 1992

Dollar coins of Liberia (1962), Zimbabwe (1980),
Gambia (1987) and Namibia (1993)

USA: dollar coins 1976, 1979, 2000, 2007 (undated, President Adams)
and 2009 (undated, President Harrison)

USA: 1 dollar treasury note, 1869

China: 10 dollar banknote, 1923

China–Canton: 1 dollar banknote, 1949

Hong Kong: 1 dollar banknote, 1957, and 1 dollar coin, 1994

Singapore: undated current 1 dollar banknote and 1 dollar coin, 1988

Taiwan: 1 dollar coin, 1960

Australia: undated 1 dollar banknote (1983), and 1 dollar coin, 1984

Galapagos Islands: 1 dollar coin, 2008

New Zealand: undated 1 dollar banknote and 1 dollar coin, 1986

Bahamas: 1 dollar banknote, 2001,
current 1 dollar coin, 1976, and gold 1 dollar coin, 1995

Fiji: 1 dollar coin, 1969

Jamaica: 1 dollar banknote, 1989, and 1 dollar coin, 1976

Cayman Islands: 1 dollar banknote

Belize: 1 dollar banknote, 1990

East Caribbean Currency:
undated 1 dollar banknote (1965), and 1 dollar coin, 1991

British Virgin Islands, 1 dollar coin 1973

Trinidad and Tobago:
undated 1 dollar banknote (1985), and 1 dollar coin, 1979

Barbados: 1 dollar coin, 1974

Guyana: undated 1 dollar banknote (1989),
and 1 dollar coins, 1970 and 1996

Tonga: undated current "1 $" banknote ("1 pa'anga")

Brunei: "1 $" banknote ("1 ringgit"), 1996

Slovenia: 1 tolar coin, 2004, and undated 1 tolar banknote

Portugal: “5 $” coin (“5 escudos”), 1988

Canada: 1 dollar banknote, 1973, and 1 dollar silver coin, 1965

USA: 1 dollar banknote, 2001

USA: 1 dollar trading silver coin ("1 troy ounce of fine silver"), 2002